Michael Godley has spent most of his long life as an actor, on stage and on TV, but he was also a pilot in the Fleet Air Arm before he went back to Pembroke College, Oxford and then the stage. When not working as an actor he spent time in retail, engineering and building.

He met and married his wife, Heather, at university and she became one of the first British Overseas Airways Corporation Stewardesses in 1950.

They had two girls and a boy, all now in the art of drama, fashion, and interior design.

By the same author

Blockade Runners

There's No Discouragement

Michael Godley

There's No Discouragement

VANGUARD PAPERBACK

A CIP catalogue record for this title is available from the British Library

ISBN 978 178 465 206 7

Vanguard is an imprint of
Pegasus Elliot MacKenzie Publishers Ltd.
www.pegasuspublishers.com

First Published in 2017

Vanguard Press
Sheraton House Castle Park
Cambridge CB3 0AX England

Printed & Bound in Great Britain

To my loving parents, Edith and Leonard.

Chapter One

He is a queer looking southerner in a steely northern city, exposed, friendless and poor. He is a refugee in an alien land. He does not understand the language; the social currency is baffling his brain. He patters towards the church on his sandalled feet.

The church is no ordinary church; it is First Church of Christ Scientist, Sheffield; a pallid hall extending the back of a pillared mansion built on the wealth of steel. Organ and voices swell to the closing hymn; He falters. Isolation cramps his steps, but he presses on to the entrance and waits for the service to end. The congregation rises for the closing hymn. The Reader beams confidently down from the lectern at the packed church and joins in the singing:

"O gentle presence, peace and joy and power;
O life divine, that owns each waiting hour."

The Reader pronounces the benediction with all the quiet certainty of light dispelling darkness:

"Through the Grace of God and the love of our fellow men,
May we fulfill the divine promise which is in us all,
Coming at last to that infinite peace of understanding."

There are a few moments of reflection, and then the organ's soft clattering murmurs, usher the congregation into the foyer, and their comforting exchanges.

It is 1933. The 1930s, like an exhausted swimmer, too far from land, is treading water and hoping that the tide will save it. Leonard, the Reader, knows the way to swim, buoyed up by his religion; Guy, the lonely visitor, feels the undertow has left him adrift. The vagaries of social currents are about to bring them together.

Leonard left the platform for the anteroom, lovingly placed his Bible and Science and Health into the small leather attached case which he carried like a communion sacrament. He put on his threadbare overcoat over his tall thin body and hurried into the foyer to mix with the congregation. The exit from the anteroom brought him close to the main entrance to the church. He noticed Guy watching bleakly as people smiled uncomprehendingly at him. Guy turned to go, alienation overwhelmed him.

Leonard intuitively absorbed the situation and spoke quickly.

"Good Morning; my name is Leonard Godley; welcome to our church."

Guy stuttered with gratitude, his soft gentleman's drawl contrasting with the broad Yorkshire vowels about him.

"How do you do – aw but – I'm afraid I wasn't able to get here in time for the service, but I wanted to see where the church was."

He spoke in a diffident stutter. Leonard was intrigued by his sandalled feet, pale corduroy trousers and bracken coloured jacket, collar-length auburn hair.

"Are you visiting Sheffield?"

"No, I've come to work here; my name is – but – Guy

Allan." he stuttered again. "I've come to help the Savilles with their boy. Do you know them?"

"Yes, I know Mrs. Saville, and John. How are they?"

"They're fine. She told me to look out for you – aw – but I'm glad you spoke to me. I was feeling a bit lost."

"I expect you do feel a bit cut off in a city like this; perhaps we could meet and talk. Would you like to come to tea next week and meet my wife and son?"

"That would be marvellous, but I'm not sure when I can get away. But – may I ring you. Are you on the phone?"

"Yes, of course." Leonard gave him the number and Guy left the church to walk the half a mile to Western Hall as if it was six steps.

***

Guy telephoned the next day and Edith Godley answered. Not before it had rung for at least a minute. She hated answering the phone because she was deaf and chronically shy. Which was the cause or which the effect of this disability was difficult to say. What with Guy's "aw but" mannerism and stutter, and Edith's repeated "Hello's," it was fortunate that Leonard arrived before one party gave up.

"Mr. Godley," Guy began. "It was so kind of you to invite me to come and visit, and I would like to, very soon. But I can't get away until next Thursday, and I wondered if you could come and have tea with me, but-, do bring Mrs. Godley and your son."

"Well that would be very nice, but I'm not sure what Edith is doing that day." Leonard hedged, knowing that Edith would rather die than meet a stranger in an even stranger house.

"Oh I see." Guy sounded disappointed.

“But I could certainly come, and bring Tony, he is home from school by half past three.”

“Please come then, about four. You know the address?”

“Yes I know the address.”

Edith looked up reluctantly from the book over which she bent her head. It was 'Science and Health with Key to the Scriptures' by Mary Baker Eddy, founder of her religion and her constant support and escape.

“That was Guy Allan; you know, the visitor I met at church yesterday.”

Edith had not been present at the service because she had the 'belief of a migraine'. Not the belief 'in' but 'of'-- the distinction was important. Her belief was in Christian Science; it was other people who believed in migraines, and the problem was that there were a lot of them, so it was difficult to overcome.

“He has invited us to tea on Thursday: would you like to go?” Edith answered by silently shaking her head and returning to Mary Baker Eddy.

Leonard didn’t argue, partly because he knew it would be useless and partly because he wanted to go alone with Tony. Conversation would be easier and he was fascinated to learn more about Guy Allan; he felt his horizons broadening.

Leonard loved Edith deeply, they were spiritually one. He had met her when they both worked together for Mr. Mather in his pawn shop on the Attercliffe Road. He had rescued her from a violent father and she had responded to his gentleness and later accepted his spiritual enlightenment. There was not a lot of it about on the Attercliffe Road in 1913, especially on a Wednesday when the flat irons were pawned to get the families through the week. The munitions factory during the war was not much lovelier, although the money was a good deal better.

At the coming together of two people in love, there seems to be an equation of giving and receiving to which there is perhaps, no final resolution except mutual enlightenment or disillusion. In the case of Leonard and Edith the resolution was mutual rejection of materialism, and a trust in the power of God to do good. But the barrier to this resolution was the body.

To Edith, the body was an inhibition; to Leonard it could have been a release from limitation. Their wedding night was a tender rape.

Leonard had chosen Llandudno for the honeymoon because it was there that his wounds had been healed after the horrors of Bapaume in 1918. Now five years later, life, not death, once more seemed a possibility. He brought his bride to 'Orme View', a boarding house of reassuring Edwardian solidity.

He stood now at the window on the top floor. The sun was setting like an Empire into the grey Atlantic. He trembled and half turned to Edith in the bed.

"Can I come to you now Edie?" Edie was silent. He looked down at her and his eyes filled with tears. She was weeping.

"What is it love, are you frightened?

"Yes."

"But I love you; how could I hurt you? You're so lovely; I only want to be part of you." Her blue watered eyes blurred with a fearful trust, gently he drew back the sheet and shivered at the sight of her taught tiny body. She did not speak. The last light of the sun caressed the shadow of her navel. With a sob that shook his body he bent to kiss the wreath of her thighs.

"Edie, my love, my love, let me, let me." Her eyes were clamped tight shut.

"I'm sorry, dear, I'm sorry, dear; I love you."

A tram clattered along the front and shattered the night.

Chapter Two

Weston House, home of the Saville family, was built four square of Derbyshire granite, now black with the smoking steel of Sheffield, but softened by the candled chestnut trees that towered above it in the acre of garden. Though destined to become the head office of an insurance group in later years, it was then, the ideal home of a third generation steel founder; a country residence in the town.

Leonard and Tony had arrived for tea and touched the large brass bell-push set in the square pillar of the portico. Through the plate-glass panelled double doors they could see the black and white tiled floor of the hall. Umbrellas and walking sticks jostled in a Ming vase; a small brass set of scales gleamed on the mahogany side table to price postal packets which such houses always seemed to be dispatching; books to the London Library perhaps, photographs to relatives, and newspapers to the colonies. A dumpy maid in black and white clattered across the tiles and wavered in the reflection of the glass.

"Mr. Godley to see Mr. Guy Allan," said Leonard as the door opened.

"Mr. Allan; someone to see you," the maid shouted up the stairs, and scooted off through the green baize door. Guy appeared on the landing.

"But, do come up. How very nice to see you."

"This is Tony," said Leonard as they mounted the polished

oak stairs.

"How do you do." Guy offered his hand formally and Tony took it, not without a little wonder.

Tony was the child of the Llandudno honeymoon eight years ago, since then, Leonard had not made love to Edith. The trauma of the wedding night had only been replaced by the discomforts of pregnancy, and a predictably difficult birth had nearly ended her life. Leonard had reared the child for the first four months and so, after a gap of a year, there was no sexual pattern to resume. Edith withdrew into deafness and 'Science and Health with Key to the Scriptures' and Leonard into building up his insurance round and the study of the Bible.

Study became his way of life. He would work very hard on his premium collections in the morning and then spend the afternoon in the Reference Library. He did enough reading for a degree in philosophy and literature. Having left school at age thirteen with a Certificate of Merit, he felt his lack of education deeply.

Tony was just becoming aware at the age of eight that his parents were different to others. Two years before, Leonard had sold his insurance round and become a Christian Science Practitioner; that is, a healer registered with the Mother Church of Christ Scientist in Boston Massachusetts. This meant that he had no other source of income than his earnings as a healer.

His account books recorded the treatments, the healings and receipts – twelve shillings, six shillings, two pounds four shillings, – his first annual total was one hundred and twenty pounds, four shillings, and the new house in Muskoka Drive, Bents Green, had to be sold to balance those books; but his 'certainty in the infinite source of good deflects any fear of want; right thinking will demonstrate this truth.' Such were the philosophical entries that were added to the double line, ruling off the total.

Tony absorbed these thoughts but winced at school when the teacher went round the class asking what your father did for a living. He would blush and lie.

"He's an insurance agent." He didn't want to be different – yet.

Guy invited them into his room where they met John.

"John, this is Tony; and this is Mr. Godley."

John was delighted and jumped forward to hug Tony. Tony accepted the hug and returned it. He had no discomfort about mental abnormality, even though he preferred his father to be a man from the Pru, he instinctively responded to the view that Man was perfect whatever the material evidence to the contrary.

"John, would you like to show Tony the garden?"

"Y-e-e-e-s," laughed John and took Tony by the hand, galloping down the stairs, baying with delight.

"We'll call you in for tea in a little while," Guy called after them.

The garden was a heaven of rhododendrons, buddleias', and magnolias. In the middle of the lawn was a wigwam.

"Wigwam, wigwam, come and see my wigwam!" John was ecstatic and Tony felt a tender joy for his imprisoned spirit.

"What a lovely boy you have." Guy watched them for a moment from the window. "Do sit down; would you like some tea now?"

"Thank you." Leonard looked around the room which Guy had made his own. The copper kettle simmered on a spirit lamp set on a small ivory inlaid table of filigreed cedar. There was a faint smell of exotic spices which mingled with the sharp smell of bay rum and cantharides which Guy used to dress his auburn hair. The desk in the window displayed silver framed photographs. One was of a Russian in a braided Cossack uniform. Haughty eyes penetrated from under a white fur hat, set at an angle of ultimate disdain. It was inscribed: "To Guy, love from Felix." Another photogragh was of a beautiful woman in a court dress, and another older woman in black, hatted and almost veiled, with no hint of a smile. There was an almost naked female figure in a Grecian dress sweeping the ground with her short hair, and there was Guy himself in the tunic and breeches of the Royal Flying Corps.

"My past," said Guy, as he saw Leonard take them in.

"Very interesting." Leonard sat down gently on the sofa draped with a loosely woven rug of un-died sheep's wool. He wondered how much Guy wanted to tell him.

Guy poured boiling water from the little copper kettle onto perfumed leaves in a terracotta teapot with a wicker handle.

"How did you become interested in Christian Science, Leonard – may I call you Leonard?"

"Yes, please do." Leonard took the offered tea in the grey glazed hand made tea cup.

"Lemon or milk," Leonard took the lemon, not having tried it before.

"Oh! I was brought up as a Methodist in a church-going family and accepted that there was a God, and He was good, and looked after you like Mum and Dad. Then I went into the army and found myself in the trenches and He didn't seem to be looking after me very well. For the first time in my life I became aware of evil and fear; and I came to the conclusion that fear was where the power lay. Banish fear and evil loses its power. So then comes the question, how do you banish fear; only by a trust in love."

"And what about the body?" Guy interrupted.

"Yes the body! The body, I suppose is the ball and chain that binds. Freeing ourselves from the body turns out to be our life's work."

"But how did you find 'Christian Science?'" persisted Guy.

"After the war, I wanted to marry Edith and so I borrowed enough money from my father to buy an insurance book. He could afford to lend it to me because war-work had been good to him as a skilled pattern maker in the steel foundries. Jacob, the man I bought the insurance book from, told me about his religion. He believed that it had helped save his son who caught polio as a small child. I suppose I wanted to know more and more because it was all about the power of divine love."

"You must have a very clear understanding to give up insurance to be a Practitioner," Guy wanted him to go on talking.

"Yes, I suppose I do have a strong sense of certainty; faith. So, what about you, Guy?" But Guy wasn't ready to talk; yet.

"We'd better give those boys some tea. I'll make some sandwiches and take them out." He went over to the sideboard and cut thin slices of brown rye-bread, spread Heinz sandwich spread on some and honey from the comb on others. Leonard carried an earthenware jug of freshly squeezed lemonade and two green pottery mugs.

"Come and see the garden."

The wigwam was empty but whoops and Indian calls from the rhododendrons suggested that an attack was imminent. The two boys whinnied to a stop at the plate of sandwiches.

"Tony's lovely," John whooped, "Can he come again?"

"Yes, I expect so," said Leonard. He could see John's eyes focus with a sudden intensity, then cloud as the concentration faded.

Guy did not reveal any more that day, but Leonard was left

with a feeling of elation, as if coming to the brow of a hill; horizons were broadening.

A few years earlier, just before Tony was born, he remembered having a similar sensation of expanding horizons when he drove Harold up to Oxford to begin his second term. Harold was the crippled child of Jacob, (Leonard's mentor in business and religion). He was now nineteen and a scholar at Oriel College. Leonard, who was five years older, rejoiced in their friendship. He drank from Harold's intellect and developing education. Together their confidence grew in argument, and what would have appeared as vanity in Harold to some, was inspiration to Leonard.

The Hobsons had a car and Leonard learnt to drive so that he could help Harold up to Oxford with his considerable luggage. A motor car might be made of matter but the freedom it gave to the limitations of the body, showed it to be an idea of God! Such was the philosophy expounded when Plato and Descartes floundered.

Oxford, on a golden October evening was Leonard's concept of earthly heaven. Classical, Gothic, and Baroque sandstone glowing in the western light; confident in knowledge and the power of truth; counterpoint of conversation beckoning to book lined rooms where that power and influence for good is nurtured. Or so it seemed to Leonard.

"Here, put this on," said Harold, handing Leonard a Commoner's short gown, as he himself struggled into his long Scholar's gown. "You're my guest in hall; just sit and listen. You may be disillusioned, then again you may not. Oxford is a world within a world and experience here is as random as anywhere."

Leonard admired Harold's massive confidence, escaping from that puny body. Leonard wondered if he would have the same confidence if he had been given the same education. How do you leap from the provincial to the universal, without some accepted badge of approval. Can you reach the infinite without going through the finite first? Leonard was confident in the infinite; his problem was the finite.

The random experience of dining in Oriel in October 1925 was to sit Leonard next to a parson's son. The college of Cardinal Newman still shed an atmosphere of earnest commitment over some undergraduates, and Jonathan Moneypenny, a parson's son, was absorbing it readily.

"This is my friend Leonard Godley, Jonathan. You can talk to him about religion." And left them to their soup while he enlarged on Somerset Maugham's latest play to one of his companions in the drama club.

"Are you going into the church?" asked Jonathan.

"I suppose I'm in a church already," Leonard hesitated.

"Oh! What is that?" Jonathan was intrigued.

"The Church of Christ Scientist; do you know anything about it?"

"I only know it started in America; tell me how does it differ from orthodox Christianity?"

This was good for Leonard who in common with most converts to an unconventional religion spoke only to the converted. He enjoyed the challenge.

"The starting point is the same; that is the philosophical strength to be found in the Bible, and in particular the teachings of Christ and the power of good demonstrated in his healings."

"Why do we need a new religion then?"

"The experience of Mary Baker Eddy was that institutionalized religion had lost the inspiration for healing, and become afraid to expect it other than through material science, which was fallible and limited to human resources." Leonard was aware of his speech sounding rehearsed and stilted. He wished he could introduce an ease that comes from confidence.

"Is a Christian Scientist infallible then?"

"To be human is to be fallible. To become infallible, man has to realize the vision of the truth about his spirituality; his unity with God; become free of this world's materiality. Life is not separate from God and because of that unity, life is indestructible. Evil draws its power from our human misunderstanding of that source of power."

"What about the eight million dead in the War?"

"It was the War that convinced me that death was a failure. All that slaughter changed nothing; it is no rational alternative to eternal life which continues in spite of what we do to each others bodies."

"So what about the short term; eternal life that's a big responsibility to bear, isn't it?"

"Bodily comfort, I suppose we would all reply; the absence of pain, a sense of peace and joy."

"It sounds like an advertisement for alcohol." Jonathan was beginning to shock himself with his incipient sense of despair.

"My concept is to understand man as spirit, not body, and life as spiritual not material," said Leonard; who was wishing he could be an undergraduate and not a Christian Science Practitioner.

The clatter of human energy around him at the crowded tables in the hall, reconciled him to some of that materiality he was trying to disperse. The journey home to the pregnant Edith, still however, found him confident of a new life.

Harold Hobson matured to become Sir Harold, drama critic of the Sunday Times.

Chapter Three

Tony was in a bit of a mess, quite literally. It was mid afternoon in Manor Road Council School. The June sunshine slanted through the high level windows of the classroom that blocked any view of the outside world with bland cream walls. The spotlight of the sun glowed on the dark pine of Miss Granger's desk from which she surveyed her class of nine-year-olds.

"Yesterday, I told you the story of the meeting of Robin Hood and Little John. Who would like to come up here and tell the class that story in their own words?"

There was a general evasive shuffle from the class, except from Tony. He shuffled with the rest but for a different reason. He longed to get up and tell the story, of which he remembered every word and more; but his bladder was as tight as a balloon and if he didn't continue to sit on it the consequence might be to his dying shame.

"Come along now, if you can't remember I shall have to assume that you don't like stories and you don't want me to tell you any more."

A general "no miss" murmur shivered across the desks and Tony's bladder suffered another surge: he could feel the drips beginning to dampen his pants. He knew he should have gone to the lavatory at the break but Tosser Tozer was following him to the lavatories and Tony knew what that meant. Tosser gloried in his erection and wanted everyone else to glory in it too.

"I bet thy cock in't as big as mine." was Tozer's taunt to anyone not yet entered into the mysteries of masturbation. The sight of Tozer's massive member delayed the joys of sexual excitement to several of his reluctantly admiring fellow students, Tony among them; hence the splitting bladder. Suddenly he realized he could wait no longer and raised his hand to ask to leave the room.

"Good, Tony, you can come and tell us the story."

He was trapped. He hadn't the courage to explain his predicament and anyway he longed to tell the story of Little John meeting Robin Hood on the log over the stream. He walked stiff legged to the front of the class, squeezed his pelvis with all his might and kept one hand in his pocket to pinch his penis between thumb and forefinger.

"Hands out of pockets now; stand up straight and speak up," snapped the heartless Miss Grainger.

At first, stage fright and the adrenalin of performance banished the pitiless pressure on his bladder until he came to the description of the water rushing under the log.

"Little John swung his ash stave once again and caught Robin a stinging blow to the side of the head; Robin groaned, staggered and fell sideways into the freezing stream as Little John roared with triumph !"

This was too much for Tony's tortured bladder. It burst; the warm relief flowed past his kneecaps into his socks and filled his shoes. The excess formed a steaming pool about his feet. His narrative squelched to stop. His tear filled eyes appealed to Miss Grainger. There was a pause as at the curtain of a great tragedy, and then the class went wild with delight at his distress. Desk lids banged, feet stamped for joy until Miss Grainger rapped them back to silence.

"Tony, I think you had better leave the room – and go straight home to change." Tony made his exit with as much dignity as his squelching shoes would allow and ran all the way home.

There another surprise met him which quickly healed his shame. Edith came to the door and instead of asking why he was home so early, said:

"Thank goodness you're here. John Saville has come looking for you." And there was John beaming away and dancing with delight at having found him. How he had found him was an extra-sensory mystery because he had never been to the Godley's before and his own house was two miles away; nor had he the available intelligence to ask anyone the way. Guy and the Savilles were frantic when they discovered he had escaped from the walled garden and had called Leonard for help and guidance. Within twenty minutes of the phone call, John banged on the door and asked "Can Tony come and play?" He had navigated busy streets to knock on the right door in this unfamiliar road.

Guy came to collect John and Tony was able to creep away and change without comment.

The consequence was several more teas at Western House and useful experience in how to conduct oneself in a county home. Sometimes Mrs. Saville would be present and tea was served in the drawing room among the glow of delicate Georgian mahogany, glazed chintz and gleaming silver. Tony marked the assurance of the Saville's older son, Michael, now eighteen and about to go to Cambridge.

"Mummy, I shan't be in to dinner this evening. I'm going to Tonight at eight-thirty – you know, Noel Coward. Is that all right?"

"You're having dinner with Noel Coward, dear. How

exciting!" Mrs Saville was not quite up to knowing about the latest sophisticated revue.

"Not exactly, Mummy. It's his latest revue, here at the Lyceum on tour."

"Yes, of course, dear; have a lovely time." It gave her such pleasure to see her healthy son developing into a young man about town. Tony made a mental note about Noel Coward who was not much talked about in the 'First Church of Christ Scientist' Sheffield. He would ask Guy about him.

On other occasions when it was Guy alone, he gradually revealed his past which fascinated like unstrung beads in a jewelry box. A private income of a few hundred pounds a year in Paris of the 1920s and the looks to attract friends with thousands more, had been a sensual bed of dilettante delights to Guy. Nancy Cunard, Prince Felix Youssoupoff, Isadora Duncan, all scorched him with their radiance and enjoyed his body. Exhausted by debauchery and penury he retreated to the sands of Juan-les-Pins and there like Job he was tortured almost to death by boils.

Guy would tell these tales (probably embroidered) as he worked on the painting that was on the easel he had in his room, yet another of his dilettante activities.

Tony noticed a deep white scar on the back of Guy's brown neck.

"Guy, what's that white scar on your neck?"

"That is where I was healed of anthrax." Guy continued to paint. "I caught it in France and would have died if I hadn't met a wonderful person who told me about Christian Science."

"Who was that?"

"Her name is Winifred and she's an artist, and perhaps you'll meet her soon, because I'm going to stay with her. She lives in Cumberland. That's one of her paintings over there."

Tony looked at the painting which he had noticed before, but assumed it to be one of Guy's. It was a cyclamen and primula on a sunlit window sill, with distant background of purple hills. It had a quality of light and vision which Guy's paintings did not.

"Tell me what happened then," Tony insisted.

Guy continued to paint but perhaps the smell of the turps released memories he had locked away.

"Well, the doctors said I may have caught this anthrax thing when I was stationed on an airfield, which was home to a lot of cattle. It was regularly bombed and the earth churned up. I don't know but that's what they said. It hangs around in you and then if you're really run down it can develop. Well, I was certainly run down after the war when I was racketing about in Paris and I began to have horrible boils. I went off to the south to rest but just got worse. That scar was where they cut me open to lance this horrid thing. But it didn't help, I got worse and really felt as if I was going to die. Then through a mutual friend I was introduced to Winifred who was down there painting. She had just been healed of a broken back and knew Christian Science would help, and it did; I got better. That is the work your Daddy does, isn't it?"

"What was it like, nearly dying?" Tony ignored the last remark; matter seemed to interest him more than the spirit at the moment.

"It was horrible, especially when you've wasted your life as much as I had just then." Tony wished he could learn more about how Guy had wasted his life!

Not long after that Guy's duties at Western House came to an end. The Savilles came to the conclusion that John was getting too difficult to be cared for at home, and sent him away. Guy wrote to Winifred and invited himself to stay on her family's estate. This was apparently what aristocratic people did; as they had lots of space they could accommodate their friends and relations without having to see too much of them. Guy was given the summer house on the home farm at Bertholme, situated below the manor house, Boothby, which itself was below the castle at Narworth. Thus was the medieval hierarchy preserved of Earls and Ladies and Esquires.

Leonard raised his eyes from the Bible on his lap and looked towards the light polishing the Cumberland fells. The rhythm of the train gave a metre to his thoughts: "Devine Love is indivisible, indestructible, infinite, impersonal, creative." Leonard was on his way to visit Winifred at Guy's suggestion. She had asked Leonard to help her adjust to the shock of her husband Ben's desertion. She still loved him deeply and her heart ached at the loss, the loss of her husband, and the father of their three children.

The cool colours of his finely balanced geometric paintings still decorated some of the white walls of their ancient windswept cottage, perched on the Roman Wall. Their serenity contradicted the impetuous passion of his seething intellect, and their universality, his self-absorption.

At first it had been unbearable to remain in that home where a life of mutual creation had brought such blissful unity. But recently, she had felt able to return and was beginning to feel harmony again, which Leonard's letters had helped her to find.

Leonard was to stay at Boothby as the guest of Lady Cecilia, and it was Grindley her chauffeur, who collected Leonard at Carlisle station. Grindley never smiled.

"Mr. Godley, sir?" he enquired as he approached Leonard's tall thin figure with the leather suitcase dangling from his serge suited arm.

"Yes, that's right." Leonard was relieved to have made the

rendezvous and smiled warmly. Grindley avoided his direct glance as he took the bag.

"Lady Cecilia's car is just here, sir." He moved towards a dark blue six cylinder Austin saloon that gleamed ahead of them.

"Thank you."

Leonard moved towards the front passenger side door, but Grindley quickly opened the rear door and Leonard found himself sitting behind the glass panel and looking at the back of Grindley, as if he were some kind of undertaker. The journey to Boothby was therefore silent but for the whine of the gearbox as it changed pitch up and down the hills and corners of the empty country road.

The manor house at Boothby was a centre for politics, philosophy, economics and art. The wide ranging discussions fitted well with the rambling house. Not more than two rooms seemed to be on the same level. Even the occupants familiar with its idiosyncrasies moved about with bent heads to avoid stunning them on a lintel or stumbling over a step.

All, that is, except Lady Cecilia. She seemed simply to appear at the dining table, in the drawing room or the garden. This impression was given partly by her beatific authority, arising out of a serene lineage, and partly because of her small stature and Victorian dress, under which her feet remained invisible.

She had come into society in the 1880s and like most of us, retained the character and dress of her early maturity. She looked, therefore, like a good tempered Queen Victoria and had the same air of destiny about her.

Lady Cecilia Roberts was the youngest daughter of The Earl of Carlisle, whose Narworth Castle rose above Boothby to dominate all the lands in the valley of the Irving. In the

1930s, the world of the Howards was still undisturbed: the castle at the top of the hill, the manor half way down, and an inn at the bottom by the pack-horse bridge over the river. On the other side, Lanercost Priory, still caring for the souls of the tenants.

Cecilia was of a more liberal disposition, however, than this lineage might suggest. This she inherited from her mother, Rosalind, the Radical Countess. A campaigner for Women's Suffrage and Temperance whose local power was so complete that that the sale of alcohol was forbidden in and around the local town of Brampton. As the Howards were the landlords of most of the local property, they forbade it in the covenant, even at the Lanercost Inn. It was not, of course, within their power to enforce abstention. As the Mafia was not known in Cumberland, the local population managed to survive without enduring the worst excesses of 'Prohibition!'

Charles, Cecilia's husband, was exactly typical of his professional middle class origins. He was the clever son of an Anglican vicar. He had done brilliantly under Jowett at Baliol and been elected as a Liberal Member of Parliament in 1906. He joined Asquith's Cabinet as Under-secretary of State for India. Now in his sixties he was Chairman of the Cumberland County Council, and carried himself with a modest stoop, born of a diplomatic disposition and an intention to avoid low lintels.

The atmosphere of the house was one of a serene continuity. It avoided grandeur and reflected flexibility, like the Cumberland light that penetrated the white painted windows on all sides. Unlike most of the other houses on the estate, Boothby was built of brick, white painted against the green of the fields and gardens. Chintzes, not antimacassars, brightened the furniture, broad polished oak boards framed

Indian rugs of exotic colours. In unexpected corners, gnarled Roman faces, distantly focused, pondered in the half-light half way up the stairs. These exiled relics, long buried, had been turned up by the plough in the fields beside Hadrian's Wall.

More recent acquisitions were portraits of the family painted by Sir William Nicholson, Ben's father. Their opulence reflected critically on the light, athletic canvases of Winifred and Ben, that hung on the opposite wall.

Winifred and Guy were waiting to receive Leonard when the Austin crunched up the steep drive. Leonard was relieved to see Guy's familiar face, and Guy was happy to return the welcome Leonard had given him in Sheffield.

"Leonard, let me introduce you to Winifred."

Winifred had a smile which always lit up her face with delight, as if she had made a wonderful discovery which she was eager to communicate.

"Leonard, how wonderful to meet you at last. I hope you had a happy journey. Do come and have some tea." Leonard immediately felt at home.

Leonard's way of helping people spiritually was one of confident affirmation, never analysis. He never wanted to know details of his patient's problems, but was receptive to their worries without encouraging self-pity. Winifred instinctively appreciated this sympathy with her privacy.

The conversation over tea was of the beauty of Cumberland and Winifred's fondness for her cottage on the Roman Wall, which they would visit tomorrow. Also of Guy's ingenuity with the Bertholme Summer House, which his domestic genius had individualized within a week of arriving. Guy had a two-stroke open two-seater with a dicky seat. In this accommodating vehicle he transferred all his memorabilia from lodging to lodging. It was a car of affectionate disposition and remarkable loyalty, whose wheezing reciprocation asked no more than two and sixpence worth of petrol every fifty miles.

"Dinner is at eight; we don't dress, you know. Come down to the drawing room at about seven thirty and I'll introduce you to Mummy and Daddy, and tomorrow you must come to Banks Head, perhaps Guy can bring you. I'll just show you to your room." And Winifred lead the way.

Leonard found his room, where his bag had been unpacked and his pyjamas neatly folded on his pillow. He sat down at the writing desk and took a sheet of crisp blue crested paper from the rack, dipped the relief pen into the silver inkwell and began a letter to Edie.

My dear Edie,

I hope all is well with you and Doris is keeping you company. Life here is very different from the one we know . Experience of it confirms that we must, and do, make our own lives within ourselves. What is around us we draw from but must not be enslaved by.

Everything is green and clean here; the conversation is smooth not jagged. There is no aggression because of their confidence in power; there is no display of affluence because everything is provided, not bought. At least that is the outward show; what is within the mind I have yet to learn.

Dearest love, I'll be home on Tuesday.

Chapter Four

Edie was putting the kettle on the gas stove in the projecting back kitchen at 92 Stafford Road. Her mother, Daisy and sister, Doris had arrived unexpectedly to get away from father for a few hours. He was out of work and practicing his verbal brutality on Daisy and Doris; Edie and Leonard's house was their refuge. They sat in the kitchen and watched Tony through the window as he played in the back garden. He was cleaning out his rabbit hutch and busying himself in the garden shed.

The kettle hissed on the gas and the cold tap dripped dejectedly into the enamel bowl. Daisy was crying silently; she was the tiniest of the three diminutive women emptied by their vulnerability. The slightest threatening gesture at that moment would have shattered them like an eggshell. Doris, Edith's younger sister, was the least vulnerable, but exhaustion from bitter fighting with their father had left her temporarily defeated, though not demoralised. It was the impossibility of escape that chafed at her ankles.

"I wish I could come and live here," Daisy voiced her thoughts like a prayer that had no hope of being answered.

"I'll look after you, mother," Doris comforted. "I won't let him hurt you."

Doris had a job at Robert's Brothers on the Sheffield Moor; a department store that stocked the basic necessities of clothing for customers of limited means. Two pounds a week she earned, selling sensible shoes to housewives and factory girls. This gave her a tenuous independence from Fred's tyranny and was a hedge against ultimate humiliation.

Doris was pretty, which made her the target for sarcasm from the bitter woman buyer, but popular with the male floor manager, who responded to her flirtatious wit. At the Locarno Dance Hall, (newly opened and optimistically named after the 1925 Peace Treaty) she was the star performer of the foxtrot and the tango, and she never lacked a partner.

"It's the tango next, Doris, may I have this dance?" The black-brown eyes of Bunny Mazoub twinkled down at her in delighted anticipation of her bodily responses. She had christened him Bunny for her very practical reason.

"What's your name?" she'd asked when they first met at the Saturday Locarno Tea Dance, not far from the University.

"Ibrahim Mazoub," he replied politely.

"Eh! What a mouthful. I can't call you that. I'll call you Bunny, come on let's dance."

Doris was always totally at ease with the foreign, in spite of never having traveled further than Blackpool or Bridlington. Also she preferred the exotic, particularly the brown exotic; they were such gentlemen and so well educated.

"Well they had to be, didn't they? To come to England and study Engineering."

"Oh yes!" Bunny had explained truthfully. "My father is an engineer; he builds railways and harbours."

"There's nobody down our yard who'd know what to do with a clockwork train. I think it sounds wonderful." Doris was nothing if not direct.

They dipped and turned to the South American beat played with all the Nordic passion of a colliery band. The marbled plaster on the Locarno's painted pillars, whirled before Doris's shining blue eyes and freed her little bird's soul to dip like a swallow preparing to migrate.

But today she was earthbound. Doris' battles with her father were not aggressive but defensive of her mother. He was not a vicious man, but he was a violent man, especially when not laying bricks. Frustration made him violent, but he was always sorry for it. "Tell your mother I'm sorry," he'd mutter to Doris when she'd stopped him in his tracks, and Daisy would always forgive him. But it left them all exhausted.

"Come on, mother, drink your tea and have a rest while you can."

Daisy dried her tears and smiled gratefully at her loving daughters. Edie did not smile. She folded her hands and closed her eyes.

"God is love," she repeated calmly. "Divine Love is protecting and guiding us all; Man is not material, but spiritual and God is omnipotent."

Edie's reaction to domestic violence had always been to deny it and turn away; hide in the bedroom, pray. Now she had escaped to Leonard who had taught her to pray properly.

Tony came in from the hut beaming with excitement. "Granny, come and see, I've got something to show you." He took Daisy's hand and lead her to the hut, opened the faded door and proudly revealed what he had been doing. The three walls opposite the dusty window were neatly covered with brown wrapping paper, pinned to the wooden walls to hide the spades, rakes, watering cans and lawn mower. The centre square was swept clean. "There, Granny, you can stay here; I've got it ready for you; you said you wanted to stay, didn't you?"

Daisy picked him up and kissed him.

"Ee! Bless you, love. I'll be all right now. I'll be one of

your rabbits."

***

Lady Cecilia, at the head of her dining table, tinkled the silver bell at her right hand, and Sissy glided across the polished floor to clear the soup plates while the conversation continued uninterrupted. Leonard was seated between Winifred and Gilbert Murray, his head buzzing with challenges.

Gilbert Murray was married to Cecilia's sister, Mary. Both sisters had chosen husbands who were Oxford Dons with liberal ideals and who placed their positions of power and influence at the disposal of society. Gilbert and Mary's daughter had married the Cambridge historian Arnold Toynbee. Leonard was deep inside the Liberal machine, but not deafened by it.

On the opposite side of the table was Wilfred, Winifred's brother, and his wife, Nan. Nan was the new woman; a mathematician from Girton, calm, detached and beautiful. Wilfred worshiped her, which helped him master his own sense of inadequacy in such a family. But perhaps his unfocussed perception was nearer to understanding that the leaders around him were rapidly losing those who would be led. He looked across at Leonard and envied his virgin intelligence. Leonard had everything to discover, while Wilfred felt himself to be at the end of his journey, even at the age of forty.

The remaining members of the party were Guy and Lady Pamela Howard, Cecilia's niece. Pamela and Guy were well matched, although half a generation apart. She had recently shocked the family by appearing in an advertisement for Pond's Face Cream. Her haughty beauty and flawless complexion was calculated to arouse the interest of all who sought aristocracy in a pot.

Guy shed his years and penury and flattered her skillfully. She was relieved to be sitting beside a non-intellectual and wallowed in his stories of Parisian debauchery, flying further and further from the truth as dinner progressed. And this was not due to the flow of wine. Alcohol was not served at Boothby, not even to visitors. Intoxication depended on wit and water. Pamela was well aware of the family tradition and had come prepared with several bottles of gin and French in her luggage. She had been a little late down for dinner but she felt the better for it. Guy enjoyed inhaling the ginny fragrance of her breath which was directed at him rather than Lady Cecilia on her left.

Cecilia was undeceived but beatific and addressed herself to Gilbert on her other side.

"Is Herr Hitler a good or a bad thing for Germany, Gilbert?"

"The bad thing for Germany is economic collapse. A good thing would be economic stability, which the Germans think he can bring them. But I fear it will be at the price of re-armament. I confess I'm not optimistic about world peace, and my beloved League of Nations is suffering from chronic impotence."

"But surely the League of Nations can contain him; the majority desire for peace will prevail, won't it?"

"This year of 1936, I'm sure, will be recorded as the deep depression that heralded the hurricane. There is civil war in Spain, Japan has invaded China, Italy, Ethiopia, and Hitler has cleared his decks by withdrawing from the League and re-militarizing the Rhineland. Meanwhile we stare at the world as if it were a cobra."

"I think the League of Nations is a dangerous waste of

time." Pamela threw in her flushed opinion. "Aren't nations like individuals, incurably selfish. Base your relationships on any other principle and you're sure to be diddled."

"What does Sheffield think about the League, Leonard?" Lady Cecilia chaired her table with diplomatic skill.

Leonard surprised himself with the materialism of his reply. "Sheffield, I fear wants employment and it makes steel for guns and battleships."

"But you don't want guns and battleship, do you?" Winifred pleaded as if Leonard was the controlling power; which perhaps in her view he was.

Her father, Charles, came to the rescue. "The other way is free trade. The world is full of needy people who don't want guns. Only governments think they need guns. We buy our guns on credit – Government Bonds – why not borrow for houses, roads, food. We can't eat and live on guns."

"I could do with some more credit for the farm." Wilfred at last felt on safer ground. "The price for barley is right down."

"I trust your barley is not being sold to brewers, Wilfred." A shadow passed over Cecilia's round face.

"Of course not, mother." But Wilfred looked a little furtive. His wife, Nan, smiled quietly to herself and calculated quickly what a ten percent increase in beer consumption would mean to them.

The next morning, Guy came to collect Leonard for the visit to Winifred at 'Banks Head.'

"The household seems to be in a bit of an uproar this morning," Leonard blurted out to Guy as he climbed into the Jowett.

"Oh really?"

"Yes, I actually heard Lady Cecilia raise her voice to Lady Pamela." Leonard was beginning to savour country house gossip. He felt a little ashamed, but rose above it.

"What was it about, could you tell?" Gossip to Guy was meat and drink.

"I gathered it was about a friend of Pamela's who was coming to stay without consultation with Lady Cecilia. She apparently didn't approve of him."

"Oh I think I know who that will be." Guy nodded. "He is a bit of a near-do-well, not to say a con-man, but very attractive and highly educated, once practiced as a psychiatrist, I believe. There will be some creaking floorboards in the night. What fun!"

"Oh dear, not disharmony I hope."

"You'd better start working on it, Leonard!" Leonard did.

Banks Head was really the rambling extension to the farm immediately next door; another on the Howard estates. Stone built from the Roman Wall it sat upon, the roofs and walls had shrugged off centuries of wind and rain to become grey as a cloud and as embedded as a crag. Winifred had recovered enough confidence to live there again without the departed Ben and with Leonard's help had been able to continue their affectionate relationship now conducted by letter. The art that had brought them together continued to unite them in correspondence.

The serene Sissy Warwick, with her red border hair, was busy in the kitchen preparing lunch with a reassuring clatter of clogs on the stone floor and iron saucepans in the sink. Sissy did everything; she served at Boothby when they needed extra help; she nannied the children when they were at home from school. She should have been married but she also devoted herself to her mother and father on the farm. There just wasn't time to get married. She was assisted by Nana the sheepdog who had succeeded in achieving the softer option of household pet and child minder, rather than sleeping in the barn and dodging the cow's kicks. Andrew, her brother, equally burnished red, had just brought in a bundle of turnips and a basket of potatoes.

"Hello, Mr. Allan," spoke up Andrew, with a cheek he reserved for non-members of their landlord's family.

"Hello, Andrew. Still on the farm then?" Guy knew it was Andrew's ambition to escape from the fell farm. His hands preferred towels to teats and dishes to sheepdogs.

"Not for long. I think I'll go to sea." Always the escape for the adventurous spirit free of responsibility.

"Tough life, Andrew." Guy was attracted to his healthy looks and confidence.

"Perhaps I could arrange for you to go to London and get some training as a waiter."

"Please, Mr. Allan, don't encourage him. Father needs him on the farm." Sissy, forever practical saw the reality.

"Oh, Siss!" They continued to banter each other in their dialect that split the vowels like chopping turnips. Hill farming was hard and needed strong, cheap legs and backs, like those little black cows that gave double cream straight from the udder.

"Come into the studio," called Winifred, and they escaped from the domestic drudgery.

The studio was upstairs. It had been extended out into the roof to panorama towards the south. Today the light brought the distant hills as close as the dry stone walls that quartered the fields below the cottage. A white canvas on a pale wood easel was showing the first signs of elusive greys and blues which would in due course absorb the eye.

"I wanted you to see my studio, Leonard. This is my world; this is where my harmony is, where my light is."

Leonard could see from the several finished paintings round the walls that her light was unique. It let the eye transcend pale colours to be delighted by the rare bright yellows and purples of thc flowers that reached towards you on the window sill.

"I'm working towards my next exhibition. I have to finish about fifty paintings by September. You can help me, Leonard, by keeping my mind calm and creative. You can see my work isn't feverish, it's harmonious. I see painting and prayer as the same thing; it is affirmation of infinity."

Some of Ben's paintings were still on the white stone walls; their solid colours and geometric angles projected a different kind of balance, intellectual, mathematical, but passionate, all immaculately executed.

"Do you like having Ben's work about you; isn't it disturbing?"

"Oh no! I like to feel he's still here. We were always very different, he was methodical, I was inspirational; he was passionate, I was romantic; his energy needed an extrovert release, mine came from contemplation. For so long we were complementary colours but then I began to fade to a paler part of the spectrum. I couldn't attract him anymore. How do you deal with sexual appetite Leonard?"

Leonard reeled a little at the directness of the question. Did Winifred guess at his personal dilemma with Edith, but she hadn't met her, how could she know, or had Guy talked to Winifred about Leonard's marriage. Leonard didn't think so, Winifred was no gossip and would never invite it. Perhaps it was that she was very perceptive. However, he had to reply.

"Do you mean incompatibility of appetite?" he countered.

"Not entirely. Perhaps I mean lack of appetite. When I first knew Ben, I fell in love with his energy, physical and intellectual. His ideas and skills which he was willing to share with me were the aphrodisiac; sex was just part of that sharing. I enjoyed giving, he enjoyed taking; we were complementary again. But then later, giving was not enough to absorb the energy, it had to be someone new."

"If you mean, how do we deal with frustration. I think it has to be redirection of energy, or even regeneration of energy when it is lacking. This usually means work: if you are an artist it is a new vision. When sexual attraction dominates, when you can't take your eyes off the object of your desire, when you can't have them, or only with disastrous personal consequences, you have to re-focus. For you it has to be locking your eye onto light in skies and plants; make them vibrant with desire for life eternal. For me it is continuing to seek spiritual enlightenment."

"That's all right if your rival isn't a fellow artist whose marble back he sculpts in adulation."

"Let's pray that the quality of his work completes the circle."

Winifred sighed and locked on to the distant, vibrant fells.

***

By the time that Leonard had arrived back at Boothby, the mysterious visitor had just arrived. Leonard saw him. He was indeed impressive, frightening even.

He was tall, had a long saturnine face, pale complexion, and white hair, long and in a page boy bob, the front was stained with nicotine. He was wearing a black fur coat, opened to show a maroon suit beneath. He was smoking as he talked to Pamela.

"You'll have to put that out, Conrad: frightful bore I know

but Aunty Cecilia is not pleased to see you. Let's get you up to your room. I'm afraid it's rather a long way from mine but that's Aunty, again!"

"Why doesn't she like me?"

"Well, I suppose it's because you stole a wallet last time you were here."

"Did I? I don't remember."

"Oh yes, you did. It was mine fortunately, so there wasn't any trouble. Do try and behave this time."

"Of course I will."

"Grindley will put your car away." His car was a vicious looking black Hispano Suiza that somehow looked borrowed.

***

Leonard was sitting in the drawing room reading the Manchester Guardian, so neatly folded just to reveal the headlines as he first picked it up. Lady Cecilia entered in some agitation.

"Oh, Leonard, what a distressing day. Pamela's brought that awful man to stay and now poor Grindley is unwell and can't drive the car."

"Can I help?"

"Well, I don't know whether you can. You see, today is the day I have arranged for the Spanish children refugees to arrive. They are orphans from Valencia caught in that horrid war and I'm billeting them on our farms. I think that's a good idea, don't you? They can help and be given a home?"

"Yes, of course; but what's the particular problem?"

"Grindley was to go to Carlisle and collect them, and Mrs. Grindley to nanny them."

"How many are there?"

“Only six.”

“Well, I can drive, and I’ll ask Pamela to come; give her something to do, she seems a bit lost. I’ve just met her Conrad and he might come too.”

“That would be marvellous, if you think you could persuade them.”

“I’m sure I could.”

As Leonard guessed, Pamela was delighted and she persuaded Conrad too. He even said he’d take his Hispano-Suiza. “Give the boys a thrill, and practice my Spanish. Also have a drink at the ‘Soldiers Return’ or whatever it’s called, by the station.”

***

The journey into Carlisle was revealing.

It was decided that the Hispano-Suiza alone would be big enough for the three adults and six starving children so off they went with Conrad at the wheel and Leonard and Pamela also sitting in the front.

“Conrad’s been to Spain, you know,” said Pamela. “He was in at the beginning of the war, weren’t you, Conrad?”

“Yes.” Conrad was reticent.

“He didn’t like it.” Pamela persisted.

Leonard didn’t know whether he should ask this, but it did seem relevant.

“Were you Republican or Nationalist?”

“Republican of course.” Conrad was quite vehement, but remained silent.

“He’s a communist, you know,” relished Pamela as if it gave him a greater sexual attraction: perhaps it did.

“Shut up, Pam.” Conrad did not want to talk, but Pamela

did.

During the rest of the half hour journey into Carlisle, Pamela revealed that Conrad had had a severe mental breakdown as a result of what happened to him, fighting for the popular front at Madrid. It was the tension between idealism, human aggression in the pursuit of power, and sheer physical horror at death, which cracked him.

He did not attempt to make Pamela shut up. He seemed to find it a relief to have it explained. Clearly, Pam had an important therapeutic function for Conrad, and indeed herself.

"I understand," said Leonard. "Much the same as my experience in France 1917. How did you get yourself out of the mental mess?"

"I had been trained as a doctor and a psychiatrist, that's why I went to Spain, to help as a doctor. I thought Communism was a benign philosophy, morally good. The trouble is that war and revolution stir scum to the top and you either sink or smother in it or climb on the rest. I did sort myself out, but only after suffering thoughts as deep and dark as hell: and other people helped me." He looked at Pam with gratitude.

"My experience was much the same except I found my peace with God."

"Yes, I can see that. You're lucky; perhaps my scientific training stunts my spirit."

"Of course not. I know Christian Scientists are supposed to resist medical science like the devil, but I never feel any conflict. If we are both trying to heal an unbalanced condition, how can there be any conflict. As a psychiatrist you no doubt agree that what heals is peace of mind. A very illusive condition."

"Oh look! There's 'The Soldier's Return', we've time for a drink. When's the train due?"

“At two-forty p.m. We’ve got twenty minutes. I’ll just go and check the arrivals, set me up with a large G & T.” With that, Pamela was off to the station. Conrad ordered the G & Ts and Leonard had his cider.

Chapter Five

Back in Sheffield Leonard had once again immersed himself in his healing practice, which was expanding rapidly because of the positive results of his clear thinking and calming presence. It wasn't faith. It was a vision of man's perfection; his divine identity, his freedom from the body. Rheumatic fever, food poisoning, bladder troubles, septicemia, depression, all receded from the patients with his help, either absent or present.

To a young man in his mid-thirties the hills of Sheffield were an exhilarating challenge, especially when assisted by the best tramways in the country. Those proud double-decker, cream coloured, sparking, singing, flanged and kissing cabled cars. Each swaying vessel driven by a gloved commander, whose majestic progress along the tram at each reversing terminus was a presence like an admiral on a quarter deck. His first lieutenant, who had no gloves, only finger mittens, was the fountain of all wisdom and good humour. His blackened fingers, raking through the coppers in his bag and pinging his silver punch, gestured like the comedian he always was.

"Come on, love; us can see y'er full on top!"

"Does yer mother know you're out?"

"Ee! He's got a bum like two duck eggs in a navvy's muffler."

But what about a car? A car can be an idea of God, to speed

his presence! Which is why Leonard went to see Mr. Handley. Mr. Handley was a motor engineer and had a garage that had a petrol pump and did repairs to cars that some would say were un-repairable. Leonard had met him at church and helped him solve financial problems about the garage; Mr. Handley had a Singer Tourer 1927 which he said would suit Leonard. Leonard went to see it.

Although nine years old it was a magnificent sight to a first time buyer. It was dark red with black solid wheels; its chassis projected aggressively at front and rear repelling collision like a tank. The black hood stretched as a faded umbrella over the scratched, black leather bench seats. The impression was that all was perfectly prepared for a bath in the open air. The engine rumbled like distant thunder, or the eight galloping horses credited as its power pack. The sum of £10 was exchanged and the car was Leonard's. A cover note was issued and a notice stuck on the windscreen to say 'License applied for' and Leonard was away like Mr. Toad.

He shot up Psalter Lane, or rather ground through all the gears to reach the top. He swept along Ringinglow Road; or rather he felt his hair streaming in the twenty-five mile an hour breeze. He screeched to a halt outside 92 Stafford Road, or rather he slowly squeezed the tyres against the granite curb. But it was true that he leapt out of the singing Singer and rattling his key in the door, called out,

"Edie, come and look. I've bought the car. Come for a ride."

But Edie shook her head and would only view it from behind net curtains. It was the only car in the road; it looked like showing off!

"Ee! I'll come and look at it. Just a minute, I'll get a scarf for me curlers."

It was Doris. She had now come to live with them after a particularly violent quarrel with her father, in defence of her mother.

"Me too," shouted Tony, appearing behind Doris. He was looking strangely feminine with a prominent wave at the front of his blonde hair. This was Doris' work. She fancied herself as a hairdresser and while doing her own hair, had set Tony's. She used her personally concocted setting lotion made from sugar and water. It was very effective and when dry, left the hair rigid in whatever shape she had created.

In this case it was a wave of such depth that it appeared to be about to break over his forehead. Tony submitted to this pampering willingly, because Doris would sit him astride her knee while she tucked and combed. This gave him a delicious feeling in those areas of his body which were now of priority interest to him at the age of twelve.

Doris and Tony and Leonard sat in the Singer. Tony pretended to drive. Doris pretended to be Ginger Rogers waving to her fans from the rear seat; Leonard beamed proudly, and recognised an idea of God when he saw one.

"Leonard, the telephone's ringing." Edith was relieved to have an excuse to get them out of the car and off the road.

"Hello! How nice to hear your voice, Madame Bronowski." Mme. Bronowski was one of Leonard's more exotic local patients. She, for want of a better term, was a 'White Russian'. She had come to Sheffield some years before, having lost her husband in the Revolution and had earned a precarious living as a teacher of music, singing and the piano. When pupils were scarce she would sell another diamond, of which she seemed to have a substantial store. Leonard treated her from time to time to alleviate her arthritis, when it affected her playing. The call was about such a problem.

"Would you like me to come and see you?" Leonard was eager to use his new car. "Yes, of course. I'll come now."

Leonard let in the clutch with great skill and dignity and pulled away from the curb, watched by the admiring Tony and Doris. Leonard bowled along tree lined Eccleshall Road avoiding the tramlines shining down each side. Clouds were turning the sky grey but no rain as yet. He tried the windscreen wiper and it worked. The tiny blade wagged a fan shaped wedge on the glass.

Mme. Bronowski lived in a large flat on the middle floor of a semi-detached Edwardian house in leafy Eccleshall. A very suitable location for a piano teacher of her distinction and elegance. Leonard rang her bell and noted the twitching of the ground floor curtains while investigation was made as to the visitor to first floor front.

Madame descended the stairs as she always did, like entering a ballroom. She always dressed in full-length lace, which added a faint rustle to her presence.

"Le-onard, do come up." She always addressed him as Leonard, giving it the intonation with her slight Russian accent, of Le-on. That she admired his dark haired, blue eyed beauty, had always been apparent, but Leonard had always remained determined to stick to spiritual matters.

The flat reflected her background and some of the photographs always reminded Leonard of Guy's collection. The grand piano dominated the room and on it were silver frames surrounding uniformed men and courtly dressed women, one of which was her. Leonard never enquired into her history, he just let Olga tell what she wanted to reveal, which was not much. She liked to give the impression that she was an escaped aristocrat, but Leonard rather thought that she had been a governess. At least she didn't claim to have a title as most White Russians did.

"You seem to be having trouble with your hands, do you? Let's talk a little and get a clear thought about the Truth."

"Will you hold them?"

"I don't need to do that. Divine Mind will do the work."

"But I know it will be a great comfort to me to feel your touch."

"Just close your eyes and think of some of your favourite music being sensitively played on your piano."

She did as she was told and Leonard escaped any greater intimacy. He talked to her for a few minutes, reminding her that touch and sensitivity was a divine attribute, part of her spiritual identity and individual expression. Her hands became relaxed and she began to play some Chopin. There was now nothing wrong with her joints, if indeed there had been before!

"Thank you, Le-onard," she smiled and looked into his eyes with something of the depth of a Russian forest. "Will you have some tea?"

Leonard did not resist this, as she always served it from a samovar, which was kept beside her, ready with hot water. Its heat, and the odour of the spirit lamp comforted the room.

"That boy of yours…"

"Yes, Tony."

"You should have his voice trained. I stood in front of him in church last Sunday. His voice has broken well; it will be a fine baritone, a bass even. I could start him off and teach him music."

"Yes he does enjoy singing, I know. I'll think about it."

"What does he want to do?"

"Well, at the moment he wants to be a naval officer, but I don't know if it will last."

"That is good. The Royal Navy is aristocratic; he can make

a social climb."

"Perhaps," said Leonard, who thought of how he had brought him up not to play with soldiers. He wouldn't let him have a fort for Christmas; he gave him a farm and a tractor.

"Well, I must be going now, I have another call to make." Leonard told his white lie to avoid further intimacy as the tea drinking came to an end. He was not indifferent to Olga's statuesque charms and Edie's sexual frigidity showed no sign of melting. He felt a disturbing vulnerability.

"I have a car now." Leonard could not help making the proud announcement.

"I am so pleased for you Leon-ard. Perhaps you would give me a ride some day!"

"Oh yes I will," said Leonard rashly, in his eagerness to get away. "Goodbye."

"Goodbye. I will see you down the stairs." And the rustling perfume enveloped him as he escaped from the front door.

She stood and waved at him as he surrendered his dignity by stooping to swing the starting handle below the brass domed radiator. The 1927 model was not equipped with an elegant electric starter! Fortunately, he had correctly adjusted the ignition and switched on, so that the tough little Singer started like its namesake the sewing machine. He climbed in, waved nonchalantly and pulled away from the curb.

It had now begun to rain quite heavily, but the hood was already up and the windscreen wiper was fanning away the raindrops, so he gathered speed confidently. The road was lined on either side by beech trees whose black shining trunks gleamed in the wet. The surface was cobblestoned and had a single track tramline in the centre.

He glanced down at the petrol gauge, wondering whether he had enough to get home: there was. His relief turned to concern when, as he looked up, he saw a tram rocking towards him down the track, splashing wet out of the rails. Concern became panic when he found that an attempt to turn to the right of the tram left the steering wheel impotent in his hands; he was stuck in tramlines as the tram loomed larger and larger in his windscreen. He wrenched again; a stubborn slide. He wrenched the other way and this time applied the brakes desperately. Success; he was free but heading directly at a beech tree which now leaped at the Singer like a wrestler.

There was a bang like a tank going over a cliff and for a fleeting instant Leonard had the image so common in Tony's comics, of a pair of wheels embracing a tree with a crumpled bonnet giving rise to a plume of smoke as a car crashed into a tree. Then his nose hit the steering wheel, his shins scored the dashboard, and all the breath went out of his body.

The next he knew was the crowd from the tram helping him out of his crumpled car and asking,

"Are you all right, we thought you were dead!"

"Yes, I'm all right." This was a challenge for Leonard to assert his faith. Into his mind came the certainty that God's protection was always with us all his healing power is omnipotent and immediate. Streaming with blood and two black eyes beginning to form, the evidence to the crowd was less than reassuring.

The tram conductor dabbed at his streaming nose with the lint from his first aid box. "Can you walk?"

"Yes, I can walk." He demonstrated by walking round to the front of the car where it embraced the tree, to see that the starting handle had penetrated the trunk like a drill.

"We'll get you an ambulance. You need a hospital for that nose."

"No, really, I'll be all right."

“Well, they won’t have you on a tram in that state. How will you get home; where do you live?” Leonard did not know quite how to deal with this problem but just then a car drew up. It was Tom Handley stopping to see if he might pick up some business with a wrecked car.

“Leonard, it’s you. Are you all right; it doesn’t look as though the Singer is. Shall I take you home?” Mr. Handley knew Leonard wouldn’t want to go to hospital.

“Oh! Please, Tom.”

“Right then. I’ll deal with this lot later.”

Leonard climbed gratefully, if painfully, into Tom Handley’s comfortable Austin Twelve and sighed with relief.

“Thanks, Tom. You’re a God send!”

“I know I am,” grinned Tom.

***

When Leonard was delivered home, bloodstained but walking, Edith and Tony and Doris all greeted him in character.

“You are God’s perfect creation; there can be no absence of protection; you are whole and complete,” said Edith.

“Ee! You look as if you’ve lost the world heavyweight championship title, Len. I’ll get you a cup of tea.” said Doris.

“Dad, where’s the Singer?” asked Tony.

Tom Handley had stopped and telephoned on the way home, so they weren’t too shocked.

“Will you come in, Tom?” asked Edie.

“Thanks, no, I’d better get on towing the Singer, thanks all the same.

“Thank you for all you’ve done, Tom; I’m glad you were there.”

“That’s all right; I expect I was guided eh?” He grinned and went off to sort things out.

"I think I want to go to bed," pleaded Leonard, and Doris took him upstairs and bathed him and put him to bed.

Leonard devoted the next few days to devout prayer and affirmation of the ever presence of God's love and protection. The swelling subsided, the stiffness relaxed, his broken nose restored its shape (as admired by Mme Bronowski) and then he began to worry about replacing the Singer.

Chapter Six

Moths fluttered like confetti in the dim beams of the Jowett's headlights. It was summer holidays again and Guy was taking Tony up to Cumberland. After shards of sun in the lakes and a setting western glow they were now burrowing through velvet darkness towards the farm where Guy had made another passing home in the summerhouse.

To relieve the boredom of the long drive Guy settled Tony on his lap and let him steer the tiny panting car. He thrilled to the challenge and gripped the wheel like a lover.

"Just keep your eyes ahead of the lights and follow the grass verge."

Tony concentrated as if he were landing a plane and Guy kept his foot on the accelerator at a steady twenty-five miles an hour.

It was midnight by the time they crunched up the drive to the house and Tony fell straight asleep in his clothes as Guy unloaded the car.

***

"What the bloody hell!" Tony woke with a start. Wilfred was ranting; cows were bellowing; the cowman was cursing and above all children were shrieking with delight in Spanish!

"Get off, get off!"

"Ole, ole."

Tony dashed out of the summerhouse towards the farmyard and saw four boys on four cows riding them like picadors and banging their sides with hazel sticks. Fortunately, the cows were of a no-horns variety so no one had been gored as yet, but one of the boys fell off, and was in danger of being badly trampled. However, he sprang up like a rabbit, unharmed, except for a massive cowpat which the panic stricken animal had expelled onto his face.

This was just what the situation needed before it became really ugly. Even the furious Wilfred burst out laughing and the cowman let fall his hay fork. The other Spanish boys collapsed too and slipped off the heaving cows.

"Mother, mother," Wilfred had recovered his anger and was bellowing in the house at Boothby.

"What is it, dear?" Lady Cecilia appeared, as she always did, from nowhere.

"Mother, I can't be doing with these Spanish kids any longer. They're ruining me; they throw stones at the chickens, they pull down my haystacks, frighten the horses and now they're riding my cows. Get rid of them."

"Please, Wilfred, calm down. You see they're very disturbed; they've been through a terrible civil war, their mothers and fathers have been killed by a brutal fascist army."

"Mother, I'm sorry, but I don't care. Get rid of them; or you may find them in a silo!"

"All right dear, I'll see what I can do."

Some weeks later, the boys who had been delivered by Hispano Suiza were returned by trailer and tractor to be repatriated to Valencia.

***

The next day was Sunday and the weekly drive from Banks Head into Carlisle and the Christian Science Church. Winifred was driving and arrived at Bertholme, Wilfred's farm, to collect Guy and Tony. Only Winifred in the family was a Christian Scientist. Her liberal parents were sympathetic but prayed to whatever power would continue to refine their intellects and be a moral force for good. Wilfred, her brother, prayed to his bankers and the gods of animals and corn; he was something of a pagan and the brilliant Nan knew that it could all be solved by equations.

What could not be solved by equations was that two minutes after Winifred arrived in her steaming Austin, with Jacob and Kate, a few moments later, in a cloud of dust, arrived Nana, the faithful sheepdog. She had followed the car down the hill and now stood panting and lolling unable to speak for lack of breath, but clearly her message was, "Why did you leave me behind; you know I like to go to church on Sunday!" So she did and sat on Tony's lap and licked his face like a lollipop.

Nana stayed in the car when they arrived at the church. Tony wanted to bring her in but was dissuaded and as compensation was seated next to Brigadier-General Shears. He was a war hero with a black eyepatch and an artificial hand. He was not in uniform but still seemed to be like a benign Captain Hook to Tony who boldly helped him find the hymns in the hymnal. He would have preferred him to be an admiral but Tony accepted him as a Christian soldier.

But the greatest excitement was to come when the Brigadier and Pauline, his pretty wife, all fox fur and feminine perfume, invited them back to Carlisle Castle where he was the Commanding Officer. They were to have drinks! What do

Christian Scientists do in such a situation? It was easy for Tony and Jacob and Kate, they had lemonade; the others had something pink that they called gin or sin. There were sandwiches as well so they didn't go hungry. Then the Brigadier had to change into his uniform for something that was going to happen in the afternoon.

"Would you like to come and help me, Tony? My batman is on leave today."

"Oh yes, please." Tony thought it meant a game of cricket but was not disappointed when he found that he had to lay out the smooth clothed khaki uniform on the bed. He arranged the gleaming medals so that they overlapped neatly. The vibrant colors of the ribbons denying the muddy carnage of their origin: the blood and blue of the D.S.O., the purple and white of the M.C., like a surplice on a priest; and the rainbow dazzle of the Mons Star, the War and the Victory medals; the 'The Great War for Civilization 1914-1919' embossed on its reverse.

"Those last three we call Pip, Squeak, and Wilfred, and that's my Sam Brown," said the Brigadier. Tony caressed the gleaming leather and the redundant brass rings that were there to hold a sword, and the studs to hold the holster for the revolver; violence tamed to ceremony. Brigadier Shears had dressed skillfully in khaki shirt and trousers; buttons surrendered to the flitting fingers of his good right hand and even his tie was loosely knotted. He just needed help with some adjustment and the settling of the jacket which Tony proudly gave.

"Would you like to be a soldier, Tony?"

"No I would not. My father doesn't like the army. I want to be a sailor."

"Your father was in the army, wasn't he?"

"Yes, he was."

"I've met him, you know; he helped me make up my mind to stay a soldier. He said I could do good work."

"Yes, he's always helping people decide what's right."

"Why do you want to be in the Royal Navy, does he approve?"

"Oh yes, he wants me to do what I want to do."

"Are you going to go to Dartmouth, then?"

"I don't know."

"Well, I hope it works out then. Thank you; you've got me ready, let's go."

***

The next excitement was when Guy had a letter from a family in Northumberland whose son was going through a severe nervous breakdown. They needed Guy's services of caring and could he come? They had heard of him through Winifred.

"Perhaps your father can help this young man; I'll introduce them."

Chapter Seven

The neo-classical elegance of Belsay Hall cast its sharp edged shadows over the embracing rhododendrons, and Leonard, once again arrived in a gleaming chauffeur driven six cylinder Austin. This car seemed to be the preferred transport for the modest aristocrat.

Mrs. Middleton was there to meet him at the porticoed steps of the entrance. She was the sane survivor of the family, mother of Laurence.

"Mr. Godley, thank you for coming. Did you have a good journey? Come and have some tea."

His bag was whisked away by a maid and the car silently melted into the stables.

"Laurence is resting upstairs just now, we'll meet him later shall we?"

"Yes of course." Leonard was glad to have time to take in this new world. The atmosphere was quite different to that at Boothby. Boothby was all buzz and intellect and cosy concern. Belsay was echoing empty, elegant despair. Mrs. Middleton addressed him as Mr. Godley; not like Winifred and her Leonard.

Tea was served in the library, a room bigger than Tony's Elementary School, and certainly holding more books. Although a cursory glance suggested that many had hardly been opened since the nineteenth century, the literary atmosphere intrigued him, and like the coal fire in the marble fireplace, flushed his face.

Somewhere on those bookshelves Leonard would have found the history of the house and family: four hundred years of border conflict. The original castle still stood hunched against the north, softened by its Jacobean additions, now occupied by the gamekeeper and family. Guns seem to suit it. In the early nineteenth century coal had been found under Sir Charles Middleton's extensive lands. The new wealth allowed the next baronet to return from his grand Tour and build an elegant classical country house. That, however, seemed to have been the last of the intellect; from then on it was the navy, the army and the air force for the reluctant non belligerent successors. This was probably the psychological problem and the trigger for collapse.

"Yes, it is good of you to come. I am rather in despair. I don't know how much Mr. Allan has told you but let me tell you about the family. Oh dear, it is so painful."

"You don't have to tell me it hasn't any power to hurt you anymore." Leonard knew that he must try to reduce her distress and fear if she and Laurence were to be helped.

"Yes, thank you I do understand. Your presence does help. All right then let's leave the past."

"Do you think I should meet Lawrence now?"

"Yes, of course. Perhaps it would be best if you went for a walk in the garden. It is so calming."

The garden was indeed a sanctuary. It was landscaped out of the nearby quarry which had provided the stone for the house. The path meandered in a gentle canyon formed by the excavation and planted with imported Himalayan trees and shrubs. Laurence was young and nervous but talked easily to Leonard about his fears. He was like a boy who didn't want to go back to boarding school.

The problem was that he knew his raging mental state was his protection from having to go back to the air force. How was he to be healed of one result without suffering the other? His derangement at Cranwell had been so violent that he had thrown himself out of the upper windows into the garden, claiming he could fly!

Leonard and Lawrence talked and walked on. Leonard sympathised and told of his own tortured experience in the trenches and how he had found a peace after the war. Lawrence uttered his fears of becoming like his elder brother and his father who had both taken their own lives. Leonard tried to separate Laurence from the power of the past.

Within a few days Laurence became secure in the knowledge that he was not to go back to the air force and that he could control his fears. Mrs. Middleton was grateful for the sense of peace that had come to the house.

"You have a son, Mr. Godley, don't you?"

"Yes I do."

"Would he like to come and stay here; it would be nice to have him here. How old is he?"

"He's thirteen now, and I'm sure he'd love to come."

"Very well, we'll arrange it."

Chapter Eight

"My dear Leonard,

Thank you for all your good work. I have the most wonderful news. Quite unexpectedly I heard from the family solicitors, that my father had died in Australia and left me a legacy of two-thousand pounds. I hadn't heard from him since he left Mother twenty years ago. I can hardly remember him and I didn't think he'd ever remember me. Well, it's all very thrilling and I'm sure it's the result of your clear thinking. I'm buying the lease on a house in Carlisle Square in Chelsea; the Sitwells live on one side and Douglas Fairbanks Junior lives on the other. I shall have to have them in! Not, I think, Sir Oswald Moseley who lives on the other side of the square! I hope there won't be any demonstrations. I'm very excited and as soon as I'm in you must come and stay. Love, Guy."

Well this was an exciting development. Guy had been brought up to be rich but had never had the substance since his father escaped to Australia with a younger woman, leaving Guy's mother (who was half blind) to live in a Pimlico basement supported by lodgers in her house above. She lived in darkness with the BBC wireless as her window on the world and her stick that rapped morse messages to her lodgers, one of whom was Guy. She had a mordant sense of humour that helped her survive and would, from time to time, ring up the BBC and enquire whether that girl who had just been singing was in dreadful pain, and could she help her. The BBC switchboard were very indulgent and came to know her well, and the girls even looked forward to her comments. When some years later she died in her sleep they even rang to ask what had happened to her.

Two-thousand pounds was hardly a fortune, even in 1937 but it did buy a short lease on a town house in Carlisle Square, Chelsea; the Sitwell's lived next door and Sir Oswald Mosely lived opposite. He opened an account with Peter Jones to fill it with his individual taste and enthusiasm. He even hired a live-in man servant in the person of Andrew from Banks Farm, Cumberland. Andrew with the red hair and the fresh face looked splendid in the tight fitting, white steward's jacket, Guy dressed him in. This was to be his training for getting away to sea.

"Come along, Edie, we're going to stay with Guy in London."

Edie shook her head and turned away. Leonard was firm and put the bags in the car. Tony was already sitting in it.

"Now come along, Edie, you know you'll like it when you are on your way." Leonard always had this terrible problem of getting her to leave the house. It was a disease; a craven fear of meeting people and experiencing new things. She knew it was wrong and irrational and that her Christian Science said it was, but she couldn't overcome her fear. She cowered into her deafness and shook her head.

Leonard simply dragged her into the car; she screamed as if scalded, and was rammed into the front seat. Tony was phlegmatic; he'd seen it all before. The broken Singer had been replaced by a beige and black bath tub with a canvas hood that called itself a Standard Big Nine. The registration letters were OG, which suited it perfectly. It was not quite the Austin six cylinder saloon of Boothby and Belsay but it was getting there.

Within half an hour down the A1, Edie was actually singing hymns and distributing sandwiches. Leonard had been quite right; she was enjoying the drive. She even continued singing hymns (though a little louder) when they hit freezing fog near Newark. Even when the windscreen wiper froze on the windscreen it was she who suggested that they open the screen on its ratchet so they could see straight into the fog.

"God is guiding us," she insisted. Tony certainly hoped he was because the headlights bounced off the fog into their eyes.

"Follow the frost on the grass verge," Tony said, remembering his vast experience driving for Guy. Fortunately it seemed that no one else was out in this terrible day so collisions were not a threat. Slowly the heat of approaching London melted the freezing and turned it just into fog. The lights of the suburbs enticed them to enter this great new world where no one knew anyone else and you could be as eccentric as you liked and no one would know.

Tony had been to London only once before, when Leonard took him on a cheap theatre trip. He began to recall that day, it helped to forget the freezing fog as it whirled past him and escaped through the cracks in the celluloid windows. It had been very wicked because it meant taking the afternoon off school using some fictitious excuse like a grandmother's funeral.

Three o'clock in the afternoon on Sheffield station was serenely calm. A puny porter with a dripping moustache, strained against the handle of his trolley piled high with mail bags, which threatened to overwhelm him. The iron wheels snapped at your toes as they passed, tickling smoke from the waiting engine sneezed up the nose. The train was almost empty (Ah! That's why the tickets are cheap.) They could have sneaked into first class but safer to stay in third, you might have to go to prison.

The fields rolled by where giant painters strode with a board on their shoulders advertising 'Hall's Distemper', (funny, I always thought distemper was what dogs had,) until another sleepy station awoke to whistles blown with pouting authority by station masters flagged like a coronation. At last it was St. Pancras; a cathedral, booming at six-thirty in the evening, with bowler hatted clerks rushing to their homes. "Some people take an hour to get to work in London," Leonard marveled.

"How wonderful," thought Tony.

"Where do we go now, to the theatre?"

"Trafalgar Square, there's a Lyons Corner House there." Leonard had been before. The Underground was an underworld of windy shrieks, snapping doors and eyeless people. 'Warren Street', how appropriate: 'Googe Street', how threatening: 'Leicester Square', how jolly, and 'Trafalgar Square', how imperial.

"It's a Cafeteria, that means 'help yourself'." explained Leonard.

"You mean you can have as much as you like?"

"Yes, but you have to pay for it."

"Oh!" A slight disappointment. "Beans on toast is the cheapest, let's have that," said Leonard. That is what the ragged man in front of them had; the man with the black fingers who paid in pennies.

The climb to the upper circle was a climb to heaven, the gods looked down on the golden court and the red velvet curtain glowed like fire. And then the play began and drew them in like Santa into a grotto. It was 'Time and the Conways', a J.B. Priestley from Bradford exploring Leonard's favourite theme, the subjectivity of Time; to Tony, a mystery, made magic by the voices of the actors.

Then it was back to the Lyons Corner House for egg on toast (almost as cheap as beans) making it last until midnight when they could set off for St. Pancras once more and the one o'clock train home. The scratchy plush of the narrow seats scrubbed Tony's naked knees but failed to lift his drowsiness that dropped like a sack of flour on his head; he slumped in the dim blue light and only awoke in smoky Sheffield. It was wonderful.

Andrew opened the door to them. Guy beamed his welcome from the first floor and invited them up. Andrew took their bags and coats with a newly learned grace. He even resisted a sneer as he took Edie's rabbit fur tippet.

"Come and have a drink. You must be exhausted." Guy was showing signs of reverting to smart society even though Science and Health and the Bible rested prominently on his new white marble coffee table; two new deluxe editions. There was, however, coffee as an alternative to whisky, gin, and sherry.

"So, you live upstairs?" Edie was puzzled.

"But, oh no. This is just how these London houses are arranged." Guy gently explained the function of the town house.

Edie remained sceptical. "What a lot of stairs." Andrew brought the coffee and Edie and Leonard sat back in the white cushioned sofas that faced each other over the white coffee table. Everything was white, even the radiogram that Guy had had specially painted to cover its brown mahogany. The walls were white, the ceilings, the window frames, the banisters, the kitchen cupboards, the wardrobes; even the telephone was white: the telephone with letters on its dial, not just numbers; Flaxman, FLA, was the exchange. "How will he keep them clean?" thought Edie.

The one exception was the front door; it was bright yellow.

"I'll show you to your rooms; you can have a rest and then I thought it would be nice if I took you out to dinner at a charming Italian restaurant I know in the King's Road." That sounded lovely Tony thought; Edie was not so sure, but she accepted the rest gratefully.

Bertorelli's was bustling with diners and the windows onto the street were steamed against the cold night air. Waiters, some very young, some incredibly ancient, balanced plates piled with spaghetti bolognese on massive silver trays, and still carried carafes of wine in their other hand. The aroma of parmesan and basil, the tang of pepper and the exciting reek of gorgonzola summoned the appetite. Oh the noise, and all these people calling each other "darling" in drawling voices, and puffing at cigarettes. Nobody called each other "love" and whispered and scraped their knives and forks on thick plates as they did in Sheffield.

"Signore Allen, your table awaits." Signore Bertorelli knew how to charm his customers and Guy was living, once again, the life he had had to leave. He glowed with pleasure. "Now, Edie won't you have a little wine: it is mentioned in the Bible you know," Guy twinkled. But Edie stuck to water. She had been too close the evils of drink not to be afraid of it. Leonard, however accepted it as evidence of abundance and generosity, so did Tony, but he was forced to have water with his.

***

Leonard and Edith had to go back to Sheffield again on the Tuesday but it was arranged that Tony would stay on with Guy. Leonard went reluctantly, Edith with glee, and Tony stayed with anticipation. He wandered round 13 Carlisle Square's white stacked stairs; he went into the basement and fantasised with Andrew about the sea and ships. Andrew did not give the impression that he was eager to exchange the ease of Chelsea, and one bachelor gentleman, for fifty seasick passengers. However, he loved the romance of the sea and he liked to talk of the discomfort of Banks Head farm from which he had escaped.

Tony played Guy's collection of Noel Coward records with the wonder of the young, assuming that these witty tunes had always existed in the adult world; quite unaware that they were there because they were the latest fashion.

Guy would be round the corner in Manresa Road at the Chelsea School of Art where he had enrolled himself and enjoyed the bohemian company. He had made a friend in Derek who was half his age and a fine painter. But that was not every day. On other days Guy would take Tony to Soho for the exotic shopping; the special coffee, the salami, the Gorganzola cheese, the wine, the rice, the mate tea. All the things that intoxicate the nostrils.

"Would you like one of my special biscuits young sir?" The oozy proprietor of the Turkish Alimentation in Greek Street beamed from behind his crowded counter. The dimness of the interior was swathed in the perfumes of Turkish Delight, pungency of coffee, the power of the salamis.

"Would you, Tony?" Guy was trying to be protective; he knew Tony wouldn't like it.

"Yes, thank you very much," said the ever eager to please Tony, and took the biscuit and bit it. The taste exploded in his mouth and dried it like a dentist's powder. He immediately wished he was a parrot as the seeds in toffee were clearly designed to please only a bird.

"Do like it?" The unctuous Turk was equally eager to please.

"Oh, yes, very much, thank you." Tony's face flushed with embarrassment at his barefaced lie and the discomfort of swallowing the rest of the vile seeds. What would happen if the Alibaba offered him more! He did; but generously gave the packet to Guy to take home. Guy bought twice as much coffee as he had intended, which after all had been the point of the little farce.

Next it was to the Charing Cross Road and the bookshops. Guy was in search of books on Bali which he said he intended to visit. Tony had read some Joseph Conrad because it had to do with sailing and the sea, so he did have an image of that far mysterious place and its undulating dancers. The pavement in front of the bookshops was half full of gaberdined and hatted men craning and peering towards the bookcases on the street and the art books in the windows. Each seemed to be lost in his personal search for a different life. It was the lunch hour and boredom and drudgery faded in their fantasies of rare editions undiscovered, sexual enlightenment unfulfilled, academic brilliance unrecognised, and the great novel still to be stimulated. Guy found his lavishly illustrated book on Bali. He paid a whole two pounds to the astrakhan collared proprietor, whose oval Turkish cigarette stuck to his lips as the pungent smoke dribbled up his nose.

They walked back towards Trafalgar Square and passed the matinee queues at Wyndham's, breached now and then by the arrival of a taxi and two or three tippet furred ladies. There they were greeted by the ex-service Commissionaire, his Pip,

Squeak, and Wilfred on his chest; that initiation into membership of the Corps of Commissionaires for a life time of salutes and a handful of coppers. But these were thoughts that had no place in Tony's mind as he sat high on the bus in Victoria Street, feeling the itch of his first long trousers against his knees.

"How do they feel?" asked Guy. "Grown up," beamed Tony.

Chapter Nine

But it was not 'The Army & Navy Stores' in Victoria Street that remained in Tony's memory, it was 'The Fifty Shilling Tailors' in Castle Gate, Sheffield. Tony had been invited to Belsay Hall by Mrs. Middleton. She had not forgotten her promise to Leonard when he was helping Lawrence out of his breakdown. Lawrence was now at forestry school in Edinburgh and doing well in a new career, and Tony was invited to Belsay for the Easter holidays.

Leonard said that in the country people wear tweeds; Tony must have tweeds: Harris Tweeds? Tony had heard of Harris Tweeds. Well no, not exactly. Harris Tweeds are rather expensive, we'll go and see what 'The Fifty Shilling Tailors' can offer. They offered a whole suit, including waistcoat, in purple hopsack, which they called heather, for fifty shillings. This price obliterated all concern about the see-through nature of the cloth, the sharpness of the shoulder pads, and the bagginess of the trousers, which were, after all, the height, (or width?) of fashion, sir.

The parcel was hugged all the way home then jumped on lovingly to mature the shoulder pads, after which it had the lived-in look. Then there was the question of the dinner jacket. At Belsay it was the custom to dress for dinner. It would have to be Leonard's own. Fortunately, Tony had grown like a weed in the last year and though only fourteen, was five feet nine inches tall. This meant that with a certain amount of acquired nonchalance, such as keeping one's hands in one's pockets as often as possible, one might disguise the fact that only one's fingernails appeared below the cuffs. The trousers were hoisted by braces until Tony's eyes watered and the general effect, in candlelight, was not bad. The effect was somewhat spoiled, however, when on the first night the maid had unpacked Tony's case in the wrong room. The result was that Tony was pleasantly surprised when dressing for dinner that his suit fitted much better than he remembered.

He was just admiring himself in the cheval mirror when Ocky, the guest next door, came into the room in his underpants and said

"I think the maid's made a mistake; I think this must be yours, it doesn't fit me."

Tony's blush almost betrayed that it did not fit him either and that the label was considerably less distinguished. However, he braved it out and laughed,

"I thought it fitted me too well!" as he reluctantly took it off.

"Sorry about that," breezed Ocky, and went back to change.

Betty the maid of all work, struck the dinner gong heartily and its echoes opened the bedroom doors of the guests who now trickled down the stairs in ones and threes. The one was Tony who was first, determined not to be late for his first dinner party and who wished to avoid too close a scrutiny of his dinner jacket. The three were Ocky with his Etonian friend Michael and Lady Sylvia. The stairs were broad enough for the boys to be either side of Sylvia who, indeed, pressed closer than the width of the stairs required. This was because Sylvia was probably the prettiest lady ever seen by these blushing young men. She had short, waved, light brown hair that showed her slender neck to perfection. The promise of smooth, pale shoulders rose from a long dress of silk georgette. It was humming bird blue and clung and floated as she swayed to each descending step.

Mrs. Middleton was presiding and inviting her guests to take sherry in the library. Tony took the offered glass and waited to see what the others would do. It seemed rather small, though beautifully cut, glowing like an amber jewel in the firelight. Would they gulp it down and throw it in the fireplace or was that only in films about Russia that Guy had taken him to see. It was just as well he waited because everyone began to sip.

"I don't think you have been properly introduced, have you? You all arrived at different times." Mrs. Middleton began to identify them. She started with Sylvia. "This is Sylvia, my niece, who is on holiday from Kenya where she is a great success but finds it a little exhausting."

"Yes, Aunt Janet, it is exhausting, and it's not the heat I can tell you."

There was a swoop of her eyelids that invited erotic speculation as to the exact nature of her exhaustion.

"This is Tony, son of my dear friend, Leonard Godley, who has helped so wonderfully with Lawrence."

Tony also swooped his eyelids but in embarrassment.

"This is Janet, my friend and Michael's aunt." Janet smiled a smile that that seemed to smother a bitterness.

"Michael and Ocky, as you know, are old school chums, now at Oxford, no doubt wasting their father's substance, but having a jolly time."

"No, we must protest, we are both very serious. I'm in the University Air Squadron…"

"And I'm in the cadet force because I'm going in the

Guards. There's going to be a war you know."

"Oh. I do hope not. Let's go and eat."

The meal had further social hurdles for Tony; there were finger bowls and local shrimps, and grapes and scissors, and a whole armoury of knives and forks, and white and red wine, and different glasses, and of course his long sleeves. But the kindness of his hostess and his companions helped him with gentle anticipation and demonstrations so that by the end of the meal even without the wine he would have been confident to eat at Buckingham Palace. Only Miss Fellowes appeared to scorn his ignorance, or envy his confidence.

The conversation at dinner was mainly about country pursuits and what to do tomorrow. Ocky, who was heading for the Guards, was horsey and had noticed that there was a Point to Point steeple chase not far away.

"I wish I had a mount here, I could have joined in."

"I think it would have been a bit late for that," Janet Middleton suggested, "But Robson has a horse he would lend you. He's my gamekeeper. At least you could ride to the meet. You look a bit heavy though, how much do you weigh?"

"I'm only thirteen stone; lean as an oak, nothing flabby about me." This remark was directed towards Sylvia who appreciated the reference with a flashing eye.

"Anyone want to come with me? I won't bother to ride if they do. What about you, Sylvia? You look as if you like a bit of jumping."

"All right then, I'll come." Ocky glowed.

"What about you, Michael?"

"Well, if you'll excuse me, I think I'd like to fish. How's the lake, Aunty?"

Pamela Fellowes was startled to be asked a question. It was Michael trying to bring her into the conversation. He knew that she fished. Sitting alone in a boat in the middle of a lake suited her sense of isolation and blank prospects; forty-six seemed terribly old.

"Oh! It's quite lively; I took a two-pound trout out the other day." She even registered a blush of pleasure as she recalled the triumph and enjoyed the opportunity to report it.

"I say, that sounds exciting, well done," said Ocky. For a moment he gave the impression that Pamela's skill had possible charms, but no, Sylvia was the catch.

"Tony, I have something special I want you to help me with. Every Easter the local Boy Scouts come and camp on the estate and they like me to inspect them. This year I thought it would be nice if you would do that for me. They are your sort of age and you did say that you wanted to go in the Royal Navy, so it would be good practice. I believe they do this sort of thing all the time."

"Well, yes, of course; if you think I can."

Tony was half thrilled and half appalled. Would they notice his hopsack tweeds and his epaulette shoulder pads, his Yorkshire accent? No they wouldn't, they were only local lads, lads just like himself. But then they would expect him to be different or it wasn't worth being inspected, was it? Perhaps just a little acting was called for and everyone would be satisfied.

The next morning after mastering the sideboard silver with its treasures of scrambled egg, crispy bacon, mushrooms, fried bread, coffee and thick white, warm toast, Tony found himself alone and free to wander about the house, to explore its slumbering rooms.

Belsay Hall was not a big house by country land owning standards. It was built strictly on the classical plan of a Greek temple. It had a central atrium lit by a vast lantern skylight from above. A gallery overlooked the marble hall on three sides and the broad stone staircase filled the other. It had only three living rooms; these were on the south side of the house and faced the terraced gardens and the lake and the wooded crag beyond. The rest of the ground floor rooms were administrative. On the first floor there were about six bedrooms arranged around the gallery.

Tony sat for a moment, alone in the library where they had gathered the night before. It had been dim then, and focused on the lamps near the marble pillared fireplace. Now in the cold northern morning light from four deep sash windows, it was cool and silent and lost. Oak and leather in rigid perpendiculars repelled the reader who would disturb the patterned library walls. He shivered and moved to the welcome of the study.

This was where the guests wrote home, or to schools, or to Africa or India. The Honduras mahogany desk glowed in its obeisance to the mother country. Tony sat in the leather bottomed seat and took up the pen with the authoritative relief nib, dipped into the blue-black ink and under the crested headed paper began… Dear Mummy and Daddy.

His excitement flowed over the paper and ended with the boast that this afternoon he was to inspect a regiment of scouts. He folded the thick paper into four and placed it like a sandwich in the equally thick envelope. He walked with it to the hall and placed it on the silver tray for collection and stamping: what luxury!

He continued on up the broad stone staircase, with its bright brass moulded handrail and went to a corner of the gallery where a swing door led to the attics and the servants' back stairs. The silence was intense. The bare treads worn into polished depressions by the timid feet of country girls, scurrying down and crawling up, to tiny bedrooms, now unused. No servants lived in the house now except Betty, the maid of all work, and she had a room on the first floor north side; the rest came in daily from the village.

In the bedroom corridor was a broad door with a bright skylight over. He opened it tentatively as if there might be no floor beyond. The light flooded over him and drew him into a room as long as the side of the house, crowded with discarded furniture and dusty artefacts. The disturbance of his presence was enough to raise a halo of dust about the full dress uniform of a lieutenant governor of the County. He boldly took the cocked hat and preened it on his head. He even drew the ceremonial sword and tapped the shoulder of the tailor's dummy which acknowledged with another puff of dust. He sat in a wheezing armchair and admired the tiny marble breasts of an eager nymph. He touched them tenderly but they did not respond. He was deflated by the chilling white of a massive bedpan and rekindled by a model yacht almost as tall as he was. It was a dream of a past life stranded on a barren shore; it was like a Jean Cocteau film that Guy had taken him to see: "La Belle et La Bete."

After dinner that evening, when Janet Middleton and Pamela Fellowes had retired (Pamela, no doubt, to read to Mrs. Middleton until she fell asleep), the boys, Ocky and Michael, proposed a game of 'Murder'. The main object of this game was to create a situation in which there was a jolly good chance of being able to kiss Sylvia. It was explained to Sylvia that she should go and hide and that the first of them to find her would murder her! Sylvia may have played this game many times before in Kenya because she seemed to understand completely and quickly left the room.

"Give her a few minutes to find a really good place," said

Ocky, "And then off we go."

A few minutes later Tony was slowly groping past a wardrobe on the gallery when the door cracked open and Sylvia's insistent whisper stopped him.

"Tony! Do you know a better place? I don't want to be caught."

Tony gulped at this unexpected intimacy, reinforced by her numbing perfume and muttered,

"Yes I do." Thinking of the swing door to the attic stairs.

"Come on then, show me." And took his hand. It was like holding a live wire. His heart was beating double in his chest and moving down his body. He led her quickly to attic stairs where they sat and giggled like theatre fans in the gallery. She kissed his cheek and said, "Thank you, I didn't want to be caught by them, only you."

Tony sighed and thought of the tiny breasts of the marble nymph.

Eventually the plaintiff cries of "We give up," from Ocky and Michael had to bring Tony's heaven to an end.

"You go first," he said, "or they'll be jealous of me."

"You sweety, all right," and she kissed him again. Tony couldn't sleep a wink that night.

The next day was the day of the inspection. His adventure with Sylvia had a significant effect on his bearing as he stood on the top step of the pillared entrance to receive the salute of the Scout Master.

"Patrol ready for inspection, Sir."

The hopsack tweeds stiffened with pride (or fear). Tony clutched his hands behind him and pouted his chest. Although descending the four deep steps to the level of the Patrol, with hands still clutched behind him, suggested an acrobat attempting a somersault on a rolling ball, dignity did not totally desert him.

He knew that he had to precede the Scout Master along the ranks of the Patrol, the newsreels of the recent coronation celebrations had been helpful in this respect. He knew that he must avoid eye contact and appear severe but appreciative of their kerchiefs and toggles. He must find a point for communication with at least three scouts. He picked on an arm vibrant with heraldry and congratulated the boy on his range of badges. He found another with a sheath knife in his stocking and asked to be shown the blade so that he praised its shine. He found another scout with particularly crisp brim to his hat and praised his appearance. He turned to the Scout Master and congratulated him on a fine body of boys, wished them a happy encampment and asked them to "Carry on."

As he returned the parting salute and watched them march away he felt there was little left to achieve in life. It was at this point that he suddenly felt dizzy and started to fall over. He realised that during the whole of this exercise he had scarcely breathed, so fierce had been the clutching of hands behind his back and the pouting of his chest. He sat on the steps with a deep sigh and was glad to see that the patrol had turned the corner out of sight. Did they see through me and my hopsack he wondered? But he decided that it didn't matter if they did, he wasn't cut out for superiority, perhaps he wouldn't be an Admiral after all, better be an actor and just play the parts.

For the rest of the holiday that is what he did; play the part of a young gentleman. The gamekeeper taught him to shoot rabbits and pigeons with alarming skill. He taught him to kill a wounded rabbit with one positive tug at the jaw. He rode a determined pony that streaked over the fells in uncontrolled glee and brought him back again like an empty sack. He was a distinguished guest at the launching of a ship and the enthronement of a Bishop: the one ascending on a throne, the other descending in a wave; one in Durham's English perpendicular, the other in Tyneside's slanting steel.

Just before he left, Michael Fellowes made Tony a wonderful promise.

"I know you're keen on the sea and sailing, well I've got a yacht and I'll take you to France in the summer; would you like that?"

"Oh yes, I would; thank you."

"All right then, I'll let you know; bye, bye."

That then was Tony's dream as the train rattled back to Sheffield.

Chapter Ten

"With fully expanded chest (shoulders relaxed) hum down the scale from A to C, prolonging the hummed 'm' on each note." Leonard was practicing his voice production in the front room.

"When from the clock's last chimmmme,
Silence beats his drummmmm,
Space with her gaunt grey eyes and her brother Timmmmme,
Wheeling and whispering commmmmme."

A Christian Science lecturer was coming on a tour from the United States and Leonard was to introduce him at the Sheffield City Hall before an expected audience of fifteen hundred people all eager to hear the healing word. This was an opportunity that he was eager to take and he had been working diligently on the content of his introductory remarks, for which he was allowed ten minutes. He knew the lecturer's reputation for spiritual inspiration and was determined to equal his perception. He would talk on the subject of 'peace', peace of mind in a world haunted by want and war.

That morning there had been a telephone call from Guy who asked Leonard for spiritual help with his finances. It seemed that his bank had written to him.

'Dear Mr. Allan, I am sure you will forgive us if we remind

you that your overdraft now stands at £1412. Perhaps you have some suggestion for reducing it.'

Their tentative politeness concealed an iron unwillingness to cash any more cheques. Leonard's advice was practical; he asked the question, "Do you have any assets?"

"I suppose I have the value of the balance of the lease," sighed the miserable Guy.

"Then sell it and clear your debts."

"But where will I live?"

"Back with Mother," said Leonard firmly.

"Oh dear," sighed Guy again.

"I'll work on it; it will work out harmoniously, just don't resent it, see it as an opportunity."

"Yes, Leonard: opportunity for what?"

"Further freedom from matter," said Leonard confidently.

Actually it did work out quite well because Guy's friend from Chelsea Art School, Derek, was the beneficiary of a family trust that gave him an income of £2.10 shillings a week. Prayer suggested to Guy that this would be sufficient to underwrite the establishment of an Art School in Mousehole, Cornwall. To begin with its reputation would be less than that of Chelsea but time would soon reverse that.

Derek had a contact in Mousehole who knew of a suitable building which had a kitchen and two rooms over a studio. The odour of pilchard would soon be eradicated by fresh air and garlic. The current price of pilchards recommended to the landlord that a rent of five shillings a week would show an increase on his income; the lease was signed and the move from Carlisle Square rapidly achieved to the satisfaction of the bank, the Cornish landlord and Guy and Derek. Also to the satisfaction of John Lambourne. John Lambourne had also retreated to Cornwall having been expelled as an unsatisfactory husband and father from his marriage to the daughter of a Lord Mayor of London. As her brilliant and handsome artist protégé, winner of the Prix de Rome, and son of a docker, he had been the centre of a glorious social experiment. Unhappily the acquisition of wealth had withered his artistic ambition so that the Lord Mayor's daughter came to the wise conclusion that it would be better for the future development of all parties if John were separated from that wealth. A small holding (very small) was provided in Cornwall. An art school would perhaps avoid the painful need for digging.

Guy's property was perfect for the enterprise. It was an empty fisherman's net store with a living space above. It was on the harbour wall and the light streamed in from four wide windows. An advertisement was placed in 'The Times':

'Summer school of art newly established in Mousehole, Cornwall, Tutors include holders of the Prix de Rome and Diplomas from Chelsea School of Art.' The only response was from a painter in St. Ives who asked to have any overflow re-directed to him. It was fortunate that Derek had his two pounds ten shillings a week and John had his cabbage plot. John decided he needed another wife, Guy said he would send for Leonard. When the invitation arrived Leonard piled the family into the car and headed west.

This was going to be Tony's great summer; he had just been invited to sail to France on Michael's yawl 'Gwenilli'. Michael had not forgotten his promise: he could not go himself but he had leant his boat to a friend who would take Tony with him, leaving on the fourth of August from Lymington.

"Could Tony get there?" Could he! He would go to Cornwall first then to France. Leonard didn't seem to be as overjoyed about the arrangement as Tony was. Perhaps it was the looming political crisis that made him seem distracted; Hitler's expansion into Chekoslovakia. But the fourteen-year-old boy's mind was full of sun and sea.

"The boats are in; would you go along the harbour and have this bag filled with pilchards. Dan will know who you are." Tony took the paper carrier bag and ran along the harbour wall to where the 'Marjorie Jane' was unloading her catch.

"Chuck your bag down, then." Tony floated it down and it was filled like a bucket with water. Strong hands threw it back up and Tony caught it like a rugby full back. His face buried into the fish that smelt still fresh from the sea. He ran like a wing-forward to the studio, up the steps and splashed them on the kitchen table. The butter was already sizzling in the pan and soon the sharp dark iron knife was slipping out the fillets into the fat. The scent of butter, fish, and new-baked bread filled the room and appetites were roused and slaked.

"Abundance", thought Leonard;

"Bliss", thought Tony;

"Must paint Dan's portrait", thought Derek; "Must ask Leonard to pay the grocer for the butter," thought Guy; Edie thought pilchards were an idea of God's!

"We've all been invited to a puppet show at the Graces," said Guy. The Graces were twins of indeterminate age and sex. They had long black/grey hair that knotted in the wind and never came unraveled. The twins had a bird sanctuary mainly devoted to the healing of injured seabirds. There never seemed to be less than ten patients who screeched at you when you made inane enquiries about their health, but were easily mollified by a pilchard. The Graces other hobby was making and performing with puppets which they designed themselves and dangled inside a sinister proscenium arch decorated with the skeletons of their less successful patients. Bones were mounted on black velvet; they glowed in the darkened room, presumably from the phosphorescence that the bones had acquired from a short lifetime of eating fish! The puppet characters were equally sinister. Neptune was all head like a sperm whale, with a trident that painfully prodded the other characters who thwarted his designs. He had a consort called Marina who had a tiny head and was all thighs. Their relationship was combative. I suppose this was in the tradition of Punch and Judy.

"We must take some food," said Guy. "They never have anything to eat except cider." "All this emphasis on food," disapproved Edie, "Some people eat to live, and some of them live to eat." But Leonard said cider was all right.

It was quite a climb to the Graces; up a rocky path along the cliff towards Lamorna Cove, but it was a calm July evening and the view over the sea to the south towards the Scilly Isles was benign; the sun was still quite high in the sky as they disturbed the darting lizards on the path. One of the Graces had fixed them with the tripod telescope and was drawing them on through the lens towards the nestling cottage.

"Hello, hello," called Guy. "These are our friends, Leonard, Edie and Tony."

"Good, good, good, how lovely, come inside: mind Colin, he's a bit bad tempered."

This, just as a crumple-winged cormorant lunged at Edie's leg. Fortunately, Colin fell over before he could make contact. "We'll just know the truth for you, Colin, and your wing will be healed," reprimanded Edie firmly.

"We've brought some pasties." Guy knew that the Graces would be relieved to know they would have a supper. This in fact was one of their strategies for survival. They were very social but had no money for entertaining. They found that it worked quite well if their friends knew this and came with food to feed them all.

"We are doing well tonight, we have some other friends here and they've brought two fruit pies and fresh baked bread with cheese," said Grace number two. The size of the pies and the pasties when piled on the oil cloth covered table revealed that the Graces were going to be fed for the week. "Here, have some cider." A big stoneware pitcher was pushed across the table and a cluster of Bernard Leach mugs. That was his contribution when he came.

But it was not Bernard tonight, it was a new family who had taken the cottage in the cove for the summer, the Sterlings.

"Hello," said Guy, as it did not appear that they would be introduced. "I'm Guy, this Derek, Leonard, Edie and Tony."

The Sterlings appeared out of the sunny shadow of the fireplace. They were very handsome. There was mother and her two daughters. Jane, eighteen and Pamela about sixteen. Both Derek and Tony were immediately stricken dumb with love! Unfortunately, Tony and Derek for the same, Jane. Derek was fastest to offer Jane a pasty and Tony ate his with Pamela, looking over her shoulder at the animated Jane.

Edie filled her mug with water from the pump at the stone kitchen sink and sat in a wicker basket chair that seemed to be on the point of collapse. However, her tiny figure was safely supported by its creaking bottom. She surveyed this social animation with head shaking suspicion. "Do you like puppet theatre?" Edie jumped in her wobbly chair. It was one of the Graces speaking from behind her. Edie thought she was consorting with a witch and was unable to respond because she didn't hear what was being said. She smiled instead; the Grace was enchanted and took her hand and said, "Come with me."

She led her out of the cottage into the back garden where a

large wooden shed, apparently built out of driftwood and painted black with tar, filled the bottom of the small holding. Grace led Edie across the sun-slanted cabbages and opened the door into the puppet theatre. Inside it was also black, but hung with dyed curtains to keep out the light that would have shone through all those chinks in the planking. The theatre was prepared for the evening performance, with paraffin lamps swaying from the ceiling and set in rows at the front of the stage. The combined odour of seabird and paraffin suggested a temple to the sea.

"I want to show you our puppets," cooed Grace, as if presenting her baby. "This is our miniature albatross, the largest bird in the sea and the bringer of doom. All his feathers are from the wings of the tern. This is the white dove, all her feathers are from a dove, and she is the bringer of love." Edie was touched by Grace's sincerity and the beauty of the puppets; she stroked them gently and they seemed to live. "There are more." Grace led her onto the stage behind the proscenium arch to where the puppeteers could stand. There, ready to be called were rows of staring characters in exquisite clothes of jeweled silks. There were kings and queens and captains and sailors and ambassadors and beautiful princesses embracing handsome princes: a whole world of fantasy.

"Where are you?" The door flew open and sunlight banished the dream. "What are you doing; you mustn't touch the dolls, they are all arranged." Grace two, (or one?) was cross. "We're all coming in now, we shall begin."

The audience arranged themselves on the planks resting across empty oil drums collected from the shore. Tony tried to sit next to Jane but lost out to Derek and had to touch thighs with Pamela. A low pitched gong vibrated through the hut and silence fell on them all. Then Bali bells thrummed until a child's xylophone tinkled an insistent tune over a gently moving wind machine and thunder sheet.

There followed a tale of glory and doom out of which came at last, true love blessings born of youth. As the tinkling died away nothing could be heard but soughing of the evening breeze around the hut and human sighs.

Jane started the clapping to disengage her hand from Derek's. The rest joined in enthusiastically; it had been an exotic dream. The two Graces came to the front of the stage and bowed gratefully. As the party began to disperse Mrs. Sterling invited them all to come the day after next to her cottage by the beach in Lamorna Cove, "Bring a picnic and we can bathe."

"We'll come by boat; we can fish," jumped in Derek, already planning to carry off Jane like the Prince in the puppet story.

"That would be fun," said Mother Sterling, but Jane looked doubtful.

"Perhaps we could release Colin if we take him out to sea," said the Graces. "If you say so," said Derek, perhaps Edie's spell was about to work.

"Until Thursday, then."

The walk back to Mousehole was an easy descent with a late setting July sun casting long warm shadows from behind them.

Chapter Eleven

Leonard had a scheme which he had been working on for some time with Edie. Their sexual conjugation was still a source of frustration to Leonard, and of fear to Edie. There had been a few bungled attempts which had ended in tears. Leonard had therefore taken out a subscription to 'Health and Efficiency' and tried to interest Edie in the photography of the female nude. It had certainly interested Tony when he found the magazine in the empty house one day.

The emphasis was on beauty; finely lit natural settings with titles such as 'September Morn' were meant to arouse only the purest of sensations; still very pleasurable, Tony found it so, and apparently so did Edie. So much so that Leonard had been able to persuade her to agree to go to a remote place and be photographed. Perhaps it was the remoteness of the project that appealed to her, but she insisted that Tony should be with them. So it was arranged.

"We are off on our own today, Guy, so you can get on with your painting and we can explore."

"Yes, of course," Guy agreed, as if he knew of the plan and may have discussed it with Leonard. "Don't forget your camera."

The Standard Big Nine whined up the hill and headed towards Land's End. The summer of 1939 was promising a perfect harvest and the sun was soporific as they spread the tartan rug on the heath looking down towards the sea.

Leonard quickly took off all his clothes and so did Tony, somehow knowing that it was expected, but kept his shoes on. Edie knew what was expected too and slowly did the same. She repeated to herself all that Leonard had told her, that familiarity with the body would drive away sexual appetite and replace it with the contemplation of beauty. I suppose he could be right, she thought. But the beauty that she still gloriously retained, (she was only thirty-five) was not in the least repulsive. Leonard concentrated on the mounting of his camera on the tripod.

"I'm going climbing," called Tony and skipped away from embarrassment.

The granite cliffs jogged down to the surf two hundred feet below and he chose a tier to the left and above him. He knew about climbing because he lived in Derbyshire and had scrambled a lot on beginners' crags with other climbers. He knew the rules; never move without three firm, comfortable holds for your four extremities. Test for firmness at each move. Keep cool and look up to your objective, not down, and preferably don't climb alone.

In the joy of sunshine, buoyant with youth and glittering like the sea with naked strength, he was ignoring half these rules. He clutched at a granite ledge that came away in his hand; he swung like door hinged on his left foot and hand, and looked down to the surf below snarling like tiger's teeth, even in the calm swell of this summer's day. Mesmerized he watched the granite shard fall silently out of sight. Keep cool, look up, he remembered.

As if blown by an invisible wind his body swung slowly back on its hinges until he could grasp again at the broken ledge. It responded with a firm hold and then his right foot found the step he had been edging towards. Three more hand and foot holds and he was lying panting on the cliff top feeling weightless.

When he cautiously approached his parents he found them fully clothed again and a cloud was crossing the sun. The journey home was silent, it seemed that nudism had been a failure.

On the beach of the harbour there was an abandoned trawler, fatally rotting on its wooden legs, victim of the economic depression and the price of fish. The village boys with the impermeability of youth felt nothing of this, and invaded the boat with romantic fantasies of raging seas, pirates, battles at sea and discovery. Tony joined them and sometimes so did Derek. Today they went aboard to borrow the dinghy that dangled from its stern. It was high tide and the dinghy was floating. They brought their own oars and the essential bailing can as a cure for leaks. Today was the day of the promised picnic with the beautiful Sterlings in Lamorna Cove. The plan was for Derek and Tony to row round to the cove and rescue the girls, they even offered to carry the picnic but Guy thought it might be rather soggy by the time it completed the voyage. They were also taking fishing lines and smelly bait to demonstrate their manly skills and win hearts. The cloud that had crossed the sun the day before had gone away and the sea was warm and calm; bathing trunks were enough cover. Derek took the oars and his broad shoulders pulled them firmly round the coast.

The others went by car and scrambled down to the cove where they found the Sterlings and the Graces and Colin who was looking sleek; not ready to fly, but he looked fit enough to swim, and if he could swim he could fish and live.

Edie was addressing him firmly. “You are just one of God’s

creatures and he is protecting you." Colin looked confused but no longer bad tempered. He edged towards the sandwiches.

"Ahoy there, ahoy." It was Derek and Tony arriving and heading for the beach where they made a soft landing on the silver sand. "Do you want to come fishing, Jane?" Derek was quick off the mark, perhaps too quick.

"I'd rather swim first."

"You can swim from the boat, you know." Derek was too eager.

"I'm not good enough for that," Jane hedged.

"Yes, all right, we'll wait." Tony was relieved, she was too beautiful to leave and his heart ached for a kind look from her.

"We think Colin is ready to go to sea and fish," said the two Graces,

"Will you take us?"

"Oh! alright then, I will," said Tony, abandoning his hopes for a glance from Jane. "Oh! let me come too, I'd love to see Colin swim away." Derek had been outmaneuvered; there wasn't room for him and the Graces and Jane and Tony. "Are you sure you can manage?" pleaded Derek to Tony.

"Oh! Certainly" said Tony pulling away before anyone could change their minds.

Guy was already arranging the picnic and charming Mrs. Sterling. Women adored Guy, I think because they sensed there was no sexual threat. Of course if you were a woman who was looking for sexual threat, this could be frustrating.

He was exotic and ingenious with food. Most of his life he had only the minimum of material resources but always contrived to live as if surrounded by luxury. His naturally aristocratic air and gentle politeness covered a stubborn determination to get what he wanted because what he wanted was on a small scale. And he could charm a duke as easily as a baker. The baker in Mousehole was by now baking wholegrain bread that Guy liked and as a consequence, so did enough others.

He was now arranging open sandwiches of anchovy and gherkin and cream cheese on blue and white checkered napkins.

The dinghy had arrived in deep water beyond the cove in open sea. The launching of Colin was about to take place. The Graces took him in their hands, one on either side; both kissed his glistening head and gently lowered him into the luminous sea. For a moment he remained still as if surprised that he still could float, remembering the embrace of cool water which he had not felt for six long weeks. Then with a toss of his head he dived and swam deep down into his element. The crew waited anxiously for him to reappear. It seemed an age, but there he was quite near, and with a fish as if to say I can do it, I can do it, thank you Graces. They wiped away a furtive tear and Tony received the glance from Jane that he had been longing for. She smiled at him with what he hoped was affection.

"I don't think we should fish; Colin could take the bait by mistake; I've seen it happen before and that would be terrible."

"Oh! Yes, that would be awful," said Jane. "Let's go back then we can picnic and bathe."

"Yes, let's." and Tony began to pull for the shore.

"Will Colin come back to see you?" Jane asked.

"He might; they sometimes do, but they soon forget and go back to their real life." The Graces looked a little sad but soon cheered up at the thought of picnic.

The sand in Lamorna Cove was silken silver and left a sheen on the smooth wet bodies of the young: on those older bodies it left patches like laddered stockings. Jane shimmered like a mermaid; a simple black bathing suit embraced the grace of her hips and breasts and she cast sensuous shadows across the grateful beach as she walked. At least that's what Tony said to himself as his heart crumpled with longing!

"Tomorrow night we're going to Minack to see 'Anthony and Cleopatra,' would you like to come too?" Tony hoped Jane didn't notice the faint tremor in his voice.

"What is Minack?" Jane asked.

"It's an open air theatre on the cliffs overlooking the sea and you sit on the rocks and watch the play as the moon rises and sets behind the actors."

"It sounds very romantic. Yes, I'd love to come."

"You'll have to bring a good cushion," Derek added with perhaps a touch of grumpiness. He was beginning to fear Tony's innocent tactics, but all was harmony again as the two of them launched the dinghy to row back to Mousehole, leaving the Stirlings to scramble up to their cottage on the cliff. Leonard, Edie and Guy followed to find the car.

'Anthony and Cleopatra' was the perfect play for this seascape setting. A tragic love story unfolding under the menace of defeat at sea. 'The barge she sat in, like burnished gold burned on the water…' just as did the setting sun. Flaming torches lit the rocks as Caesar's envoys advanced in triumph to discover the dead lovers. A perfect introduction to Shakespeare, although to Tony it was no introduction, he had already studied the play for his school certificate. He was enthralled almost as much as he was with Jane; whose profile he studied in the reflected glow.

Chapter Twelve

But if Tony was in a state of romantic bliss, Leonard was in the gloom of depression: a depression oozing out of the political crisis and threat of war. He had arranged to cut short the Cornish holiday and spend a week in a caravan at Charmouth in Dorset. The excuse was that he wanted the family to have a week on their own before Tony went sailing off to France. The gloom really arose out of those fears suppressed by his faith; faith in the power of God. Fears originating in the death and destruction of the war he had been through, and that now threatened to destroy again.

Tony was sitting in the back of the car savouring the exquisite loss of his first love. He projected the vision of Jane's golden beauty on the window glass beyond which the gold and white glory of the Dorset coast dazzled the sea. Leonard gripped the steering wheel and wrestled with his fears, seeing only dark clouds on the horizon. Edie was reading 'Science and Health' and asserting harmony about the caravan and it's toilet facilities.

The caravan was one of only four in the sloping field on the headland. It had been jacked up into an almost horizontal level, but felt alarmingly insecure as they climbed into it. It began to rain. The car had to be left in the car park at the bottom of the hill as it was too steep to drive to the caravan. They were isolated in what was rapidly becoming a submarine about to submerge. The view was magnificent if you could have seen it.

"Have we got anything to eat, Edie?" asked Leonard uncertainly.

"There is a tin of sardines and some bread." Edie felt uncharacteristically strong and positive. This was indeed sufficient unto the day. In her opinion, some people eat to live and some live to eat. She was firmly of the first option.

"Can we make some toast?" Leonard looked gloomily round the rocking box for some electricity but of course, there was none.

"There are these two Primus Stoves." Tony fiddled with the methylated spirits and the pump until he had a roaring blue flame heating the steaming space they were now bathing in.

"But how do we make toast?" Leonard gloomed.

"We can't." Edie was not gloomy. "But we can fry the bread in the frying pan in some of the sardine oil." This was an amazing leap of imagination for Edie whose interest in food could only ever be metaphysical. Perhaps it was the egg-like context of the caravan that stimulated her. In any case they were soon gratefully eating sardines on fried bread and Edie sang hymns in delight.

The clouds cleared and the sun came out to show the glory of Lyme Bay. Across the horizon in a grey frieze, steamed columns of warships, heading east towards Portland, Aldis lamps chattering signals.

"Can we go and see them, Dad?"

"Yes; better than soldiers, I suppose." Leonard was resigning himself to the gathering menace, Tony was embracing his romantic notions of becoming a naval officer and saw his French sailing holiday as a splendid preparation for the service.

Weymouth was awash with sailors. Blue, pale-scrubbed collars laundered the brisk air with their three white border stripes. Nelson's great victories? Tony had always gobbled up any naval myth. Gold braid glinted in the sun; pinnaces, whalers and cutters crossed and re-crossed the frothing water between the great Portland harbour and the Weymouth landings. Impregnable battleships, haughty cruisers and destroyers rode in confident imperial peace. Anyway, that is how Tony saw it, through the eyes of the bold midshipman who deftly brought his cutter to the stone stairs. Leonard wondered how many of those steel graves would end up on the bottom. Thank goodness Tony was only fourteen. The holiday-makers simply enjoyed the spectacle.

"I suppose we'd better get you to Lymington." Leonard was looking at the map. "If we allow three hours, that should be all right."

"Yes we arranged to meet at the Master Builder Hotel at about one."

"Right, then we'll leave about nine-thirty in the morning."

The parting at the hotel was unemotional; they were not a very vocal or tactile family, they just entrusted each other to God and left. Tony went to seek out his new skipper.

The Master Builder Hotel glowed in the August sunshine; its mellow red brick retreating shyly behind the flirting wisteria, now all green lace with the odd purple tress of a second blooming. Once the residence of the master shipwright who commanded the yard on the banks of the Beaulieu River, slipways busy with Nelson's navy, it was now the refuge of gentlemen yachtsmen, recovering from, or anticipating the damp discomforts of their virile hobby.

Tony stepped tentatively into the cool shaded entrance hall, gleaming with brass and mahogany. It was empty except for a sleeping sheep dog who didn't even stir when Tony pinged the clapper of the ship's bell on the counter. The insistent vibration may not have disturbed the collie dog but Tony feared that he had started a half-finished frigate to slide down the slipway into the river below. Before the vibration had subsided, however, a ship's steward, pale from a lifetime below decks, but fat from the missing stores, appeared as if by lift from behind the counter.

"I am meeting Mr. James Blackburn here. Is he in?"

"Yes, sir, he is expecting you. He is in the lounge; I will take you through. May I have your name sir?" Tony gave his name, relieved that James Blackburn was expecting him. The fat steward waddled his penguin feet towards the lounge, curtsying and bowing as he dodged beams and changing floor levels.

Blackburn looked at him, Tony thought; there was no beaming smile and hearty handshake.

"Ah! Hello (slight pause), Tony." As if in disapproval of his name (Tony rather agreed with him, he had decided to get rid of it as soon as he could) "Steward, can we have some tea? You'd like some tea, wouldn't you?"

"Oh yes please, thank you."

Tony began to guess that James Blackburn (one of Michael Middleton's chums from Oxford) was less than enthusiastic about having Michael's protégé on board as a condition of being lent the boat. That's all right, thought Tony, I don't mind having to prove myself, I know I can do it. As they waited for tea to be served, James quizzed Tony about his background and his sailing pedigree, neither of which seemed to be satisfactory to Blackburn, although being a gentleman, he did not say so. Tony replied honestly and of course did not cross-examine Blackburn. He knew, however, from Michael, who had given him a helpful briefing, that James was an Oxford Physicist now teaching at Mill Hill School; that he was a Roman Catholic and that Tony could expect some antipathy because Michael had explained how they met at Belsay through Christian Science. Michael had become bonded with him in the University Air Squadron and assured Michael that he was a very fine pilot and sailor, and that he would come to admire him. Tony was only too happy to let it happen.

The silver tea pot emptied, cucumber sandwiches and Victoria sponge cake consumed and the remaining crumbs shaken onto the carpet, James seemed more relaxed and said, "Let me show you the boat; we'll sleep on board tonight, it'll be cheaper and she's all provisioned. Another two friends of Michael's join us tomorrow morning, then we'll set sail on the afternoon tide."

Four of them, then it must be quite a big boat. Indeed it was; a forty foot yawl of very dignified aspect. She was riding at anchor comfortably in the Beaulieu River and looked as though she was never going to be hurried. Her name was 'Gwenilli', no doubt named after some substantial Welsh maiden.

Tony was first on board up the rope ladder that hung over her side and to him she seemed like a three-masted schooner.

"Yes, go on explore; your bunk's up forward, as you're the youngest."

A yawl has two masts; the main forward of midships and the mizzen aft of the tiller post; they are both gaff-rigged so there was a lot of timber about and a lot of hard work to do getting them up and down. All of which Tony thought splendid and ducked out of the cockpit into the charthouse/engine room with a bunk either side. Then he rattled down the two steps into the main saloon where on each side were two substantial larders; beyond was the big mahogany table and either side of that two big bunks with stowage above. Further forward, nestling either side of the mainmast were the galley and the lavatory, no doubt conveniently placed for being seasick. Tucked up in the bows were two canvas cots where he was to sleep; splendid, he had lots of room, very cosy.

Tony could not believe he had never been on a boat bigger than a dingy ever before, it all seemed so familiar from his reading and imagining. Nor could James believe it when he listened to Tony's nautical vocabulary and saw his quick response to the order to take the covers off the sails and stow in the locker.

"It's set fair, take them off; it'll be something less to do tomorrow. Let's start the engine." James opened up the mahogany engine cover and revealed the Morris Vedette Marine petrol engine. He took the starting handle from its clips and fitted it snugly on the shaft; first a few turns to lubricate and prime, then switch on the magneto and with one strong pull she chugged away at her contented one thousand r.p.m.

"Now that is really sweet: we shall be glad of her when we're in the Alderney Race." Are we ocean racing, Tony wondered; hope so; but didn't think you were allowed to use your engine; curious?"

"Go and make your bunk up, then: you brought your sleeping bag, didn't you?"

"Oh yes."

"Good, do that then. We'll go back on shore and have a drink then come back aboard and open a tin of Irish stew."

"Sounds good," responded Tony, looking forward with interest to being initiated into 'drinking.'

The evening passed pleasantly with James sizing up this Christian Science Grammar School boy and Tony enjoying acting the public schoolboy, although he knew his accent kept slipping. They knew quite a lot about each other by the time that the Irish stew had been washed down with bottled beer. Tony felt decidedly woozy but as he rolled into his bunk and said his prayers he was pleasantly relieved to find he had not been struck dead!

Chapter Thirteen

Leonard had gripped the steering wheel until his knuckles were white. The journey back to Sheffield had felt like a flight from doom. He felt the German take-over of Austria and now Czechoslovakia, to be physical weight crushing his shoulders. His Christian thought forbad it, but he felt that war was now inevitable: suddenly the vortex was sucking him back into the whirlpool he had escaped only twenty years before. He must resist despair.

When he arrived home, there was some relief to be had from a letter from the Mother Church assuring the Christian Science Churches in Britain that, in the event of war, it was their intention to set up an organisation supplying food and clothing and financial help to the people of Britain. Here was something positive he could do. He replied immediately that he would work with his colleagues to set up a working committee. They would be ready.

The telephone rang.

"Oh Leonard, I so glad you're back, Mary is not well."

"Hello, Steven, how nice to hear your voice; what's the problem?"

Steven and Mary were close friends from the church and Leonard had given them healing help before.

"Well, it's a claim of what appears to be rheumatic fever. She was working in the garden yesterday in the rain and had now developed this fever and swelling and raging pain."

"Thank you for letting me know, Steven. Let's not dwell on the material evidence, let's concentrate on Mary's spiritual perfection, let's banish fear. You go and hold her hand and I will find a clear thought about her. But ring me up at any time, day or night if you need more support to banish fear. I don't feel that you will."

"Thank you Leonard, it is good to know you're there. Good night."

Leonard's own self-indulgence immediately left him, he joyed in the work he knew he had to do, and could do. He shut himself in his study and let his mind clear; making himself receptive to the truth that man is spiritual, not material. The body is not a prison of limitation, vulnerable, decaying, it is a means of demonstrating infinite life and divine energy. There was no further call from Steven and Leonard went to bed with his healing thoughts.

Suddenly he sat up in the dark, was that telephone? No, it wasn't ringing but something was ringing in his head; it was Mary and Steven; they needed help. He concentrated on the infinite strength of God's love and the peace it can always give, and with that peace the power of matter to frighten with corruption, is banished.

"Shall I ring them? No, if I'm mistaken, it will only disturb them, if I am right about their crisis, the healing is complete now, and there never was an assault on Mary's perfect health."

In the morning the telephone did ring and it was Steven.

"I nearly rang you last night: Mary suddenly became icy cold and was gasping for breath. I held her hand and fought to banish fear by trusting in divine love. She let go my hand and began to breath easily and I fell asleep, this morning she is weak but well and confident, and so am I. Thank you, Leonard;

thank you for banishing my fear."

"Steven, you have done it yourself; this experience has moved you on in our spiritual journey. You won't slip back now. Give Mary my love, and I'll come and see her this afternoon; if you would like me to."

"Yes, please do, about four – for tea, yes?"

"Yes please. Thank you."

As he hung up the telephone receiver, it rang again. It was another call for help. And so the loving work went on and Leonard's depression was banished, for the time being. There was plenty to do and he wasn't missing Tony quite as much as he had been before.

Tony was very happy at the helm of "Gwenilli" watching Harry and Tim, the other two members of the crew, being sick. He was noting with a sinfully smug dispassion, the signs of on-coming retching. 'Retching', the perfect term for this curse. First the victim falls silent; they become grave and distant, observing the sky, hoping to escape the heaving of the sea. But the sky simply emphasises the rolling of the horizon. Their Adam's apple begins to twitch, faster and faster until with the desperation of a suicide they dive for the side and vomit themselves empty of everything, slumping to their bunks transparent and grey.

This was Harry, he was a bad case; he should never have stepped on a boat, staring at a wobbly jelly brought on a nausea for him. Tim was different; he would simply break off a fascinating conversation with "Excuse me!" position himself over the ship's side and evacuate, then say, "Sorry about that; feeling better now. What was I saying?" But Tim was a laconic American whereas Harry was a melancholic Englishman. These were the two friends of Michael's that came with the boat. Tim needed a lift to France, on his way to Paris (his geography was indistinct, but all were glad to have his wit with them to Brittany.) Harry, it seemed had an ambition to join the Merchant Navy, which surely, if his luck held he would be cured of before the holiday was over – he was.

Tony was feeling smug because he didn't feel sick and because James had shown him how to hold a course and not luff up, then trusted him to the helm through the night watch.

"Keep a sharp look out for other craft; there won't be many, or I wouldn't leave you here. If you do see anything just alter course away from them. Flash this torch on the mainsail, then come back on course when you've lost them. During the night we are well away from land so you can't come to any harm. The wind is steady

At three to four knots westerly, you should be able to hold our course with this setting. Lash the tiller if you like. If you drop off she'll luff into wind, flap and wake you up. I'll pop out from time to time to see how you're getting on. He never did, he must have felt confident of Tony's cadet skills. Tony grew inches and years entrusted with that watch.

After rounding Cape de la Hague, James took the helm. They were entering the Alderney Race. Tony now found out what it was, a tidal race that funnels between Alderney and the French mainland. Catch at the right time and it is like going down a ski slope and sweeps you on your way south.

"Start the engine, Tony; we must have good steerage way to hold a straight course." The Morris Vedette responded to Tony's swing and the screw pushed a good positive thrust past the rudder. "That's better."

Tony could see what James meant. The speed of the current was almost the speed of the boat under sail, so that there was little positive flow over the rudder. They needed the engine to give them a positive helm. It really was amazing, just like bath water running out; terrifying if it started to take you towards the rocks. It was quite a relief to come out of it and ease towards Sark. You felt that you were in control again. Carantec was their destination. James knew it well and was friendly with a French family who spent all their summers in their villa on the shore of the Bay of Morlaix.

"Carantec dries out at low water, and there is no harbour as such, so get the legs ready to bolt on. I haven't got the local tide tables so I don't know how far we'll be able to get in when we arrive." James was making his preparations for landing.

As it happened, it was high water and they sailed well in shore; near enough to the villa to be greeted with a wave and bravos from the family Piry. The whole scene made Tony feel as if he was in the middle of a Monet. And though they were nearly halfway through the twentieth century, nothing much had changed in Brittany since the end of the nineteenth. Perhaps the dresses were shorter and there was more flesh to see, at least on the bodies of the holiday makers; the local peasants were still in bonnets and long dark skirts.

James spoke French fluently, 'sans accent'. How wonderful to be as clever as that, thought Tony, as he watched him joking with the extended Piry family, while Tony stuttered his School Certificate French to Claude and Claudine, the fourteen-year-old twins. Perhaps if he drank a lot of French wine his fluency would improve. The opportunity was about to be given him.

James had made a 'Petit arrangement', (as he had done in previous years), with the Restaurant Leclerc, opposite the church in the centre of Carantec. Their entry into the restaurant was greeted by the family Leclerc with a roar of affection that moistened the eyes even more than the aroma of onions browning on the hob.

Melting embraces by the patron and his femme, christened

the crew like so many prodigal sons with the perfume of garlic, Gauloise, fresh bread, fresh herbs, eau de cologne and persperation.

"Voilà votre table messieurs, bon appétit," and he plonked a massive earthenware flagon of wine in the middle of the table so that it shook and splashed red, on the stiff white cloth.

So began Tony's introduction to sensuality, and you could see James exulting in his seduction: oysters swallowed like a salty tongue; cassoulet delved and devoured as once he gobbled strawberry jam, and crème brule chomped like chocolate; the whole absorbed with white wine, red wine, coffee and cognac. Tony felt himself growing and his French improving.

"What is all this costing?"

"Never you mind; we'll sort it out at the end of the holiday,"

"Thanks," burped Tony, and accepted the offer of another crepe with calvados.

So the blissful weeks passed. Tim had gone on to be an American in Paris, but Harry was with them for the return voyage. He was enjoying the eating and drinking and, from what Tony was meant to hear from Harry and James' slanted remarks, the local brothel. They were obviously discussing whether it was time for Tony to be initiated: they couldn't quite decide whether he would be thrilled, terrified, or outraged by the prospect. Much to Harry's disappointment, James decided that for the time being, sailing was more important, and anyway they had their obligations to the family Piry. They took them out in 'Gwenilli' every other day, to swim and picnic in secluded coves; that is if the weather was fine, which it usually was that summer, but they were also promised a longer trip to the Isle de Brehat. It would take all day and meant setting off early, catching the tide.

The tide had played a trick on them, or at least on Harry. Harry had been specifically told by James that he must have the dinghy alongside the 'Gwenilli' in the morning, when the tide would be up, and his job was to go and fetch the Piry's.

"Now you know that means you will have to stay on board tonight while Tony and I dine ashore; you will have to row us in and go back to the boat, because when we come back about ten, the tide will be out and we shall walk out to the boat. Got it?"

"Aye, aye Skipper, I could do with an early night."

"Good."

Tony was elated that he had been excused this duty; he felt that he had graduated in James' estimation. He wondered if, perhaps, James was planning an evening in the brothel for him; but in fact nothing happened, they just entertained the Montaignes to repay some of their hospitality.

But when they were saying good night to the Montaignes outside their villa on the beach, James noticed that their dinghy was still there, high and dry.

"Oh bugger, I'll bet Harry's gone off to the broth–bistro and forgotten the tide. I'll give him hell, and he can bloody well swim back here for the dinghy in the morning, that'll teach him."

The walk out to 'Gwenilli' was silent: James was genuinely furious. If he found him asleep on board, Tony was afraid he might kick him. He wasn't; he still had to come back. Tony climbed quickly into his cot and shut his ears and went to sleep feeling glad he wasn't Harry.

Tony was awakened by the angry shouts of James bellowing at Harry to get up and fetch the dinghy. Harry was intensifying James' frustration by moaning that he had a terrible headache and couldn't get up.

"If I do I shall be sick."

"You're always bloody well sick. Get out of bed or I'll chuck you in the water myself." And he began to drag Harry on to the deck.

"I'll fetch it, James, I'll fetch the dinghy." Tony couldn't bear the bullying any longer, although he felt Harry deserved it. Anyway he wanted to continue to impress James.

"You shouldn't let him get away with it, Tony, but thanks anyway."

As Tony went out onto the deck, naked in the cold morning air, the sun only just above the horizon, a faint mist over the sea and his breath adding to it, he wondered whether he had done the right thing. The sea was as calm as glass, and looked as solid. Would it shatter in his face as he dived in, or close over the top of him and seal him under? He dived and gasped for breath as the cold water crushed him, but six strokes later he felt like a fish, streaking through his own phosphorescence.

As he reached the shore and the dinghy, his extremities had shrivelled to so small a size, that sitting on seat, and on them, caused no discomfort at all!

At least Harry had not forgotten to put out an anchor; the dinghy had not floated away on the morning tide. Tony rowed it back to 'Gwenilli' like a champion sculler, glorying in the straight wake that followed him over the mirrored surface.

"Hey, steady on, you're going to ram us," yelled James; and Tony backed his oars just in time, falling into the bottom of the dinghy with his bottom in the air.

"Come on, bum boy, throw me a line. Well done." James was pleased.

It was not Harry's day: but then it never was. James had a rather nerve wracking technique for leaving harbour smartly when the wind was favourable. His method was to set all sails, luffed up into the wind, then let them fill and gather forward speed while his crew hauled in the anchor at breakneck speed. The idea was that the forward motion cancelled out the heaving on the anchor and it was only a matter of coiling in the chain. The snag with the system was that if the crew didn't gather the chain in fast enough and get the anchor clear of the bottom before the boat overtook it, you suddenly came to a sliding, slewing halt with perhaps a couple of crew overboard looking for their wrenched off arms.

Tony and Harry were the anchor men up in the bows.

"Haul away," shouted James, showing off to his French friends.

The boat began to make weigh, Tony started to haul on the anchor chain with Harry behind him taking the strain as well. Speed was essential and Tony heaving the chain hand over hand without looking behind him at Harry. Harry, the lubber, instead of adding his weight to the hauling, was frantically letting the arriving chain gather in his arms like a housewife skeining wool. There was a loud howl from Harry who had arrived at the point when he couldn't hold all the chain he had gathered any longer, and let it drop on his feet.

"For God's sake, Harry; keep hauling, it's nearly vertical; we've got to get off the bottom!" No help there; Harry was doing a war dance on his damaged feet. With four more frantic wrenches Tony felt the anchor swing free just as they passed over the holding point.

"Anchor aweigh, Skipper." And James smirked with satisfaction to his effete French friends. Thank goodness the 'Gwenilli' was long enough for James not to see what had been going on up forward, or poor limping Harry might have been keel hauled!

It was a wonderful day at the Isle de Brehat, bathing and

picnicking on fresh bread and local coarse pate, peaches and grapes and warm red wine. Harry got a lot of sympathy for his bruised toes from pretty little Claudine and so felt it was all worthwhile, this sailing lark.

The international crisis had been ignored by the Piry's and James, whose attitude was probably typical over most of Europe: war is inevitable; let's enjoy this wonderful summer. But the morning after returning from Isle de Brehat, it was not possible to ignore it anymore. On the Prefecture, the Bureau de Poste, the Mairie, there had appeared the 'Avis', calling all reservists to the Colours.

"I expect a similar notice is waiting for me in London, from the Royal Air Force Volunteer Reserve. I must get back." Suddenly it was all very real and serious. It wouldn't be long before James would be flying his plane in anger. The next two days seemed to empty the town and the beaches. Half the fishermen went off to their Navy; all the young men went off to their Army; James said goodbye to the Piry's who went back to Paris looking glum; James told Tony and Harry to lash up and stow while he went to settle the bill at the restaurant. There was no sense of elation or confident patriotism that traditionally greets a declaration of war; memories of last time were too recent; there was just depression.

"We'll sail tonight," said James decisively. "The tide is right and it'll save us twelve hours. There'll be a steady south-easterly when we get clear of land."

They started the engine and set out, a full set of sails flapping gently over the calm water, until they were well out of the bay and picking up the breeze. Their white, red and green navigation lights reflected a naïve, childlike pattern on the calm, dark, water; competing with the diamond stars and the rising moon. Then the breeze took over, ruffled the water and the pattern faded into broken glass; the glow from the binnacle bathed the helmsman's face and seemed like a crystal ball revealing the future.

The passage across the Channel was swift and uneventful, even Harry was able to swallow his nausea. They made a landfall off Salcombe, Start Point, which was satisfactory, and decided to go in for a rest and to clear customs.

Dinner at the Salcombe Hotel was a bit of a shock after the Restaurant Carantec; grey food at twice the price, beer instead of wine. And still no one discussed the political crisis; just looked gloomy. But none of this stopped them from having a good night's sleep on board in the harbor, which prepared them for their next leg, up the coast to Lymington.

This did not turn out to be a smooth passage. Crossing Lyme Bay they were hit by a severe squall, caught with all sails set.

"Damn, I should have seen that coming." James was cross with himself; the wind was now force six or seven, healing 'Gwenilli' alarmingly and blowing them towards the shore. He put her into wind to get her upright. Meanwhile, Harry, of course, had gone below in a state of collapse. It takes three to reef; one on the helm keeping her into wind; one on the halyards letting down the sail, and another reefing and stowing the sail.

"Harry; get up here," James yelled below. No response. "Harry, you've got to come up here or you drown." Still no response.

"Tony, take the helm; keep her into wind." James went below and immediately reappeared with the luckless Harry who looked like a corpse.

"You've got to take the helm and keep us in to wind while we reef." Harry wretched an empty wretch as James threw him onto the rear seat of the cockpit and put his arm over the tiller. Tony let go and scrambled to the mainmast and the main halyard.

"Into the wind, remember, just as it is now. got it?" Harry just went greener, his eyes looked sightless; he wretched another dry wretch. James scrambled onto the top of the deckhouse and gave the order, "Lower away." Tony unhitched the main halyard, took a couple of turns round the cleat for safety and began to drop the main gaff and the sail. James embraced the slackened sail and reached for the highest reef tails and started to tie his reef knots under the boom. The boat was bucking like a bronco, pitching her head into the waves, now heading into wind.

"Oh Christ! Harry keep her into wind." Harry had collapsed and was no longer on the helm; he seemed to be praying in a corner of the cockpit while the 'Gwenilli' swung off wind and the main boom was trying to sweep James overboard. Tony quickly took a hitch on the halyard cleat and dived into the cockpit, grabbed the tiller, and brought her back into wind. She steadied up but began to pitch again. He hauled Harry out of his corner and draped him over the tiller.

"Stay like that or you'll drown," said Tony repeating James' warning. Harry's wretching body remained draped over the tiller, keeping it in the same position; the wind direction remained constant and reefing of the mainsail was completed. James was able to go back to the helm and roll the unconscious Harry below.

"Get the foresail down, leave the jib. I'm letting the sheet go." Tony stretched himself between the foresail halyard and the luff of the foresail, let the halyard go and did a flying tackle as the sail came down. He managed to smother it without falling overboard and stuffed it down the fore hatch. Phew!

They were under control again and making a heading that would clear Portland Bill.

The weather moderated but remained dull and wet all the way to the Isle of White. They motored up the Beaulieu River to return to their mooring. It was Sunday morning, the third of September. The river was deserted; a fine grey drizzle hid a feeble sun that was failing miserably to break through. As Tony rowed them ashore an eerie silence exaggerated the rhythmic creek of the oars in the rowlocks. Out of the gloom on the landing stage appeared the figure of a man with the face of a potato; a wart on his nose dripped drops of collected drizzle.

He spoke; there was no greeting, only:

"The Germans have marched into Poland, the war starts at eleven a.m." He took the line and made it fast to the bollard, then turned and disappeared into the mist. Did he ever exist?

"Well that's that," said James as he heaved his kitbag on shore.

They trudged to the 'Master Builder' and Harry rang for a taxi to take him to Southampton.

"Can I give anyone a lift?"

"No thanks, Harry, I've got my car here. You can come with me Tony," he said quickly, rescuing Tony from an embarrassing ride with poor Harry who was in deep depression at his failure to become a sailor.

The taxi arrived quickly, there being no customers that morning, and muttered goodbyes and "Good lucks" were said, cold hands were shaken, and relief was felt as the taxi whined away.

"Come on, I'll buy you breakfast in the 'Builder', would you like that?"

"I certainly would, but I haven't settled my share of the

Carantec expenses yet, let me do that first."

"Please, have it all on me. If I hadn't had you with me, I dread to think what might have happened in Lyme Bay, and anyway, believe me, it was not a big bill."

"Well, thank you, that is very generous; I appreciate it very much. But let me at least pay for our breakfast."

"All right then, it's a deal; come on I'm hungry," and they took their seats in the dining room, which was empty.

I don't think that either of them ever forgot the modest luxury of that meal and the comfort of its surroundings. The depravations that came after, made it an implant on the memory. The toast was so white and thick, and cosied under starched white napkins; the coffee poured black and elegant, into deep white, gleaming breakfast cups, blanched with hot milk from its smaller silver pot. The bacon was pink and white with sweet fat; the eggs were yellow and poached, deep as muffins; they sat on golden fried bread that cut like cake. The marmalade was dark, sharp and chompy; the butter ran on the toast because it was still hot under its napkin. They sighed with content, only a little disturbed by the thought that they might have had kippers. This doubt vanished when they heard that kippers were 'off' that morning.

James had a conventional fighter pilot's open sports car of ancient vintage. It was a Wolsey. Named by Wolsey, 'Hornet', to give it an air of menace, its lines were low and thin and long; its front wheels were detached from the long bonnet to allow your cornering to be dashing. The menace and the dash were slightly diminished when James turned on the ignition with the aid of a toothless comb that he kept in a pocket in the door.

The ride was stimulating, as the wheels were as narrow as a Hansom cab's, and the tyres as thin as paper. The drive to Southampton did not take long and they were soon shaking hands and saying goodbye, knowing that they were unlikely to be seeing each other again. They looked into each other's eyes with mutual respect and wished each other luck. Tony, being a Christian Scientist, didn't believe in luck, and while speaking the convention, mentally commended him to God's eternal protection. James, being a Catholic, mentally crossed himself.

(James Blackburn had a good war, he survived, became a Wing Commander, one of the most decorated, two DSOs, two DFCs, an American Airforce Cross; was torpedoed in a troopship, captured by the German submarine, escaped after being imprisoned and continued his war!)

Chapter Fourteen

When the political crisis gathered momentum after Leonard had gone off to Dorset, Guy and Derek decided quickly, to pack up Cornwall and go back to London. They returned to Guy's mother's house in Pimlico, there to await events and to volunteer for the armed forces, in the hope of becoming gainfully employed. Guy found that at the age of forty-three he was not wanted by the London Scottish Regiment and had to settle for becoming an ambulance driver with the London County Council. Derek, aged twenty-one was snapped up by the Royal Artillery (London Artists Battalion), to be trained on anti-aircraft guns.

Tony rang his parents in Sheffield to tell them he was safe and well and would spend the night in London with Guy in Pimlico.

Leonard fought back his mounting fears of immediate bombing.

"Don't stay too long; Mummy misses you."

"Yes, all right Dad; I'll be home on Tuesday."

Fourteen Clarendon Street was not exactly Carlisle Square; Pimlico was not Chelsea. It was decidedly dingy and dark. Guy's mother lived in the basement of this narrow terrace house and never came out. Behind her almost sightless eyes and dark glasses, she communicated with a red slash of lips that seemed to be operated by remote ventriloquist control, and the aid of a walking stick that rapped messages on the ceiling.

Guy greeted Tony in his dark blue blouse and trousers of the ambulance driver. He had already re-tailored each garment to give him a stylish fit.

"How nice that you can stay; sorry Derek's not here, he's at his training camp in Kent."

"Who've you got there, Guy?" The shriek came up from the basement, emphasised by a smart rap on the ceiling and the yap of a dog.

"It's Tony, mother. You remember Tony. I'll bring him to see you in a little while." This seemed to satisfy her.

"She will be your only company tonight. I've got to go on night duty, so you will sleeping alone. I hope you don't mind."

"No, not at all; I've got a lot of sleep to catch up."

"Yes, how was your trip, good fun?"

"It was the most wonderful experience in so many ways. I shall never forget it – particularly the food. What's for supper?"

"Coq au vin, you're probably bored with that now. "

"Never."

"It's a good dish; it goes on and on."

"Yes, I can smell it."

"Not too strong is it? It is its first night."

"No, no, I was just talking about the herbs."

"Oh good, well let's eat then."

Guy brought the pot in from his tiny kitchen and set it on a brass trivet on the reclaimed marble pub table; then a bowl of rice and sweet chutneys, also a green salad dressed and aromatic.

"Try this wine, it's Retzina; it's Greek. You might not like it. It tastes of turpentine, but it's strong and unusual."

Tony knew that Sheffield was going to be pretty dull after

all this. Tony found that Retzina did taste like paint stripper at first, but very quickly got used to it and refilled his glass. Tony told Guy about his adventures in France and Lyme Bay and time passed happily until Guy had to go on duty.

"If there's an air raid warning go down to the basement with Mother, keep each other company. She has a powerful line in German abuse that will amuse you.

I'm finding ambulance driving a bit boring; I've put in a request for transfer to the water ambulances; that'll be more fun. They operate from Westminster pier, I hope I get it. Bye, bye. See you tomorrow before you go home." And he rode off in the blackout to his ambulance station in the King's Road on his rickety ladies bike, with its fluorescent mudguards.

Tony didn't have to wait long for his first air raid warning; it came shortly after Guy had left. There had been one that morning, almost immediately after Chamberlain's broadcast, telling the nation they were at war. It turned out to be a false alarm but its accelerating wail had turned over a few stomachs. Tony now experienced the stomach churning, but being young it was more from anticipation than fear. But the sound of bicycling policemen riding the darkened streets outside, blowing their whistles and calling, "Take cover," that did seem sinister, because it was human.

"Are you all right Mrs. Allan?" Tony called down to Guy's mother.

"Come and talk to me," she said; so he went down to the basement.

It was dark, he could hardly see his way. Mrs. Allan, being almost blind had no need of light; the blackout regulations were no bother to her. In her room, the only light was from the glow from the single bar of a two bar radiator; fortunately, heavily guarded from her long black Edwardian skirts. Tony was relieved to see that, or he feared that he might have witnessed a conflagration like Miss Faversham's. Her bed was also in the room, its bedding also seemed to be black and it seemed to stir. Tony felt that this might be from its own pungency, because the atmosphere was certainly weighty with a sweet scent, soured by body odour. But it really did stir, to reveal a black Pomeranian dog. It yawned, and its little pink mouth caught the glow of the fire; that was the only move it made.

"Come and talk to me, tell me who you are. Guy never tells me anything."

"My name is Tony and I am the son of Guy's friend Leonard, who lives in Sheffield. Do you know about him?"

"No, I don't, Guy never tells me anything. What does your father do?" Oh dear, was he going to have to tell his father's life story?

"He is a Christian Science Healer in Sheffield."

"Christian Science: that, Guy did tell me about. Said I should try it. I told him it was American and cranky; Americans are cranky, you know."

"Oh: are they, why do you say that?"

"Because my husband ran off with an American floozy; she was cranky, must have been, to run off with my husband."

"Are you frightened of these air raids?"

"Not these air raids; there are no bombs. I remember the last war. We had proper bombs from Zeppelins. They killed hundreds of people. I was chaperoning Guy's sister at a house in Belgrave Square when we had to stop dancing because of the air raid. The Prince of Wales was there and he went off with that hussy, Freda Dudley Ward, who only came in to shelter. Quite appalling. What are you going to do when you grow up?"

"I don't know. I did want to go into the Royal Navy, but now I think I want to go to Oxford."

"I expect that you'll go into the Royal Navy now; you won't have any option, because the war will go on, they always do. Will you mind?"

"No. I think I'll join the Fleet Air Arm, I'd like to fly."

"Yes, that's what Guy did: but he never tells me anything; he seemed to spend all his time in Paris with Prince Yusupov."

A steady wail rose from the siren signalling the 'All Clear'.

"That's the 'All Clear', we can go to bed."

"Yes, you go to bed. I shall listen to the Wireless, it tells me everything. Good night, and thank you for talking to me."

"Oh, it was very interesting; I'm going tomorrow, or we could talk again."

"Good night. I hope you go to Oxford, but you'll be in the navy first."

"Yes, I expect so. Good night."

Chapter Fifteen

When Leonard and Edie arrived home after seeing Tony off to France they had some news that lifted the gloom of approaching war.

"I'm getting married, Leonard, Edie."

Doris was still living with them after her flight from father, although she had mended relations with him and visited her mother every week, giving her moral support.

"Oh he's not so bad," Daisy would say. "As long as he's not got the drink in him, and he's working. He brings me my housekeeping, which is more than you can say for half the husbands down our yard. The missus has to go down the pub to get it!"

"Oh that's lovely, Doris. Is it Fred?"

"Yes, it is. Fred with the legs."

Fred was known as legs because he walked everywhere; no one had ever seen him on a bus or a tram, but he had been to Bridlington on a train. They had met in in the Rambling Club. Doris had good legs, which she mainly used for dancing and standing on in the shoe department at Robert's Brothers, but she also loved walking in the Derbyshire countryside, which is why she joined the Rambling Club and why she met Fred.

"You know, Leonard, he's impotent," she had told Leonard during one of their intimate exchanges. Leonard found comfort with Doris in his sexual frustration which Doris knew about and understood.

"I can always relieve you Len, whenever you feel you need to," she had generously offered, and meant it. Whether it had ever been necessary, nobody would ever know, but he was grateful for the offer.

"It's daft, isn't it; my Fred's impotent and our Edith's frigid; and you and me go short." Doris's logic was irrefutable.

"Are you sure it's going to work?" Leonard had asked when marriage was first suggested.

"Oh yes, he's a loving man who needs to get away from his smothering mother. He's forty-five, you know, and I'm thirty nine. He won't have the responsibility of children and I'll have someone to look after. And he's got a good job, you know; he works in the Share Department at United Steels. He's ever so clever at figures; he can add up six rows in his head and always get it right. I think it must be something to do with his eyesight, because he's just as good at billiards and snooker. He's been banned from the Locarno Billiard Hall because he always wins. They play for money, you know."

"Do you think he'll take his pipe out of his mouth on his wedding night?"

Leonard was getting skittish; it was nice to see.

"I don't expect so," laughed Doris.

"So when is it to be?" asked Leonard while Edie gave her an affectionate kiss.

"We're going to the Registry Office on Thursday. It's half day closing and I'm taking the day off, so is he. We've got somewhere to live, very convenient, near Hunter's Bar, and Fred works at Broom hill. Mind you, it wouldn't matter to him where it was, he'd walk to Neeps End. It's got a kitchen and a living room downstairs and two bedrooms up. The lav's in the yard and the bath is in the kitchen, but it's got all you need. It'll be wonderful to have a place of our own for seven and six a week. Fred's bought some furniture, we've got something to sit on and sleep in."

"Have you got something to eat off? Let us buy you that for your wedding present."

"Not much, that would be lovely, thank you. We're having a bit of a party after the ceremony at our place, 14 Gordon Road, there won't be many, not enough room, any way we don't know anybody!"

"Yes, we'll come Doris, won't we Edie?" Edie looked away, but didn't shake her head.

***

It was the day of the wedding; the telephone rang;

"It's for you Doris; I think it's Fred; he sounds a bit funny," said Leonard as hen handed the receiver to Doris.

"Yes,Fred?" Doris intonation seemed to anticipate a problem which she was not about to accept.

"Doris?" squeaked a muffled voice, "I can't come. I've broken my teeth."

"What do you mean, you've broken your teeth?"

"I put'em on my bedside table and knocked 'em off, then got up and trod on them. They're smashed."

"I'm sorry about that, love but what do you mean, you can't come?"

"I can't get married without any teeth."

"I'm not marrying you for your teeth. Don't you try to get out of this because of your teeth. You get there to the Registry Office at eleven o'clock or it'll be more than your teeth that get smashed."

"But Doris!"

"Is your mother there?"

"Yes."

"Let me speak to her."

"Yes, Doris Mother, Doris wants to speak to you. Come on, quick, she's cross."

"Hello, Doris," said mother cautiously.

"What's all this about Fred's teeth stopping him getting married?"

"Is that what he says, don't you worry, I'll get him there. I expect what he's really worried about is that he won't be able to hold his filthy pipe in his mouth. He hasn't got a best man, has he; or he could get him to hold it with the ring. You're taking the ring, aren't you?"

"Yes, I am," said Doris firmly, "You get him there. Did you get all that?" said Doris, turning to Leonard.

"Yes, I did. Well done Doris, he won't get away now. Do you think I should go and get him in the car and let you and Edie go in a taxi?"

"No, it's all right, his mother will get him there."

Mother did get him there and the ceremony went off smoothly, apart from the alarm when the right hand pocket of Fred's suit began to smoulder and smoke, as he was toothlessly mouthing his eternal vows. He felt the heat, reached into his pocket and dashed his pipe to the floor in a shower of sparks. It had the effect of emphasising the passion of his sincerity, and fortunately did not activate the fire alarm, although it did activate the Registrar who accelerated the ceremony to a swift conclusion. Fred's suit had a brown mark on the right hand pocket for the rest of its (and Fred's) life. Fred said it didn't matter because it was a brown suit. Doris was remarkably calm, if not a little triumphant at having secured her man. She carried him off to their cottage in Gordon Road in the back of Leonard's car, waving to the indifferent population as she passed. Fred re-lit his pipe; Edith coughed.

Left: Leonard and Edie on their wedding day, 1924
Right: Edith as a young girl

Left: Dorris sitting outside their first house
Right: Leonard's mother, father and brothers

The Bents Green, Sheffield suburban semi; going up in the world

Boothby Manor

Leonard and Edie outside their miracle houses, 1955

Chipping Campden, 1946

The Austin Big 12, a ‘Doctor’s car’, 1943

Daphne Robinson, Headmistress of Woodhouse Grammar School, Sheffield, 1943.

Doris and Fred on their wedding day, 1940

Leonard, Edie and 'Tony', outside one of Guy's many temporary homes, usually a borrowed summer house.

'Aunty' Peg, outside her ramshackle welcoming home.

Guy as a Royal Navy Petty Officer, talking to his fashionable sister, 1940, Battle of Brittain.

Michael and his old Sunday school friend Brian; both pilots.

A better view of Peg's 'Lodge Farm'

Derek with his anti-aircraft gun at Kenley fighter aerodrome.

Guy with his ambulance.

Leonard and Edie at Creek House, Teddington, 1971

Guy in his natural habitat, The Studios, Glebe Place, Chelsea.

Chapter Sixteen

The 'Phoney War' had passed into the real war and a real winter. Leonard was feeling it, and struggling hard to keep his nerve. This struggle was aggravated, but to some extent helped, by relentless work. There were nightly air raid warnings which broke his sleep (though not deaf, Edie). So far the raids were not intensive, and only modest damage was done to the city and its steel works, but the cumulative effect was exhausting. Leonard was now registered as a Minister of Religion, under the Direction of Employment Regulations. This meant that he had extra rations of petrol to carry out his duties but it also meant that he had to travel every month a hundred miles up the A1 to Catterick Army Camp in north Yorkshire. There he conducted a Christian Science service for those troops who wanted it.

Catterick was a vast military training base, as it had been even under the Romans, and even such a minority religion as Christian Science raised a significant congregation. One of his flock was Doris's Fred who had been called up into the Army Pay Corps. Although not a member of his church, Fred looked forward to meeting a friend in this bleak military city, and was glad to come to his services, even if it meant putting his pipe out!

Guy had succeeded in transferring to the Thames River Ambulance Service, just as it was taken over by the Royal

Navy. He was now a Petty Officer and Harbour Master at Loch Fyne, the combined operations training base in Scotland. The compensation was that on his evenings off, he contrived to dine with his acquaintance, the Duke of Argyle.

Derek had been posted, with his fellow artists and their anti-aircraft guns, to Kenley Fighter Base in Kent, and been lucky to survive the Luftwaffe's determined attacks during the Battle of Britain.

Michael at his Grammar School, a bus ride away, was preening himself as Flight-Sergeant of the school Air Training Corps. He had been accepted for the Fleet Air Arm and was waiting to be eighteen and called up. The fortunes of war were now juggling with all their lives and every ball was in the air.

One of these fortunes was the higher income this brought to Leonard because of the strains of life in the 1940s. More people seemed to need more healing work; there was plenty to occupy his mind in those night-waking hours; perhaps too much. An increasing affluence meant that he could have a better car. The original 'Singer' had, of course ended up embracing a tree; its replacement had been a lumbering bathtub, known as a Standard Big Nine. This was a euphemism for being under powered. It was cold in winter but sunny in summer when the hood was down. Now he could afford a proper 'doctor's' car, a black Austin Twelve saloon, with brown leather seats and a heater! It was not new, of course, but it looked as if it was. It was his joy. He was a bit ashamed of himself for allowing this material object to lift his spirit; but it was easy to rationalise into it being a manifestation of divine substance, and he was, after all, doing God's work with it. Anyway this is how he felt as he sped up the A1 towards Catterick. The large slim steering wheel caressed his hands with its sensitive tremor, the heater pushed warm air across his face, the black bonnet lead the way with its winged wheel badge, and the leather seat hugged his back, and the day was bright.

But a gloom began to settle on him when stopped at the guardhouse. There his identity was challenged; he surrendered it and was accepted.

"To the intersection, sir, and turn right into Bapaume Road; you spot it with its cross sticking out the top."

Bapaume was where he had been wounded in May 1918. To him, the well drilled lines of Nissen huts, dressing to the horizon, seemed like a million tombs, repeating into distant Flanders as a million bone bleached headstones.

This Nissen city was anonymous and automaton; all white lines and marching men, prodded by shouts from thick necked sergeants. On this crisp Sunday morning the muscular brass music of conventional church parades could be heard from those marching to the garrison Anglican Church.

He found his chapel and its Christian cross rising above the domed hump. 'Non-denominational Christian chapel' it said on the door. He parked and went inside, there to be greeted by a grinning Fred.

"Hello, Len, bit of a surprise eh! Doris told me you were coming, so I wangled myself as your steward for the day. Hope that's all right?" He suddenly looked a bit sheepish; perhaps he'd been too cheeky.

"Of course it is, Fred. How nice to see your friendly face. How are you getting on, anyway?"

"Oh not so bad; of course I hate it but it could be worse. It was worse when I did my basic training. I was hopeless; I couldn't keep up, I fell over my rifle and my teeth fell out. Didn't break them this time though. Now I'm settled in my pay office job and they think I'm marvellous; it's being good at sums, you know. I get to know everything that's going on and can wangle anything, that's why I'm here. But if they're down to me to use a gun I'll tell you, we've lost!" He grinned again. "Peter, Peter Lee will be here in a minute to play your hymns; he got your letter and he's been practicing."

"Yes, he's the son of a friend of mine. It was good that he was here, but I suppose he'll be posted soon. I'll have to find another pianist won't I, how about you?"

"Me? I can't play; the only thing I can play is snooker!"

"No, I meant, are you going to be posted?"

"Not if I can help it; anyway my chief accountant major seems to need me, and I intend to keep it that way."

"Well done, Fred, that's the way to survive. Be positive and keep laughing as you always do. You'll be all right."

***

Christian Science is rather a centralised religion. The Mother Church in Boston, Massachusetts, issues a programme of daily readings from the Bible linked with the relevant readings from 'Science and Health with Key to the Scriptures' by Mary Baker Eddy, the founder of the religion. The Sunday service repeats these 'lessons', but in addition the local Reader prefaces it with a selection of his own readings from the same source. There is no sermon as such. No danger of a cult of personality here, and no one Reader serves for more than one consecutive year. Some of the congregation find this helpful, but some find it remote and often seek out the Reader later, especially if he is a Practitioner of Healing. This was Leonard's experience which gratifyingly expanded his practice but was an extensive responsibility. When the service was over he announced that he would be available for a further hour to those who might want to talk. It was two o'clock before he was free again. Fred had had to go away and smoke his pipe and have his dinner, but he loyally came back to find out if Leonard was all right.

"You must be hungry, Len. Let me take you the Officers' Mess; they'll have something for you there. You're the equivalent of a Padre, you know, they're officers."

"No, no, Fred, take me to the mess hall with the men, it's more relaxing."

"All right then; I hope they've still got that sausage and mash I had, it was really good, with rhubarb and custard to follow. The food's really good here, you know, they buy it locally and it's good Yorkshire stuff. No, I'm definitely not going to get posted from here."

There was plenty left and Leonard enjoyed it. He lost a little of his lingering fear of the army. But outside it had begun to snow. He was glad of his heater and his flashing windscreen wipers and his broad deep tyres. It was already three o'clock and the snow-heavy clouds were hurrying on the dusk. Passing the army green three-toners and their sullen loads, he headed south through Wetherby and Knottingley, hoping to get to familiar Doncaster before the snow drifted. It had been a long day, setting off at six-thirty, conducting the service, comforting his flock, eating sausage and mash (that was the best bit) and now squinting down his headlights into the snow. Now it was Rotherham and the furnaces of the steel works seemed to be holding off the snowflakes. A rumble along the cobbles of Attercliffe Bottom and he was nearly home. He slid to a halt, exhausted, at 92 Stafford Road. It was nine-thirty p.m., fifteen hours since he had left that morning. His was the only car in the white trackless street.

"Hello love", Edith looked up from her 'Science and Health' but didn't move from her chair. "I've been knowing the Truth for you, Leonard," she said." "Do you want anything to eat?"

"No, I'm too tired to eat, and my teeth are hurting. I think I'll just go to bed." He kissed her cheek and went upstairs.

Chapter Seventeen

The stomach-churning wail of the air raid warning woke Leonard. It was eleven thirty, the luminous alarm clock told him so. He looked across at Edith; she was still asleep. Across the landing in his bedroom, Tony turned over and immediately went to sleep again. He knew it was not his duty night as a bicycle messenger boy at the Air Raid Post along the road. Mr. Berisford, their next door neighbour, was already there at the stone built Methodist Church, where a steel reinforced vestry provided a robust command post.

Mr. Berisford was Chief Warden, a full time evening occupation. The small additional income that came with this responsibility eased the penury of his earnings as a salesman of paper bags to small shopkeepers. It also gave him a well-deserved dignity. He looked imposing under his black steel helmet, 'Warden' painted on the front in white, and emerging from under it, his 1914-18 Kitchener moustache. Recently he had been issued with a black boiler suit. It had epaulettes with his rank on; this was better than paper bags.

Beryl and Minnie Berisford, daughter and wife, were already treading downstairs to the cellar, with their eiderdowns, torches and sandwiches and flask of coffee. They were obeying Mr. Berisford's standing instructions in the event of a warning. "I will not be able to carry out my duties efficiently if I cannot be sure that you are following the correct procedure."

Therefore, they conscientiously obeyed, however slight the raid might be. Tonight it was going to devastating. There was a bomber's moon and no cloud. The rhythmic beat of German aero engines triggered the anti-aircraft barrage and you could hear the shrapnel of their exploding shells rattling back down onto the slate roofs of the surrounding houses, smashing their way into the loft.

The bombs began to fall, but not too near; presumably they were aiming for the steel works in the east end of the city. The first wave passed, but was immediately followed by another whose bombs landed much nearer. Tony leaped out of bed and looked out of the window; there were fires started about a mile away in the main shopping street. That would be quite near John Saville's house where Guy used to work.

At that moment Leonard came out onto the landing with Edith. "This is a bad one, we'd better go down to the cellar." Edith was clutching her Science and Health; Leonard was wrapping her in the blankets.

Tony said, "I'll just get dressed first and get my homework, it'll be something to do."

The guns in Norfolk Park were now in constant barrage; the tremor of their recoil could be felt all along the road to the cellar. For some reason the bombers now seemed to be concentrating on this western part of the city. Leonard and Edie were sitting in the striped deckchairs as if on summer holiday on the beach, except that they were wrapped in blankets. Edie just continued to read her 'Science and Health', Leonard looked transparent with a fear he was determined to control: "Fear is loss of faith in God to love and protect and that can never be." This was the thought he was hanging onto, trying to stifle the memory of all those Flanders' dawn bombardments, rising like vomit from his stomach. Tony with the blissful ignorance of youth, felt only an eager excitement as he looked up when each new explosion shook the house. His essay on the Treaty of Utrecht did, however, gain a certain intensity as the cellar steps shuddered under him, and he did wear his A.R.P. helmet. "They say you never hear the one that kills you," he might have said, but even that did not occur to him.

They certainly heard the next one. The noise was totally enveloping, dust and soot grew out of the walls, glass shattered somewhere above, slates smashed into the street and the blast sucked air out of their lungs and lifted them out of their seats. A glow began to reach them down the whitewashed cellar steps. It had become strangely quiet, except for a tinkling of broken glass and dribbling of rubble as if sliding down from a tipping lorry. Tony dashed upstairs to see the damage; they had not been hit, it was the house across the road. It was blazing brightly in the frosty night. The gas main was fractured, the wooden floors were crackling merrily. Tony knew it was empty, like so many houses at that time; nobody wanted them and families were split up. There was no sound of a fire engine, they had more desperate work to do.

"Dad, it's all right; it's the empty house across the road. It's on fire, but we've only lost our windows. I'd better run down to the A.R.P. post and tell Mr. Berisford." He grabbed his tin hat and dashed away before anyone could stop him. Not that Leonard made any attempt to do so, he just asserted Tony's divine protection.

"I'm glad you've come, Tony. I need some extra help. It's been a hell of a night. It seems that there was mist over the east end and they went for the west end. The whole of the Moor's gone and Fitzallen Square and Fargate. There shouldn't have been too many casualties; they've hit mainly empty shops and offices."

"Yes. I've just come to tell you that the empty house opposite us has been hit; yours and ours are all right, just slates and windows gone. We're all all right. Have they finished yet, do you think?"

As he asked the question, the 'All Clear' sounded. Then it was hot drinks all round and assess the damage. The bombed house was detached, and as there was no wind, it was able to burn itself out without lighting anything else; certainly no fire engine was able to come, and you couldn't do anything with a stirrup pump. Tony helped by filling in the damage report for the street and hoped the war damage team would not be too long coming with their boards and tarpaulins. It was cold in the house. At eight o'clock he went to his bus stop to go to school and to his amazement it came. He delivered his essay on the 'Treaty of Utrecht' to Mr Beynon, the history master, with a certain smug satisfaction.

"I didn't expect to see you this morning, and certainly not your essay. How did you get on?"

"Oh! It wasn't too bad."

What it is to be young, thought Mr. Beynon, another survivor of 1914-18. I suppose we'll all be just summed up in a peace treaty some day.

Chapter Eighteen

The damage to 92 Stafford Road was not extensive. It was certainly habitable, once the glass and slates were replaced, but Leonard's increased income allowed him to think of renting a nicer house in a nicer area. He found one on the Manchester Road at Cross Pool. Cross Pool was on the edge of the Derbyshire countryside. It had a view over Rivelin Valley, a garage, and a garden that backed onto fields. A Dentist lived next door; a professional man: he worked for the Education Committee. The bombing had blown them up the hill.

It was true that Tony was now twice as far from his school as before, but even this turned out to be an advantage. The bus that he used, actually started from the Cross Pool terminus. It meant he left earlier but could finish his homework on the journey, but there was an even greater advantage.

"I see you have changed your address to come and live near me." This was Miss Robinson speaking, her shining grey eyes twinkling with amusement. Miss Robinson was the senior English teacher at this mixed, boys and girls grammar school, and its youthful headmistress. She was thirty-three. Tony was already half in love with her. She was his favourite teacher of his favourite subject, English. She produced all the plays for the school, in which Tony was always cast in the lead, and she was pretty.

"I'm sorry?" She had asked him to come to her study and he was blushing and slow to understand.

"I live just round the corner from you in Nether Lane, the road that goes up to Lodge Moor Hospital. Do you drive now you're seventeen?"

"Yes, I do." He continued to be baffled.

"Then you can drive me to school." He nearly fainted with anticipation. "You can drive me home after rehearsal this afternoon."

They were currently preparing Shaw's play about the American War of Independence. 'The Devil's Disciple.' He was playing Dick Dudgeon.

"It will be a pleasure," and he really meant it. This was the beginning of the enrichment of a relationship that survived to the end her life and guided him in what to look for in a wife.

He had by now definitely decided that he wanted to get to Oxford, to follow in the path of Harold Hobson, Leonard's friend. He knew it would be a great joy for his father, if he could achieve it. For himself, he was now thinking of acting with the OUDS at the university, and going on the stage as a career. However there was a war on, and he was committed to joining the Fleet Air Arm.

The school, in its patriotic enthusiasm, had formed a squadron of the Air Training Corps, but in addition to that, it was fielding an athletics team to run in the county championships for cadet military organisations. Tony was running in the quarter mile. The senior officer presenting the awards was none other than Major-General Shears, the one-armed officer that Tony had helped to dress at Carlisle Castle, back in 1937. He was now Officer Commanding Northern Command.

"I wonder if he will recognise me, if I win, and he hands

me a cup?" Tony savoured the curious situation which was like something out of an Edwardian Boy's Own novel. It gave him an even greater incentive to win.

Athletics meetings in wartime were primitive in the extreme. They were usually run on grass and because of the difficulty of getting spiked running shoes, either because of shortages, or lack of money, every competitor wore plimsolls to make all things equal. All the competitors had been instructed that, in the event of them winning a trophy, they were to return it to the steward immediately after having been presented. It was quickly replaced on the trophy table for the next hero but two, to receive it at the hands of (or, as in this case,) from the one hand of the Brigadier!

Tony did win the 440 and received his trophy, which was really quite warm from so much handling. There was no flicker of recognition from the brigadier amid the flurry of saluting. There was no 'stage door' where Tony could go and stand, so the sentimental moment passed. After all there was a huge gulf of maturity between twelve and seventeen!

Chapter Nineteen

The aftermath of the blitz was more and more work for Leonard. There was the distribution of the clothing sent by the Christian Science Church from Boston, U.S.A., there was more demand for healing work, most of which was re-assurance rather than bodily ills; there were the continued journeys to Catterick.

It was all very well for him to constantly assert to himself the infinite capacity of Devine Love to energise all his work, but there was no doubt that in the terms of this material world, he was running down fast. His condition found the weak spot, his teeth. His mouth was bleeding, he had advanced gingivitis. He consulted with Mr. Guisburn, his next door neighbour, the dentist, who told him he must have all his teeth extracted, and recommended a practice not far away. He was rather ashamed to go but knew he couldn't continue as he was.

"Come in Mr. Godley, Mr. Guisburn gave us an idea of your problem. Just sit in the chair and I'll take a look." Leonard sat in the mahogany and leather chair that was cranked back to prostrate him into a vulnerable position. A bright light blinded him and Mr. Spiers prodded and poked painfully, sighing more and more deeply.

"Have them all out, that's the answer. Have a set of false ones and there's an end to your troubles."

"You think so, do you?"

"Oh yes, certainly; we can do it for you on Thursday."

"Oh! I see. How long will it take for me to recover and fit false teeth?"

"In two weeks we should be able to fit you with a temporary set and then a personally moulded set two weeks after that. Completely sorted out in a month."

"A month. I'll think about it; there are certain duties I have that would have to be fitted in. I'll let you know." And he leaped out of the recumbent chair feeling he had escaped obliteration.

"Well, let us know soon, so we can fit you in at your convenience; we're very busy you see." This, patently, was not true; the telephone had remained silent and there was clearly no need for a receptionist. Leonard could see there was a metaphorical rubbing of hands at the prospect of a substantial transaction.

"And how much will it cost?"

"Oh! Not a lot when you consider it means you never have to go at dentist again."

"How much?"

"Twenty pounds," said Mr. Spiers quickly.

"Does that include the false teeth?"

Mr. Spiers read Leonard's caution correctly and merely added, "Guineas; twenty guineas, total."

"Thank you, I'll let you know." He felt better already, knowing that it was not the way to go. The next few days he concentrated on trying to heal his condition, asserting that his body was no more than a convenient carapace within which to continue our spiritual destiny within the limitations of this material world. At least the bleeding stopped.

Chapter Twenty

"If you want to get into Oxford, we'd better do something positive about applying to a college. Have you thought about which college?" Tony was driving Miss Robinson to school one morning when she raised the subject.

"Yes, I've chosen Pembroke."

"Why is that?"

"I loved the way you taught 'Boswell's Life of Johnson', and he went there."

"And had to leave because he couldn't afford to stay!"

"Does that mean I can't afford it?"

"No, I don't think so. Colleges organise themselves into groups. You choose a group and apply to a specific college. There are three things that decide your tactics: one, your chances of winning a scholarship awarded by a particular college; two, the size of the college; large usually means expensive living costs (rent of rooms, service, board, they call them 'Battels') and the third and last, (rather ironically), is the subject you are studying. Does the college have a scholarship in that subject; does it have its own tutors in that subject? Now you are going to read English Literature, but there are not many scholarships in English Literature. Oxford doesn't regard it as a significant subject worthy of serious study. In fact, except that you are mad keen on Oxford as a place, I would point you in the direction of Cambridge for English Literature. But I can see that you are not going to be an academic; you want to be an actor, don't you?"

"Is that silly?"

"No; it's not silly if you get a degree behind you in the likely case that it won't provide you with a living. You'd make a splendid teacher, you know!"

"But I don't want to be a teacher, saving your presence; couldn't live up to your standards, you see. My spelling's awful!"

"All right then, but bear it in mind, and stop flattering me," she smiled.

Now let's continue. I don't think you would win a scholarship; you have insight but not academic discipline. No flattery from me then! However I still think you should take a scholarship exam; the papers are wide ranging and will give you the chance to shine on some of them. It puts you in a higher category of applicant and will lead to being offered a place. The offer of a place will mean you will be given a Sheffield City scholarship. Pembroke is a good choice from the size point of view; it's small. I looked it up when you mentioned it once before: it only has one English Don, and he's the world authority on Anglo-Saxon in general and 'Beowulf' in particular. That's hardly your cup of tea. It has no scholarship in English to apply for but it does have one in History. I suggest you try that. You're good at History, so I'm told. Go on, try that. And another thing I found out is that McGowan, the History tutor, is an authority on the American War of Independence. That's your subject, isn't it, playing as you are, Dick Dudgeon in 'The Devil's Disciple'.

"All right, then, let's write today."

The little Morris Eight ticked to a halt in front of Miss Robinson's study: they smiled a conspiratorial smile at each other and went their separate ways.

Chapter Twenty-One

Pembroke College in November 1942 was about as gloomy as the war news, disaster and defeat in all theatres. As the college was occupied by the Intelligence Corps (much to the smug amusement of the dons) there were no undergraduates in residence, but there was enough accommodation for the few taking the entrance and scholarship examinations. Among the khaki uniforms, schoolboys looking pale and worried, as they plodded the quadrangles and staircases muttering facts into their school scarves.

Tony, lacking that academic discipline remarked upon by Miss Robinson, was wallowing guiltlessly in the academic atmosphere, which he saw in more romantic terms. He did have a book open as he luxuriated in a basket chair that was as deep as a bath, but he found it difficult to concentrate as his eyes wandered round the empty walls which he mentally decorated with paintings from his home.

The night was very dark; there was, of course, the blackout in force, but the November gloom emphasised the darkness. He had been invited to go and dine in hall and he groped his way down the staircase into the quad. Suddenly, through the archway leading to the Master's Lodging, came a low flying white feathered owl, or so it seemed. This was the Master on his way to chapel. He was lit by his own white surplice, fluttering over his long Doctor's gown. On top of his white head, above a beaked face and piercing eyes, was balanced a mortarboard of seemingly gigantic proportions. This was generating such aeronautical energy that it seemed to be elevating him above the flagstones as he swept along. Could he be real, or was he an Oxford phantom come to warn the Intelligence Corps of yet another disaster? He could have been from any century since the college was built.

The apparition urged Tony to greater efforts of revising later in the evening. Meanwhile he followed in the wake of the Master, bypassing the chapel and going straight to the great Hall. Here was more magic. To comply with the blackout regulations without attempting the impossible task of blacking out the twenty-foot-high stained glass windows, the college was allowed to use candlelight. It was confidently assumed that no light would escape into the sky to attract any German airman beastly enough to want to bomb Oxford. The candlesticks were glowing silver and even the beakers filled with temperance drinking water, were seventeenth century silver. Presumably the governing Fellows had made another confident assumption; that no member of the Intelligence Corps could possibly be tempted to pocket his beaker.

The examination papers next day were not too terrifying and, as Miss Robinson had predicted, allowed him to demonstrate his wider reading on the subject of the American War of Independence. His interview with McGowan seemed to go fluently and he left Oxford confident that he would return.

Some two weeks later there arrived, a chubby, high quality envelope, bearing the engraved crest in pink, of Pembroke College.

"You open it, Dad," said Tony; partly out of trepidation, but also hoping that what it contained would wipe away all his father's troubles. Edith sat still in her chair, eyes closed, praying. Although, how at that late stage, prayer could alter the contents, Tony could not imagine.

The look on Leonard's face told it all. He flushed with pride and joy and a tear came into one eye, quickly blinked away as emotion was suppressed. "Yes, they've offered you a place, to be taken up when you are released from service. Well done, well done: oh what joy this gives me, Tony." He handed him the letter and Tony saw it confirmed, signed by H.L.Drake, the Senior Tutor. "You know you could go next October, if you wanted to; they will defer you a year if you have a place at university."

"Yes, I know, but I wouldn't want to interrupt the Oxford experience, and by volunteering for the Fleet Air Arm I get my choice of service. I don't want to go into the Army and have a rotten time like you did, and if you wait to be called up, that's what can happen."

"Yes, I suppose you're right." But Leonard looked doubtful.

"Don't worry, Dad, it's a long training."

"Let's hope so. I wish it was all over." And for a moment he looked desperate.

"I must ring Miss Robinson, she'll be thrilled, I know."

It was the weekend and no school until Monday, so he went to the telephone. Miss Robinson lived with her uncle who was a widower some twenty years older than his niece. He had a daughter who was already at Oxford reading Politics, Philosophy and Economics. On the few occasions when Tony had called to deliver something to the house, it was always her uncle, the Doctor of Music, whose forbidding presence opened the door. Tony sensed resentment at his popularity with Miss Robinson. Whether the fierce doctor disapproved because he felt it was professionally indiscrete, or straight forward jealousy, Tony had not given it much thought. The arrogance of youth could afford to ignore it.

It was Dr. Linfoot who answered the phone. “Yes?” His tone, as always was negative.

“This is Tony Godley; is it possible to speak to Miss Robinson, please?”

“No, she’s not available.”

“May I leave a message?” A pause that Tony felt might be followed with a firm “No.”

“Yes?”

“Could you tell her that I have been offered a place at Pembroke?” Another pause that seemed to suggest disapproval of Pembroke’s judgement; no hint of congratulation there.

“If I see her, I will tell her, goodbye.” The receiver went down and never did the true meaning of ‘goodbye’ seem more cynically betrayed.

***

On Monday morning the beep, beep, from Miss Robinson’s car, rushed Tony from his breakfast. He grabbed his school bag and ran down into the road to where his teacher was just moving over to the passenger street. As he opened the driver’s door he blurted out, “Did you get my message?”

“No, what message?”

“I left it with your uncle on the phone. I’ve been offered a place by Pembroke!”

“Oh! How wonderful, congratulations.” And he could see she nearly kissed him. ‘I wish she had,’ he thought. “Your parents must be so pleased; aren’t they?” She checked herself with this domestic interjection.

"Yes, they are; it's a joy to see, but of course I'm thrilled myself, and a bit shaken by my complacency that it was bound to happen. It's just that I have this strong feeling that the right things will fall into place. Tell me not to be so smug," he said allowing himself an intimate glance into her smiling face.

"Oh life will soon start to tell you that, without me starting now. Just hang on to your confidence and be glad. Anyway you've got to take your Higher School Certificate papers next term. That will wipe the smile off your face."

"And it's my call up papers after that." For a moment he thought of raising the matter of her uncle's boorish behaviour, but he instinctively realised that it was none of his business; so didn't mention it.

He thought of something even more personal to say as he wizzed the little Morris Eight across the city.

"I don't like my name."

"Your name. What's wrong with Godley?"

"No; not that bit. The other bit, Tony. I think it sounds weak, and I just don't like diminutives."

"What then?"

"Michael, my second name. I like that, and it is my name. Silly not to use it."

"But people love a diminutive; you'll be called Mike, and that's much worse than Tony."

"No they won't; I won't allow it."

"Well why don't you disallow Tony, and insist on Anthony?"

"Too late, and I don't like Anthony much either."

"Well, I never guessed all this was going on in your head; thank goodness I always call you Godley."

"Yes, I like that, and I always think of you as Miss Robinson, even though I know your first name, which I think is so pretty."

"I think we had better change the subject."

"Yes, I agree, except to say that the reason I raised the subject is that when I go into the navy, I shall have the chance to change it: no one will know me and they will say, "What's your name?" and I can reply Michael, and there, it's done."

"I don't think your Chief Petty Officer is going to be much concerned; you'll be Godley to him, if not just a rank, the lowest of the low, and anyway, if he notices you at all, it's bad news."

"I say, you seem to know a lot about naval life."

"I do. My father was a commander in the Royal Navy, but I hardly knew him. He was drowned in the Great War; I was only seven. And another thing, I have a fiancé in the navy now, he's also a Commander R.N."

Tony felt a blow to his stomach as if struck by a football. Somehow he had never assumed that she belonged to someone else: she was his, and his alone; certainly not to that horrid uncle, who Tony had assumed was the only other man in her life. Oh, the arrogance of youth. Was this the beginning of life knocking over his complacency?

"Ah! I see." He was floundering. "Where is he serving?"

"He's in the Mediterranean, on a destroyer. My letters come from Alexandria."

Their conversation flagged after that and Miss Robinson knew she had wounded him. She knew she should have told him before, but somehow their affectionate friendship had just crept up on them like sunshine. She didn't want to dispel a warmth that was so hard to sustain with a destroyer in the Med.

Chapter Twenty-Two

'Report to H.M.S. St. Vincent, Gosport, Hants before 1600 hours, 8th August 1943. Travel warrant is enclosed.'

This was an order, the first order he had ever received; the end of freedom; the end of option. Such thoughts, however, did not occur to him because he was happy to comply. For Leonard it was quite different; he was the one who felt the sanction, the power behind the order, the loss of freedom; he had to surrender his only son. He fought the deadening sense of loss; he affirmed the unity of man and God, that there could be no separation in the divine mind: but his efforts to rise above the limitations of his earthly love of child, seemed puny.

Tony was soon to be Michael and exhilarated by the prospect. His enthusiasm stabbed at Leonard; uncharacteristically he wished to crush it.

"Well, there it is, Dad, I'll be off in three weeks from today. It just gives me time to run for the school in the finals; we stand a good chance of winning, we're strong at all distances."

"I don't want you to go." Leonard's eyes were suddenly blazing.

"But, Dad, I have to go; it's an order."

"I don't mean go into the navy, I mean to the athletics. We've only got you for a few more days and I don't want you to be away in Leeds."

"But, Dad, they're depending on me in the quarter mile; I

can't let them down."

"Let them down; let them down! That's nothing but personal pride and pitiful tribalism." Leonard couldn't believe he was saying this, but he knew that that is what he felt: family love was more important than tribalism. "I forbid you to go."

Tony was stunned. He had never seen his father like this before, was he going mad? Something told him that he might be; he didn't argue.

"All right, I'll tell them I can't go."

Leonard collapsed with temporary relief. "Thank you."

Tony wondered how he would break it to Mr. Barnes: Mr. Barnes, the Physics master, who, being too old to be called up, had devoted himself passionately to establishing the Air Training Corps and its athletic team. He felt it to be a patriotic duty, and he was so proud of his boys and their future glory. It was, of course emphasised by the fact that he had no children of his own and he drew great strength from the admiration and loyalty generated among these innocently enthusiastic boys.

Tony wanted to discuss it with Miss Robinson on the way to school, but he found her strangely cold this morning.

"I've had my call up papers," he said, hoping to start the discussion.

"Oh! Your parents must be sad," she said and lapsed into silence until the end of the journey. Tony parked the car, turned and smiled at her; she looked up, unsmiling, and said, "I'm sorry I've been so quiet this morning, but I've had some sad news. My fiancé has been killed: his ship was sunk in the Med."

Tony wanted to hold her, comfort her, love her. But he could do no more than say, "I'm so sorry." They looked into each other's eyes for a fleeting moment, and she did take some slight comfort from his loving look, but she, like Leonard, did not want him to go.

Flight Lieutenant Barnes took Tony's bad news surprisingly sympathetically. "I quite understand," he said, and Tony sensed that he did. Perhaps he wished he had a son to love like that.

Chapter Twenty-Three

The goodbyes, when they came were easier than the build up to them. After all he wasn't going straight off to the front exactly. He was off to Portsmouth and the world of the Royal Navy for which he had had a romantic attachment since he was about eight, and at one stage wanted to make it his whole life. Here was a chance to find out whether he would really like it. A buoyant boy in tweed jacket and grey flannel trousers squeezed himself onto the crowded train on the London platform. All trains were crowded in wartime, everyone seemed to be ordered to move about, and with a kitbag as big as another person. The corridors were as jammed as the compartments, and going to the lavatory required desperation. Ticket inspection was an assault course, the inspectors (when there were any) were popped out at stopping stations like champagne corks. But then most people were travelling on government warrants rather than a cheap workman's morning they were trying to pass off as a monthly return.

There was no one to see him off at the station; he had had no opposition to his insistence on that. Stuffed into the train, he already felt he had made a break with the past.

The morning took him to London; the train stopped at every town. Then it was down the labyrinthine tube at St. Pancras, across to Waterloo and its massive stairs from the river. The Portsmouth train was a haze of blue and white; it seemed that khaki soldiers (except for the odd marine) were banned. It was in the corridor again, but the kitbags were white. Although Tony had by then, been to London several times, it had always been to Chelsea and Westminster; he had never seen the sprawl of suburbia. Now he did, as the train screeched and ground over the points of Clapham Junction, Surbiton, and Worcester Park, before bowing into gentry Surrey.

He suddenly realised how hungry he was when he was wedged on his way to Portsmouth. He hadn't eaten since a massive breakfast that must have taken most of the rations for the week. He should have bought a sandwich at Waterloo but he heard 'report before 1600hrs' ringing in his ears, as he bumped across the station.

He looked about him to see if he could spot any other tweed jackets, but no, just jolly and miserable tars. Until a tweed jacket with a full bladder came bulging down the corridor, like a fish going down a gannet's neck.

"Excuse me, excuse me, desperate!" He kept saying, in convincing tones. To have tried to engage him in conversation just then would have been useless and cruel. Tony would wait until he returned relieved.

This he did and as their faces more or less, kissed in the crush, Tony spluttered out. "Not going to St. Vincent, are you, by any chance?"

"Yes I am, and you too?" And he squeezed in beside Tony to continue the conversation. Tony nodded as vigorously as he could in the space available.

"Fifty-five Pilots Course, yes?"

"That's right."

"My name's Douglas; what's yours?"

This was it then; this was good bye to Tony, this was the beginning of Michael. Tony took a deep breath, he hoped was not obvious and said, "Michael, Michael Godley." It was really quite easy once you'd said it.

"Douglas Hurd, how do. Can't shake hands, no room. 'G' for Godley, 'H' for Hurd. That's good. next in the alphabet; we'll probably see a lot of each other."

By the time they reached Portsmouth Harbour, and had taken the ferry to Gosport, they knew all about each other. Douglas had highly recommended himself to Michael by revealing that he had just completed two terms at RADA, and was set on a stage career. They became firm friends in the short time fate kept them together.

H.M.S. St.Vincent was, as they say in the navy, a 'Stone Frigate.' That is to say, it was a shore establishment run like a ship, from which you were allowed 'Liberty' from time to time. "Liberty men, fall in." the Pipe would say and a metaphorical liberty boat would pull away from the guardhouse to return before the allotted four hours had expired. An organisation that has a secret language makes for a warm belonging. On the other hand the convention may enrage you. Michael found it amusing and boyish.

The building itself, had been erected in the end of the eighteenth century to house French prisoners captured during the Napoleonic Wars: it was, in fact a prison but a productive prison. It had really been a factory; the prisoners were put to work. They probably found it much more congenial than serving under Napoleon, and many a British tar would gladly have exchanged his hammock on the 'Victory' for a bunk in 'St. Vincent.'

It really hadn't changed much for these aspiring airmen, as they collected their bell-bottomed, blue collared uniforms, lanyards and flat caps, and doubled across the vast parade ground. Tradition was even more vigorously imbued by the training staff; the Warrant Officer, the Chief Petty Officers, the Petty Officers and the Leading Seamen, all of whom were too old for active service and so had started their careers as boys soon after the turn of the century. The Leading Seaman who taught the mysteries of the bowline and the clove hitch seemed to be part of the 'Boyhood of Raleigh'. the Petty Officer who marched them on the rifle range wore the Polar Medal from Scott's last expedition. He also had a finely honed filthy sexual wit that made his young gentlemen blush. At least they were supposed to be young gentlemen, because trainee naval aviators were officer cadets, ranked as Leading Airmen and wore a white cap bands to inhibit their behaviour.

There were, of course less traditional officers recruited into the Royal Naval Volunteer Reserve. One lieutenant in particular whose peace time career had been in the theatre. He had volunteered for the navy because he liked sailors, and his skill at handling parade grounds of them was legendary. Even the Warrant Officer admitted his admiration for this 'bugger'.

A couple of months after they had joined, it was Trafalgar Day and an excuse for some 'Skylarking'. Lieutenant Theatre borrowed a Wren Officer's uniform, her tri-corn hat was perched on his red, beautifully coiffeured wig. He toured the mess decks as an exquisite pantomime dame, bantering with his boys as if it were Boxing Day at the Opera House in Manchester. Michael and Douglas were delighted and shortly afterwards were recruited into the cast of his nativity play. Michael was the Angel Gabriel and Douglas was Joseph. There can't have been many naval barracks where it was possible to see a nativity play before going on leave for Christmas 1943.

Perhaps learning to fly with the U.S. Navy would be a little different.

Chapter Twenty-Four

Christmas leave was embarkation leave before sailing for the United States; this cast a gloom on home in Sheffield. Leonard was razor thin with overwork and the loss of Michael. He was disappointed with himself for not being able to rise above this separation and fear for the future. He asserted the unity of the Divine Spirit, protecting and guiding as in the comforting phrases in the Twenty-Third Psalm, 'Yea, though I walk through the valley of the shadow of death, I shall fear no evil; for thou art with me,' But why couldn't he be as sanguine as some other fathers who consigned their sons to God, and left it at that. His friend Stephen (who with Mary he had healed several times of other troubles) and whose son Bryan was now flying bombing raids over Germany. All I can say to myself, is; though I suffer, others shall not. This is how he left it with himself.

Michael was sensitive to his father's torment but couldn't help but feel happy with his own lot. That is really what Leonard wanted to achieve and was glad to see it in Michael. Anyway, there was a distraction, Guy was coming for Christmas. Guy was not on embarkation leave; he was on sick leave, prior to demobilization. Guy was now nearly fifty and had developed high blood pressure, for which in a very un-Christian Science way, he was very grateful; he was to be invalided out of the service. Whether this hypertension had been brought on by his responsibilities for Pier Number Three on Loch Fyne or the generosity of the Duke of Argyle at dinner, nobody seemed to care, but Guy was glad to return to Bohemia, trusting that God would provide. The provisions he brought from Scotland were shockingly sumptuous: a ham, a bottle of fine old malt whisky, chocolates, and heather scented toilet water. Guy's efforts to rise above the appetites of the flesh were nostalgic, to say the least. Leonard cheered up in the presence of his sensuous friend.

"Come on, Leonard, you need a little grounding; too much spirituality makes you light headed: your balloon starts tugging at its moorings. Here have a whisky!"

"That will certainly make me light headed. No, I think I'll have a chocolate; are there any creams?" Creams wouldn't hurt his gums.

"Here, Michael, you have a whisky." (Guy had always called him Michael; it was he who put the idea of a name change into his head.) "This is a single malt whisky, fifteen years old, out of the Duke of Argyle's cellar. This is as smooth as a baby's bottom, try it; it's only made of wholesome highland water flowing through the rye."

"All right then." He found his first sip so seductive that it was some two years before he drank any alcohol again; it all tasted so horrible after that malt whisky.

Michael tried to ring Miss Robinson, but only received from her uncle, the glacial information that she was away for the holiday. Michael might not have believed him, but a stifled sigh at the end of the message suggested that he was missing her too.

They were sorry to see Guy go back to London. Michael drove him to the station and they embraced affectionately on the platform. Some eyebrows were raised at this vision of a

Petty Officer hugging a Leading Aircraftsman, but then, there was a war on.

The parting from Leonard was not so easy but it had to come when then Movement Order came with Michael's warrant for the train to Greenock on the Clyde where he was to join the liner Queen Mary for a swift dash across the Atlantic to Halifax, Nova Scotia. It was easy saying goodbye to Edie, her faith was simple and total. 'The Lord is thy shepherd,' was enough to allay any fears for both of them. But for Leonard it was a test of his own faith; it was a spiritual crisis which he did not want to involve Michael, whose confidence was supreme, and lack of fear, total. That must not be threatened. The actual parting, therefore, was emotionless. No embrace, just a handshake, a momentary look of understanding as to what was going on behind the eyes. "I'll be all right, Dad, don't you worry; you've taught me how to protect myself." Then a heave of the kitbag into the train; a slamming of the carriage door, a swift wave out of the open window, and Michael felt a guilty joy at his approaching adventure.

Out in the Clyde the 'three funnels of the 'Queen Mary' dematerialised in the Scottish mist as the tender chugged them out to cliff sided liner, painted battleship grey in her wartime livery. There were about fifty passengers clambering up the gangway into the hole in the side of E deck, but no one that Michael knew. They were mainly American airmen returning home after shattering tours of duty over Europe. He felt isolated for the first time.

This sense of alienation and dream-like isolation continued when he followed the directions of the Quartermaster to find his cabin. The liner had, of course, been stripped of all her luxury when she was prepared for war service, but there still remained the perfect, pale oak panelling, along the endless corridors connecting the functional parts of the ship. To look down a hundred yards of a bereft, but gleaming tunnel, sent a shiver of unreality down his spine. He thought he heard the roar of the fifteen thousand American troops that would fill the ship on her return journey mingling with the vapid laughter of the passengers that the liner had been built for.

When he found his cabin it became clear how it was possible for the 'Mary' to carry fifteen thousand men and their equipment. The cabin, originally designed to accommodate two people in luxury now accommodated ten in layers like a slave ship. Later he was glad to be allocated to look out duty on the boat deck, rather than be slotted on his shelf. The sense of isolation lifted suddenly when the rest of his draft appeared in the mess hall, having arrived on later trains.

"I say. Isn't it creepy, this ship." Douglas was feeling the same. "Plenty of room in the lifeboats, though, eh?"

"At thirty knots, no U Boat can catch her, so we can concentrate on the food," said Michael. "Haven't seen a spread like this since 1939; no wonder the Americans are bigger than us: eggs over, eggs sunnyside, eggs scrambled, eggs boiled, soft, hard, bacon fat, bacon lean, ham thick, ham thin, frankfurters, hamburgers, waffles, maple syrup, corn flakes, cream, pancakes, jams, grapefruit, oranges, orange juice, grapes, fruit salad, toast, rye bread, bagels, muffins, milk, iced tea, hot tea, coffee, chocolate!

"Go on, ask for something they haven't got; go on."

"Can't think of anything; yes I can, marmalade. I don't think he would think it was funny," said Douglas, eyeing the twenty stone, black, all-in wrestler waving his spoon.

Chapter Twenty-Five

Leonard was toying with a piece of grey bread which he dipped into a glass of milk just a quarter full. Most of the rations for the week had gone on entertaining Michael and Guy. Leonard didn't mind, he couldn't eat anyway because his teeth hurt. Suddenly he got up from the table and went to the telephone. He scrabbled through the directory to find the dentists number. He jabbed his fingers angrily at the dialling ring.

"Dental Surgury, Spiers speaking."

"Leonard Godley here. I came to see you about having my teeth out."

"Yes?" Mr Spiers' voice rose expectantly.

"I'd like it done as soon as possible."

"Let me see now; we could do it this afternoon."

"I'll come," snapped Leonard.

"Very well. I suggest that you do not come by car as you may be still feeling the effects of the anaesthetic by the time you leave."

"I see; when shall I come then?"

"Now, if you wish."

"I'll be there in half an hour."

He slammed down the telephone and set off to walk the mile to the dentist, without saying a word to Edith. As he walked his mind rampaged round his head, his spiritual assertions battling with his bodily agonies. "The body is merely a carapace of convenience for the soul; it is not a prison of oppression. Man is free of human limitation released by his unity with God." His pace increased with his mental struggle, until he was almost running by the time he reached Spiers' surgery.

"We are all ready for you; this is my brother who will administer the anaesthetic so that you will be quite comfortable. Shall I take your coat?"

Leonard was standing there stunned. "Yes, thank you." He relaxed and let his coat slip from his shoulders.

"In here, please."

Once more he found himself among the threatening mahogany, the clamping leather, the piercing brass, and smell of disinfectant with its smug superiority to disease. The room was dark except for the directional light penetrating the mouth and pinning his head to the chair.

"Now I have your dental details from your first visit; I assume you wish me to remove all the teeth as previously discussed." Leonard nodded and closed his eyes.

"My brother is now going to place the mask over your mouth and nose, and all you have to do is breathe deeply and gently until you are asleep. When you awake you will be sore but relieved of the pain and discomfort you have been suffering. Now just breathe deeply."

Leonard did as he was told and he could feel his body falling away under him, sinking into the chair like a coat of mail or a diver's leaden suit.

The connection between his brain and muscles was severed; he had lost control. But he felt the canvas strap being tightened round his head, securing him to the chair. He tried to open his eyes, but he could not; he tried to open his mouth and speak, but he could not. He felt the first tooth pulled and opened his lungs to scream, but no sound came. The second tooth tore his head apart; he screamed, but no sound came. And so it continued until he felt his head was severed and rising and rising and he looked down, swimming in an inverted ecstasy of pain, and then it left him and he was suspended over his own body slumped in the bloodied chair.

The brothers Spiers were bowed over him and muttering.

"I think he's a gonner; what shall we do?

"Is there a pulse?"

"I can't tell, I think so."

"Let's leave him a few minutes and see if he recovers." And Leonard watched them from above as they shuffled off into the other room.

Then He descended and inhabited his body again; and the pain returned, but bearable. He could move, he could speak, he moaned as the brothers returned ringing their hands in relief.

"We just left you to rest a little. How are you feeling?" Leonard moaned again.

"You continue to rest; we'll call you a taxi to take you home. Is your wife there?" Leonard nodded. They left the room again. Leonard tried to leave the hateful chair but was too weak; he sank back and swooned.

"The taxi is here, let me help you, I've given him your address and paid him. You'll soon be home: just go straight to bed and take these pills I've put in your pocket, and keep washing your mouth out with salt water. I'll see you next week to see about your new set."

Leonard was helped into the taxi and was relieved to find that his feet made meaningful contact with the floor.

"Had your teeth out, have you? You never regret it, had

mine out ten years ago. Ee! It's lovely taking them out at night and popping them in that glass." Leonard dozed as the driver continued to enthuse about dentures. "That's what I gave my daughter for her wedding present. All her teeth out; ee! She was that pleased."

The driver stopped enthusing long enough to help Leonard into the house where Edith was appalled at his appearance. His mouth was hanging open and misshapen like an idiot. Saliva and blood dribbled down his chin and stained his shirt. He was pale as paper and trembled. "Put me to bed, Edie," he pleaded.

In bed his head began to swim; his brain boiled; he felt that his re-entry to his body had been incomplete and misdirected as if he had landed mentally sideways. He began to repeat the pain of the operation, but detached from its bodily impact. It developed a resentment, an anger, that made him aggressive and depraved. "Fuck off you useless bitch," were the words that came out of his mouth, though not in his head, when Edith patted his head and tried to soothe him. It was as if boiling water had been thrown over her.

She shrieked and recoiled as tears sprang from her eyes. She saw a vision of her drunken father indulging his frustrations on his family. She controlled herself and recovered slightly; she tried again. "Can I get you anything, Leonard; shall I read to you?"

"Fucking well leave me alone, as you've always done, you useless bitch."

This time she ran trembling from the bedroom and crumpled into her chair sobbing. It was not Leonard speaking: he was in the reverse situation to that in the dentist's chair. Words were issuing from his mouth and lungs beyond his control: he was possessed! He writhed about among the bed clothes; he clutched at his penis which he found erect, but without sensation. Was this the source of the evil? Should he cut it off? The pain experience surged again and distracted him.

"There is no fucking God." He howled in despair: Edith heard him and shuddered again. She reached for her 'Science and Health', and began to intone the Lord's Prayer as interpreted in Christian Science:

"Our Father which art in heaven,
Our Father-Mother god, all harmonious
Hallowed be thy name,
Adorable One
Thy kingdom come
Thy kingdom is come."

Leonard continued to rave: now it was the War again, the first war.

"Eddie! Where's Eddie? Eddie's dead! No he's not, I just saw him; Eddie's not dead.

Come on get out; thank Christ they're letting us retreat. Look out here's another, get down. I'm going back; Eddie's not dead. You daft bugger; let him be: Eddie's better off dead. Eddie! Eddie! Eddie! I'm coming, Eddie. There you are, Eddie: give us your arm, Eddie; over my back, Eddie, over my back; hang on, Eddie; you're not dead, Eddie; you're my mate, Eddie; you're my fate, Eddie; come on, Eddie; we can't wait, Eddie. You're alive, Eddie; you're alive, Eddie!

He seemed calmer now: Edith reached for the telephone, she wished she could ring Doris, but Doris had no telephone. She wished she could ring Michael but he was halfway across the Atlantic. She dialled the number for Mrs. Battle. Mrs. Battle was the only other Christian Science Practitioner of

Healing in Sheffield. Leonard found her antipathetic. She was a dominant woman who Leonard felt achieved her healings by willpower rather than love. "Now pull yourself together, you know very well from your reading of Science and Health with key to the Scriptures by our leader Mary Baker Eddy, that there is no sickness in the mind of God. I shall come and see you again in a week's time and I expect you to have improved." It was more than their health was worth not to have improved: if they had not improved, they rang up Leonard Godley, rather than face Mrs. Battle again. Mrs. Battle knew this and was equally anti pathetic towards Leonard Godley.

"Hello, Maude Battle here; can I help you?"

"This is Edith Godley."

"Ye-e-es." There was an audible application of brakes as Maude relented on the "Can I help you?"

"Leonard has a belief of mental collapse. He needs help; can you come?"

Maude suppressed a tendency to gloat. "What appear to be the manifestations?"

"He is raving and shouting obscenities." Edith did not know how she could repeat these words; it was evidence of her desperation and isolation from her beloved Leonard

"Is he physically violent?"

"He thrashes about in his bed, but hasn't lashed out."

"I will come round immediately; do not approach him."

"Thank you." Edith wondered whether she had done the right thing.

Maude Battle immediately rang a general practitioner of her acquaintance.

"Doctor Quayle, good afternoon. This is Maude Battle here; I wonder if you could advise me."

"Good afternoon, Mrs. Battle; I trust you are well." He knew better than to expect her to say otherwise. "Certainly; if I am able."

"A colleague of mine, Leonard Godley, I think you know him, seems to have had a severe mental breakdown. I have not seen him yet but have a description from his wife which is alarming; he is raving wildly and shouting obscenities. I think it may be necessary to section him for her safety and his well-being. Would you be able and willing to come and see him with me?"

"Is he violent?"

"I believe he is."

"Very well, I'll come; give the address and I'll meet you there. You know I shall bring some sedatives to inject."

"Yes."

"I'll take you to him." Edith was alarmed to be introduced to Doctor Quayle, although she knew Leonard knew him, and he was a sympathetic man. As she struggled up the stairs, desperately tired with worry, she began to explain about the extraction of the teeth that had brought on the collapse.

"Let's have a look at him." Doctor Quayle had his bag open already and Maude un-characteristically stepped behind. Edith approached Leonard first. "Leonard, Leonard?"

Leonard who had his head buried into the pillow, swung round and started up. "What the fuck do you want, piss off!"

"Leonard Godley, control yourself." Maude Battle tried her technique powerfully.

"There is no fucking God, so you can fuck off for start, Maude Medler."

"Well, at least he recognises me." She did not know whether to be appalled or flattered.

"Mr. Godley; do you know me. I've come to help you?" He

was approaching with his syringe full, and at the ready.

"Get away from me you're a bloody dentist, aren't you? Look what you've done to me." And he opened his mouth wide; it was raw red, dribbling hole."

Quayle was clever; he said, "No, I am a doctor and want to see what they've done to you, so they can be punished: may I look?" It worked; Leonard let him approach and as the doctor peered into the mouth, he stuck the syringe into Leonard's forearm. He stepped back and Leonard started to thrash about like a hooked fish until he, at last, relaxed. He did not become unconscious, he just looked dazed.

"He seems very resistant to sedatives; that was a massive dose, but at least he's calmer now." Doctor Quayle turned to Edith and spoke gently. "I am sure, Mrs. Godley you want Leonard to be cared for, so I am going to arrange for him to go to a home where they are familiar with these conditions, and they will soon make him happy again. It's just that he has had a terrible physical shock. Do you understand?" Edith nodded dumbly.

Quayle turned to Maude Battle and explained, "I'm going straight back to my surgery and making arrangements for him to be taken to the Wharncliffe. I don't believe that he needs to be sectioned at this stage, provided he goes quietly. That injection should last two hours; I'll tell them it's an emergency and they'll come straight away with an ambulance and two male nurses. Can you stay with Mrs. Godley until then? I don't want to make the arrangements here, in front of her: after all it is the lunatic asylum."

"Yes, I will, and thank you so much Doctor Quayle for your kind help. Please send your account to my address, will you?"

"I will, and thank you for acting so practically." A fleeting glance of mutual understanding fluttered between them, and he was gone.

Maude stayed with the shattered Edith until the ambulance came half an hour later, and showed a tenderness that Leonard would not have expected.

"Give me your Doris's address, and I'll go and fetch her for you, so you won't be alone."

Chapter Twenty-Six

'The Wharncliffe Asylum' might have been named after some sinister character in a Bronte novel. It was on the Derbyshire moors, outside the city limits, remote enough to avoid any contagion from madness or to hear wails of distress. Even the ambulances used were a self-effacing black, more suited to the criminal. At least the day was sunny, though cold, when Leonard was brought to the eight-foot iron gates, hinged between two massive granite pillars that marked the end of the hospital's embracing walls. The guardhouse oozed its jailer from his snuggery, the smoke of his illicit cigarette following him to the gate, which he opened quickly to avoid its extinction in the ash tray.

As Leonard had come quietly he was able to enter the building with some dignity, though firmly supported by two muscular male nurses. He was calm now, whether from the effect of Dr. Quayle's drug, or because the mental storm had passed, it was difficult to tell. Leonard himself felt that the walls of the corridor were congealing behind him, sealing him inside. The impermeability of the dark green tiles, glinted sanitary indifference at the inmates.

"I must get myself out of here, out of here, out of here." Every thought Leonard had seemed to echo in his head. "Out of here, yes." But he also felt a sense of security creeping over him; a shedding of responsibility, which was refreshing but alarming in the consequence of surrender to madness; a disastrous retreat from life.

He found himself standing naked; every orifice was examined (his mouth produced a gasp) his eyes were bored with lights, his reflexes were tested, he was questioned obliquely.

"Why is this man here?"

"Admitted by Dr. Quayle as being of unsound mind, verbally abusive to his wife whom he did not recognise. He may be suffering the trauma of having all his teeth removed with inadequate anaesthetic."

"What is your name?"

"Leonard Godley; Leonard Godley; Leonard Godley." "Did I say that three times or only once?"

"Do you know who I am?"

"No." The doctor paused, appeared to begin another question, but then stopped and continued with another question.

"How old are you?"

"Twelve."

"What is your address?"

"Fifty-four Carnaby Road." (The doctor shook his head, checking it with the registration form.)

"What is your occupation?"

"Delivery boy." (The doctor shook his head again but decided to follow where his patient might lead.)

"Where did you go to school?"

"Morley Street Council."

"Where are you now?"

"I am working at Mr. Dobson's greengrocer's."

"Do you feel ill?"

"No."

"Why are you here?"
"I don't know."
"Do you want to go home?"
"Yes."
"Who will look after you?"
"My mother and father and my sister Agnes."
"Do you know where you are now?"
"In hospital." ("At least we have a basis of fact at last!")
"We will make you better, will you help me do that?"
"Yes"

"Give him a single room; feed him, and let's see how he gets on. No sedatives." Leonard was led away, his head still echoing.

The door clanged shut on him and his tray of food; he devoured it ravenously in spite of his sore mouth, he drank a pint of water at a gulp. Suddenly the lights went out and only a dim blue bulb leered through a cage on the wall. He crawled into bed and dropped a thousand feet into unconsciousness.

There was a massive explosion that threw him out of bed. The bombardment continued, the earth shook around him and made the crouching figures beside him tremble. Steel helmets rattled on rifles as they shrank like tortoises along the trench to the rear.

"Hold on, Eddie, we're nearly there." The body on his back twitched an answer.

"Roll call: sing out when you hear your name." Corporal Anson cleared his throat.

"Corporal, there's only three of us left: Godley, Love, and Devine."

"Where's the rest?"

"Dead, Corporal, and Eddie was left for dead but we've brought him in. Can we get him to the field ambulance quick, corporal?"

"Godley, Love and Devine, the only ones left. Blimey, it's enough to make you a fucking believer. I'm going to change my name to fucking Angel! Get on then, get Love to the ambulance." Leonard climbed back into bed.

"You're all right now, Eddie." He slept again.

"Can I see Edith, my wife?"

"Do you love your wife?" Doctor Dent was proceeding cautiously.

"Of course I do."

"Good: then we'll arrange it in a few days; you need to rest still." Leonard accepted it. He knew he was travelling through a mental journey and he wasn't there yet.

"Jacob, tell me about this Christian Science, then."

"Yes; well, that's a tall order, but what I can say with certainty, is that it has taught us how to pray; pray and be protected. I suppose the starting point is the affirmation that God is Love and prayer is affirmation, not supplication. God already knows what we need; it is up to us, to connect with his spiritual power by purity of thought and acceptance that man is spiritual, not material."

"So, God is the source of infinite energy to do good; if we can connect with it?"

"Yes."

Leonard was suddenly aware of his surroundings for the first time since he came out of the dentist's chair. The echoing in his head had subsided; the light reflecting from the tiles illuminated rather than threatened, his mind was clearing, but nothing was familiar. Where was home; where was Edith?" He tried the handle of the door out of his room, it was locked. He tried to look through the observation window in the door, but it was opaque from inside. He looked around for a bell to summon help; there was none. He had no idea of what time it was, what day it was, how long he had been there, and how he got there. There was a curtained window; he drew the curtain aside, the window was barred. The sky outside was black and starless; there was a sound of bombers' engines. They were not German engines; they did not have that menacing beat. They were flying very low; it sounded like a whole squadron. Then they were gone and the silence was greater, until they returned, but higher this time and not bunched together. Leonard remembered now; he had heard it before; it was the Lancaster bombers training over the dams in Derbyshire. He must be in the Wharncliffe Lunatic Asylum. It was under their flight path out on the moor.

The shock of realisation stung him but stimulated him: they were saying he was mad; they had locked him up. He stifled a wave of panic.

"I must prove my sanity; I must not frighten them; madmen make us afraid. I must banish fear, my fear, their fear. Who put me here; what have I done to make them afraid? I must write a letter to Edith, a loving letter that they can read; but first I have to speak to them; where are they? They will come if I shout, but they will think I am raving. I must wait until they come in the morning, for now it is night and dark. I must sleep and be peaceful, then they will accept that I am not mad." He smoothed his rumpled bed, plumped up his pillow, lay down and went to sleep.

"You wanted to see me?" The doctor looked expectant, they were alone.

"Yes: I want to say that my mind is clearer now: I know who, and where I am."

"Tell me then."

"I am Leonard Godley, I am a Christian Science

Practitioner of healing and I am in the Wharncliffe Lunatic Asylum."

"Do you know who I am?"

"You are the doctor in charge."

"Yes, but do you recognise me: do you know my name and remember where we met?" Leonard stumbled; he knew this was a hurdle he must jump to be free, but he didn't know what the hurdle was. The doctor smiled. "Let me help you. Let me say Spanish refugees; Boothby, Cumberland."

"Nineteen thirty six!" Leonard bared his gums in an exultant, toothless grin. "You are Doctor Conrad Bronsky, with your Hispano Suiza and Pamela. Where is Pamela now?" Leonard was vital and clear again; he savoured his elation.

"I must say you have recovered well, haven't you? You've penetrated my disguise."

"Yes; you had long white hair that was brown with nicotine; now it's short and black."

"I needed a job, so I changed my appearance, and it worked. I got this appointment, hardly a distinguished one, but I quite like the isolation. I live here you see. I remembered that you came from Sheffield but I was too scared to get in touch with you: after all you don't believe in all my mumbo jumbo, do you?"

"I do, if it alleviates distress: we're all trying to help, aren't we? I hope I shan't need your mumbo jumbo now, but what happened to Pamela?"

"Pamela is having a high old time. She's in the A.T.S, driving some sugar daddy general around the country. You might know him from the Carlisle days, Shears; General Shears."

"Good heavens, what a coincidence."

"Not really. Pamela knew him from those days and pulled

a few strings, she's very good at that. Are you still in touch with Winifred?"

"Oh yes we correspond regularly and speak on the phone; she's still living at Bank's Head and preparing for her next exhibition."

"Well you've passed your sanity test and I've lost another patient. I must say I thought you were a lifer when you first arrived. We've got plenty in here escaping from what we call reality. Well done, we'll see about getting you home. Edith is on the telephone, I assume. It would be nice if you rang her. I'll arrange a taxi, you don't want to arrive in an ambulance, it's bad for your business!" Doctor Bronsky grinned, and they were friends. "We do have a dentist attached to this hospital; I'll arrange for him to fit you with new teeth; all part of the mumbo jumbo treatment, what!"

"Oh thank you, Conrad; it will be a relief."

"Well false teeth must be an 'idea of God; part of Devine Intelligence', eh?"

"I see you've been doing some research, Conrad, good for you." And they both laughed.

"But don't work so hard, Leonard. Haven't you got a hobby that doesn't entail reading and thinking?"

"What else is there?"

"Gardening; building a rabbit hutch; painting like Winifred."

"I wish I could."

"Well, try: it will help to keep you sane."

"All right I'll try."

"And get Edie on the embroidery."

"Thank you for all you've done. I'm sure God brought you here."

"Maybe he did; goodbye."

Chapter Twenty-Seven

Michael of course was totally unaware of his father's breakdown and recovery; in fact, with all the enviable arrogance and optimism of youth, he was thinking only of himself and the first banana he was about to eat for four years. There were two of them nestling on his aluminium sectioned tray as he passed along the 'Chow' line on the Queen Elizabeth.

"Can you remember when you last had a banana, Douglas?"

"No, I can't: nobody told me it would be my last, so there was no reason to remember."

"I think my last banana was just about the same time as my last spoon of sugar in my tea. I can remember that. It was at school, after a tennis match and we were having a cup of tea and a bun in the girls' domestic science lab. And there wasn't enough sugar to go round, and I said I didn't want any; and I have never had sugar in my tea since then; so it's about four years ago."

"That was terribly decent of you."

"No it wasn't. I kept doing things like that. I remember when I was about seven and stealing apples from a garden. They'd seen us and sent for the policeman. He caught me on my next raid and said I'd go to prison and live on bread and water, to which I replied, "I like bread and water", so he let me off!"

"I had no idea I was making friends with a criminal." Douglas finished his hamburger steak and two bananas, and swigged his coffee.

"Come on finish up; we're on watch in ten minutes and it'll take all that time to get onto the boat deck in this great cathedral."

The boat deck, one above the promenade deck was nevertheless swept by freezing spray on the windward side which Michael had drawn. It was blowing a stiff force six from the north west and the 'Queen' was shouldering into it as she raced across the north Atlantic. She was rearing and sliding in the swell in spite of her vast tonnage. Michael wasn't sure what he was looking out for because no U-Boat could catch her twenty knots, and the German battle cruisers were either sunk or skulking in Norway by this time of the war. There were, however, the Northern Lights. They were; radiant in the ionosphere, dancing like veiled Salomes, indigo and red; white and straw. The Lorreli of the north, beckoning to oblivion. Michael would have missed a battle cruiser had it chosen that moment to appear; or indeed the next moment when the motion of the swell vomited (without nausea) his bananas onto the deck: fortunately to be swept overboard by the next dash of spray stinging and cleaning his face.

***

"Anyone caught outside not wearing his balaclava, will be put on a charge." The leading seaman was enjoying terrifying his charges with tales of frozen ears snapping off your head in temperature of thirty below. They were waiting in the dispersal camp at Monkton, Canada, to be sent to their flight training schools and it was still January. There was, however, the diversion of the sports store and its skiing equipment. Sign a chit and learn to ski. A group of them did, and numbed their bottoms on the nursery slopes. Fears of frostbite in vital areas forced them back to camp, there to lie about their newly acquired skills as downhill racers.

"Will you take us tomorrow, Mike?"

"Sorry, boys, I'm being posted tomorrow."

Indeed they were (but not the next day) to the United States Naval Air Station, St. Louis, Missouri. The weather wasn't much warmer there, and all the aircraft were grounded. So it was Ground School: Meteorology, navigation, aircraft recognition, warship recognition, and athletics. The United States Navy was keen to keep its young airmen fit, and so had them swimming, boxing, wrestling. Each physical activity was supervised by a sadist, expert in the sport being taught. They were retired prize fighters and wrestlers, given the rank of Lieutenant Commanders. They couldn't believe their luck; or rather, they could and proceeded to increase in weight exponentially. The physical differences between the British and American cadets was startling. The Americans were twice the weight and a head taller than the British, except for the odd Australian or Scot who had had access to beef in his childhood.

"O.K., now hear this; I'm going to show you how to break a man's back." That certainly got the cadet's attention. The instructor, who would enjoy a post war career as a Hollywood gangster, and had previously, as a wrestler, dislocated more necks than a chicken farmer, called over the weedy ten stone Michael.

"On your knees, Cadet. No; there's no need to pray: it's too late. On your knees, and on your elbows." Michael dumbly obeyed, assuming that it would be irrational for the navy to mutilate its elite at this stage in their careers. Lieutenant Commander Thug then sat astride Michel's back settling his seventeen stone on a refined spine. Michael began to think that rational reasoning was not to be relied on.

"O.K., here's what you do. I tuck my legs inside his: I tuck my arms inside his, and I do this." At which point he straightened his body like a swimmer beginning a race. Michael's body was elevated for a split second as all support was dashed away, then crashed that eighteen inches to the floor that expelled every gasp of breath from his body, and for a split second he seemed to lose consciousness. He hoped that he had not heard the crack of bone as he did so.

"O.K. Cadet; now you can try it on me." These were the next words he was able to hear. He staggered to bestride the elephant, almost split his groin in the attempt,, tucked in his legs and arms, attempted to straighten, failed and dismounted.

"It's just that you gotta be taken by surprise. O.K., shove off, cadet; no hard feelings: just go and find someone your own size. Who's next?" The expression "Shove off", was used officially as a sign of dismissal, calculated to imbue the subordinate with a naval tradition associated with sea and boats, not easily achieved in St. Louis, Missouri, some fifteen hundred miles from the nearest ocean.

And so it continued with the boxing. There, at least, protection was provided by a helmet, but that simply seemed to make the target bigger and exaggerate the pain of the blows. Thank goodness there were signs of spring and the runways were clearing.

Ensign A.J.King, U.S.N., was a quiet American and a gentle instructor amongst a training staff of some twenty pilots who daily took their novice pupils into the air for the first time. Daily they suppressed panic and uttered that imperative,

"Hands off, I've got her," as they aborted a landing, take off or uncontrolled spin. Many longed to go back to combat flying to avoid the tension. Michael was fortunate to have Ensign King as his teacher, he never heard him swear, or raise his voice. Some of the other instructors' obscenities were cherished by their pupils and saved for desperate occasions, when they proved to be quite capable of bringing salvation.

The Boeing Stearman biplane would have been envied by Biggles as a 'Hot ship'. She was powerful, positive, sturdy, and forgiving. Safe for clumsy flying, responsive to skilled flying, rather like Ensign King. The thrill of climbing into her rear cockpit, that first day was never to be surpassed, until the thrill of climbing out of the front seat after his first solo flight.

For the next three months Michael recorded in his log book, take-offs, landings, spins, wing-overs, slips and 'S' turns to circle, rolls, chandelles, inverted spins, loops, falling leaves, Immelmans, snap rolls, cartwheels and night flying. It was an intense time for all of them: June the sixth, 'D Day', passed without any thought for the two hundred thousand men who were scrambling ashore in Normandy. With all his flight checks passed he felt safe to get his wings, but there was still another six months to go and things could go wrong. The failure rate was high in that Primary Training Squadron; they wanted to weed you out before they had invested too much time and money on your potential.

Douglas had 'Dipped'; he had not passed his B Stage Check. Sadly it was not unusual, some fifty percent of those starting the course would not reach the standard for award of Flying Badge, and it was not unusual to find the 'Dipped' pilots in tears. To console them was impossible: a glorious death in battle was all they now longed for. How would they tell their parents and their girlfriends; it was no comfort to them that the news would be greeted with relief.

"Dougie, please don't take it so hard; it is just bad luck; it's not you; you just had a particularly tough egg of an Instructor on a day he was in a bad temper; and anyway he probably felt he was doing you a favour; he didn't want you to kill yourself."

"Or somebody else, more like."

"There are lots of other things you can do in the navy."

"Such as?"

"Well, if it happened to me I'd be glad to go back to sea: you like the sea, don't you?"

"No."

"Well, why did you join the Navy?"

"I wanted to fly in the Fleet Air Arm."

"You should have put the Navy first."

"Michael, you are sounding like a vicar at a wedding."

"Sorry, I'd better shut up. Come on let's get a milk-shake and go and watch Rita Hayworth in 'Cover Girl'."

"How's that going to help?"

"Well, if you concentrate on her auburn hair and glorious breasts, you could find it a substitute for flying."

"Grrr!"

So it was goodbye to Dougie, and sadly after a few letters, as between lovers, he faded out of Michael's life. Now his mate was Ted. Ted the giggler, who seemed to think Michael was hilarious. They had now moved on to Pensacola and the Harvard trainer, which was a joy to fly, but seemed quite technical with its flaps and retractable undercarriage and variable pitch propeller. Pensacola was a vast, old established U.S. Naval air station, deep in the heart of Florida where customs were different from St. Louis.

Michael was travelling into town to have his photograph taken in his new uniform as a midshipman. Having progressed thus far in his flying, but still only nineteen, he could only be commissioned as a midshipman; you had to be twenty to be a sub-lieutenant. He didn't mind, it felt rather unique and Nelsonian; he was very naïve. This was demonstrated when, seeing an old fat negro granny get on the bus, he stood up to offer his seat to her. She looked panic stricken and scuttered as fast as her weight would allow, to the black part of the bus. Everyone, black and white, looked at him as if he was mad. He hardly left the base again after that.

But that was some time ago and he had become indifferent; he now had his wings and was a sub-lieutenant and was flying Avenger Torpedo Bombers whose technicalities now seemed simple.

Chapter Twenty-Eight

Leonard had made good progress in restoring his balance of mind since graduating from Wharncliffe Lunatic Asylum. The talks he had had with Conrad Bronsky had re-introduced him to a world outside his intense spiritual hothouse. He lost none of his certainty that Man is a spiritual being but that there is a necessity for that spirituality to be interpreted in material terms. His intense burden of healing work on top of the physical stresses of travelling, administration and separation from Michael, had brought his mind to boiling point, and he had found it impossible to switch the kettle off. Edith, who loved him dearly, and he her, was remote in her prayer, and and her support was withdrawal not physical love. So intensity was never released and sleep was never deep, only exhausted. Bronsky had pointed this out to him, for which he was grateful, but there was no easy solution to Leonard's way of life as he began his healing work again, responding to the demand.

Doris continued to live with them, off and on, Fred being away in the army. This, at least, enlivened the atmosphere in the home; she was irrepressible; she was now deeply enthusiastic about Spiritualism, to a comic extent. She found it easier to comprehend than Christian Science. Leonard was sympathetic but tried to point out that there was little spiritual progress in communicating with a human spirit world. Doris was not deterred and her abundant sense of humour made her accounts of communication from her wise old Indian Chief, quite hilarious, and sometimes relevant.

It was, however, a relief to be invited by Winifred, to stay for a week in Cumberland. She was preparing her next exhibition and would appreciate some spiritual guidance. This would be a relief from isolation for both of them. On the journey he was re-reading letters from Michael. They were interesting and positive, and Leonard's spirits lifted as the curtain of steam drifted across his carriage window, to show the fells and tarns of Cumberland, washed by that cool northern light that Winifred captured so perfectly in her paintings.

"You have not been well, Leonard, have you? I spoke to Edith while you were away; she told me about your troubles. I felt we should talk and help each other. I think we both feel very lonely at times."

"Perhaps not as lonely as a Roman soldier pacing this wall we're sitting on."

Leonard was trying to make light of it. It takes time to admit to what he felt, was a failure.

"You mustn't feel that you've failed, Leonard. You must see it as an opportunity to grow in strength. 'There's no discouragement', as you always say, remember."

Suddenly he was overwhelmed by a shudder of yearning. An immense sob split his chest and tears literally spouted from his eyes, streaming down his cheeks in the May sunshine. The distant hills of the Lake District glistening to the south, lost their focus.

Winifred instinctively put her arm about his shoulder. "Weep it away, Leonard, weep it away: that's what I do." She gently kissed the top of his head and he experienced a surrendering joy, and dissolving of anxiety.

During the rest of the stay with Winifred, Leonard became more of the artist and she more of the healer.

"The Arts are the material manifestation of the man's spirituality; the artist creates from immaterial concepts. Not all art is spiritual, but it is conceptual, and so free of the limitation of what we call reality. It is up to the artist to aspire to, and inspire, enlightenment or despair." This was Leonard speaking.

"Detachment from human reality must remain a conscious act, or it becomes an unproductive trance: our upward steps towards spiritual progress are in seeing only goodness and beauty about us. To deny this world is to deny the good that it can teach us, the grounding it can give us. Leonard, I think that you are in need of grounding just now. Let's go and see farmer Warwick and ask him about his cows and pigs, that will ground you soon enough. Perhaps I should paint his cows and pigs, but I never do: too much ground perhaps."

The sight of the sow with nine ravenous piglets to feed soon grounded Leonard, and he spent the rest of his stay rescuing the piglets from their steam roller mother, who felt that her own survival was more important than her piglets.

When he was back in Sheffield his physical and spiritual energy returned and his work prospered. However, he remembered Winifred's advice and looked for grounding. It came in the shape of Doris.

Doris was a champion ballroom dancer, already the holder of gold, silver, and bronze medals, won in the competitions at the City Hall.

"Come on, Leonard, come dancing with me. It'll take you out of yourself."

"I'm sure it would; I can't dance."

"I'll teach you soon enough, I'm a champion, I've got

medals to prove it."

"What do you think, Edie?" Edie shook her head, but not in disapproval, only disbelief.

"Last year you gave a Christian Science lecture in that hall; what are they going to think of you?"

"I don't suppose there'll be many of the same people doing the tango, Edie. Anyway it's in a different hall. Come on, Len, it'll be a Tea Dance; it won't be full of licentious soldiery."

"All right then, come on, when is it?"

"This afternoon. Have you got the right shoes?"

"Oh, yes. My Sunday shoes are light and shiny and black and I'll feel safe in those." So he went, and loved it. Doris was a strict disciplinarian: you had to get the steps right; the concentration it needed was absorbing, and the result was exhilarating.

"Now come on, Len, relax; put your right leg inside mine, and pivot, just feel we're one flesh! There, you feel better for that, don't you Len?"

"Yes I do." It was fortunate that his mental illness had banished his libido.

But still he found it difficult to sleep, and still the healing work made its demands and he needed the work, because his savings were dwindling, but he was encouraged by a letter from Michael.

U.S. Naval Air Station,
Fort Lauderdale, Florida. Tuesday, 26th Feb. '45

Dear Mum and Dad,

I had Mum's letter yesterday, telling me about all the troubles you've had. You should have told me before when they were going on: I can pray effectively too, you know; the way you taught me, but I know you just didn't want to worry me. I assure you I don't worry, that's something else you taught me! What have I got to worry about? I've got my wings; I'm a Sub/lieutenant, I'm flying my torpedo bomber; I'm 'inboard', as we say in the Navy. Let me do some worrying for you, if there's any to be done.

I've arranged for my pay allocation to you to be increased to £4 a week, I get £8 a week and all found. I don't drink, I don't smoke, I don't go out with girls; sounds boring but it isn't, not in lovely Fort Lauderdale with generous hospitality from a lovely family, who have a grand-daughter who's keen on me! Don't worry; not about to settle here. We're off back to the Royal Navy in Maine next week and I hope to be back in England in two months.

Keep resting, Dad; you're still a young man and have a great future; we'll work something out together.

Love,
Michael.

The last parade at U.S. Naval Air Station, Fort Lauderdale, Florida, was the sad occasion of the sudden death of President Franklin Delano Roosevelt. He had died on April 12th; missing by about a month, the German surrender on May the 8th. He was probably held in greater universal affection in Britain than in the United States, where many U.S. citizens saw him as having dangerously socialist tendencies. Michael was rather surprised at the perfunctory acknowledgements of Roosevelt's achievements by the U.S. Vice-Admiral, commanding the base.

The course ended on the 18th of April, and they were sent on leave to New York en route to Brunswick in Maine. This found them celebrating V.E. Day in Billy Rose's Diamond Horseshoe night club; not without a sense of guilt which was quickly subdued in the sensualities of wine, legs and tantalising feathers. Their war wasn't over; their war was in the Pacific and still to be won.

Although Brunswick, Maine was a U.S. Naval Base, they were now firmly back under the command of the Royal Navy, which they found congenial; irony was once again the prevailing culture.

"The weather looks as though it's going to be bloody awful, so you'd better get off on a navex and find out about dirty weather again." The flight commander was referring to the reputation of the U.S. Navy (wrongly) that they never flew off if there was a cloud in the sky.

So it was it was off into the dull, grey yonder, and three legs of a navigation exercise. Michael now had his crew; an observer/navigator, Geoffrey and a wireless operator/air gunner, Jim. He felt quite secure. Until, twenty minutes later, when a terse call from base, ordered immediate return as fog was closing in. The tone of the message was that we should have known better than to go up on a day like this, thought Michael. Oh well; it's always 'pilot error'. Geoffrey gave him a course for base.

It took two attempts to find the runway and land in that Cape Cod fog, then he had to receive a reprimand from the flight commander for being dilatory. All of which he accepted as the need for the commander to relieve his guilt about sending them up in the first place. He had by now completely forgotten what it was like to be a civilian. If you didn't like it: 'you shouldn't have joined'. There was that inevitable irony again. Fortunately, he did like it.

Squadron morale was high; they had been selected to join

the 'Illustrious' in Rosyth next month and they were to 'work up' at Crail in Fife.

But they still had to be cleared for deck landings before they could call themselves a Fleet Air Arm Pilot. They had practiced enough with their ADDLS, as they called them; Attempted, Dummy Deck Landings. These were practices on dry land under the control of the Batts Officer. He had the unenviable responsibility of signalling to each pilot with his 'ping pong' bats how he should control his height, his attitude, his speed, and eventually, when to cut his engine and so pick up the arrester wire on the flight deck, or if the pilot had not responded accurately, cancel the landing, wave him off, and send him round again. Nasty mistakes at the last moment put 'Batts' in danger of decapitation. He took his job very seriously; he was, of course a pilot himself.

The great day had arrived and they were to fly down to Norfolk, Virginia, where a small escort carrier, the U.S.S. Charger was ready for landing on, in Chesapeake Bay. Just four successful landings to be qualified for deck landings, not too difficult in fine weather, with all that training behind them. And so it turned out to be for all but one unlucky boy who failed to take a 'wave off' properly. He didn't raise his undercarriage, caught the top of the crash barrier, tipped over the bows of the short little carrier and drowned, trapped under his canopy which had jammed forward on impact. Michael didn't know about it; he had qualified before it happened but some had to continue after the accident, which was tense. The poor 'Batts' Officer got very drunk that night; he blamed himself, but it wasn't his fault. It was 'pilot error'.

Soon after this incident the squadron was sailing in the Queen Elizabeth, returning to England, or rather, Scotland, the Clyde and Glasgow. This vast ship was almost empty again because now the American troops were coming in the opposite direction, going home. On this crossing they didn't have to keep watch for submarines any more.

Everything in that small British island, looked tiny after eighteen months in America, the trains; the fields, the houses; the people seemed like toys.

The squadron was hoping for some home leave but the rumour was that they were to go straight to the Naval Air Station at Crail, Fifeshire; and so it turned out to be true. It was also true that they were to join 'Illustious', ready for them in Rosyth.

"If we going onto 'Illustrious', that means the Pacific, and they've got to give us leave." Ted was confident.

"They don't have to do anything; they can do what they like with us." Michael was ambivalent about leave; he slightly dreaded what he might find at home. He had telephoned when they arrived at Greenock and the conversation with his father had been strained.

"How are you, Dad?"

"Oh, how good it is to hear your voice; when are you coming home?"

"Not sure yet, Dad. We're on our way to Crail and they'll tell us there about leave; shouldn't be long."

"Where are you going after that?"

"The Pacific, I expect." Michael wished he hadn't said that, but it was pretty obvious.

"Oh!" There was, what seemed like a long silence.

"It takes a long time to sail to the Pacific, Dad." There was still silence.

"Dad; are you all right?"

"Yes, I'm getting better. I'm regaining my spiritual strength. I wish this war was over." Michael heard the anguished sigh in his voice.

"Dad, I've got to go now, the train's leaving, I'll call you from Crail." The train wasn't leaving for another hour; he felt awful, but what could he say?

Ted countered on. "They've got to give us 'passionate leave', I've got a girlfriend who needs seeing to; it's been eighteen months." Not for Ted, it hasn't thought Michael. Oh it's so simple for some people.

Intensive torpedo exercises against tired old Destroyers taking evasive action, was the order of each day. The squadron had now been strengthened by veteran flight commanders who looked pretty sullen and resentful of these gleaming young boys: they reckoned, they needed scaring. They lead them in tight formations, low over the target ships. Michael was glad to see the ship's crew shake their fists at them. He, himself, defied his leader, when he felt for certain that the consequence of following, would be to tangle with the ships funnel. Better a 'bollocking' than a nasty mess. His leader didn't seem to notice as he rejoined the formation a few moments later. Oh dear, this didn't look happy for the future.

***

The future came rather suddenly when he was given a telegram. It was from Aunty Doris, it read: "Come home, Father in prison."

He immediately rang home. Doris answered the phone.

"What's happening, Doris?" He was glad it was Doris, there was no spiritual beating about the bush with Doris.

"Leonard went out of the house yesterday shouting at Edie that he had to go and see Guy in London. She couldn't stop him. He just ran off, without even his hat and coat. The next thing she knew was a policeman calling at the house to tell her that Len was in prison at King's Cross in London for stealing a suitcase and he would be up before the magistrate on Monday, that's the day after tomorrow."

"That's at King's Cross, is it?"

"Yes; can you get there?"

"I'll get there: I'll stay with Guy. Does Guy know what's happened?"

"No, he's not on the phone."

"Oh dear: I'll get away tonight. Thank you, Doris, for letting me know, and for looking after Mum. I'll keep in touch."

"Of course you must go. Take as much time as you need: we shan't be joining 'Illustrious' for two or three weeks." The squadron commander was sympathetic and gave Michael leave. He grabbed an overnight bag and got a lift to the station, waiting at Edinburgh for the first train to London. He telegrammed Guy that he was on his way.

Although the war in Europe had been over three months, the trains were still as full as before with servicemen and essential travellers. If he hadn't been one of the first to get on the train he would never have had a seat all the way. As he was travelling at his own expense, he was not travelling first class. He crouched next to the window, crushed by the rough khaki shoulder of a sergeant in the Gordon Highlanders, whose brewery breath confirmed a riotous farewell. Opposite, with lisle covered legs conveniently spread, was a WAAF corporal with lipstick lips, smeared askew. As the journey shunted through the night, the Black Watch and the WAAF regained tumescence and began to flirt heavily. It was like the conjunction of a bomber and a tank. Michael was glad gallantly to surrender his corner seat for hers, so that they could fuse their bodies without disturbing the rest of the compartment.

Michael had other things to think about. What had Leonard actually done: the stealing of a suitcase must be a mistake of some kind. Was he deranged or just absent minded. Most likely he was in one of his manic moods. Would he have any legal representation; would Michael be able to see him before the hearing; would Leonard be fit to plead? It would be better if he was regarded as unfit; yes, let's hang on to that for a bit.

The town and country that the train passed through, was still surprisingly dark, dim as the lighting in the compartment. Although the blackout restrictions were lifted, the austerity restrictions were not, still all was gloom. At last dawn glimmered blearily above London's smog and they shuddered into King's Cross.

"Can you direct me to the police station, please?" Michael asked the policeman at the barrier.

"Can I help you, sir?"

"No thank you, I have to meet someone there." The policeman looked doubtful, but gave Michael the directions. He was a naval officer, after all. It was only five minutes' walk away.

The building had rather a comfortable aspect; it was mid-Victorian castellated, it only needed a drawbridge to complete its look of having been drawn by a child. It suggested that it was full of 'Bobbies' who only wanted to take your name and address. Michael felt re-assured. The sergeant at the desk looked promisingly avuncular.

"I believe you are holding my father, Leonard Godley; may I see him?"

The sergeant instantly connected with this unusually gentle case. King's Cross was a tough area with two seething stations and a prison up the Pentonville Road; gentleness was rare.

"Yes, sir, I will arrange it. May I have your identity card?" Michael was ready with his naval identity card which the sergeant made a note of in his day book.

"I am sorry to say, sir, that we are very short of space; we don't have an interview room. I shall have to take you to his cell." The Sergeant frowned as if he was reluctant to reveal the primitive conditions that Mr. Godley senior was confined in. "Constable, will you show this gentleman to Mr. Godley in number four." Michael was grateful for his commission; it aroused greater respect out of the navy than in it. Here he was being treated as a guest at the Savoy; it would not have been the same in the naval prison in Portsmouth. There they knew just how lowly a Sub-lieutenant was.

The Constable led him down worn stone stairs to a corridor of iron caged doors; the immediate impression was of a zoo. There were growls, groans, and oaths; the sound of rattling metal and wracking coughs. These beasts behind the bars seemed to have been there since the early nineteenth century, but not in the least eager to get out. The Constable stopped at number four and turned the key. Even before the gate swung inwards, Michael connected with the pathetic sight of his father rising from the rough grey bunk with arms outstretched towards his son, like a prodigal father returning home. The constable withdrew quickly without locking the gate; he was confused by a feeling that he was the warder of a sepulchre.

"Oh, Michael, I knew you would come. I'll be all right now." He embraced and kissed his son. Michael felt the grizzled four-day growth scour his own soft chin. Tears filled both their eyes. They sat together on the bunk.

"What happened, Dad?" Michael was eager to find out whether Leonard was thinking rationally and yet on the other hand he wanted to convince the magistrate of his father's mental instability.

"I don't remember anything until that women yelled out "Stop thief!" on the platform. To me it sounded so comic, like something out of Toy Town. I just stopped and turned to see what it was about. Then a policeman took my arm and my bag and this woman caught up with us and said I'd stolen her bag, and they brought me here and charged me with theft."

"Yes, well it is clear that you were not well and not thinking clearly. Can you remember getting on the train in Sheffield?"

"No."

"Well, we will just tell the truth to the magistrate tomorrow; just as you have told it to me now. When they ask you 'how do you plead' say, 'not guilty' and they will dismiss the case and you can come home. I'm staying in London with Guy…"

"Yes, Guy. That's why I came to London. I wanted to see him."

"Yes, you will see him. I will come tomorrow and help you with the magistrate. I'm going now. Try to rest, and here, I've brought you a Science and Health, the little pocket one you gave me to take away; it will comfort you; there." And he pressed it into his hand. Leonard's look of gratitude collapsed Michael's lungs like a blow to the solar plexus. "Remember, 'not guilty'. Remember, Dad; "Stone walls do not a prison make, nor iron bars a cage."

Leonard smiled wanly; "Ye shall know the truth, and the truth shall make you free."

Michael squeezed his father's arm, turned, and left. The constable at the end of the corridor came to lock Leonard in.

"Thank you, Constable; I'll be back tomorrow for the hearing."

"Yes sir; he's not well, is he? Anyone can see that; they'll let him off, you'll see sir."

"I hope so. I do hope so. Where is the Clerk of the court's office, I need to go and see them?"

"It is in this building, sir. If you go outside and turn right, you'll see the entrance on the side of the building, marked with a brass plate." How compact the Victorian world was, thought Michael, and Pentonville prison just up the road.

The brass plate gleamed with importance and warned him of its dignity. He caught the blurred reflection of the crown on his cap badge as he entered. He thought he saw it coincide for a moment, with the crown on the brass plate. He felt re-assured again. He was directed into a large room with a large desk and a thin boy behind it. It was by now late in the morning and the clerk to the court (perhaps he was he the clerk to the clerk of the court?) was just about to open his packet of sandwiches so carefully prepared by his admiring wife. She loved him for the security he represented. All this was apparent from the neatness of the parcel he was unfolding. Michael apologised for calling at an inconvenient time and offered to withdraw.

"Not at all, not at all, they can wait." As if it was the sandwiches who would be disappointed; and he slid them into a drawer, together with a copy of the Sporting News.

"How can I help you?"

"I am Sub-lieutenant Michael Godley and my father, Leonard Godley, is to appear before the magistrate tomorrow morning."

"Ah yes I have the list of runners here… I do beg your pardon, I'm afraid I'm mixing up my hobby with my sandwiches: it's my lunch hour you know."

"Then it is very good of you to see me." Michael was warming to him quickly.

"Yes, down for eleven o'clock, before Messrs Honk,

Devine, and Shepherd. Leonard Godley, yes, I should say he stands a good chance of getting off under Devine." He guffawed at his own wit and immediately begged for forgiveness. "I do beg your pardon, yes please forgive me. Your father, you say; yes very distressing."

Fortunately, Michael had a ready sense of humour himself and forgave him immediately, but did begin to think he had walked through the Looking Glass.

"Will he be represented?" He became solemn again.

"I wish to represent him. I also wish to enter a plea of 'not guilty'."

"I will enter that fact and you will be called."

"Thank you. May I ask you…"

"Please do: what?" The clerk settled back in his mahogany chair, put his thumbs in his waistcoat pockets and prepared to give a legal opinion. Michael was beginning to realise that Mr. Clerk the clerk was a fantasist and saw himself as a high court judge, far above the crumbs of sandwiches and Sporting Life.

"In your vast experience of the law, what are the chances of a man being acquitted of a charge of theft, if he has no recollection of the event and can show evidence of previous mental illness?"

"I would say that it would depend entirely on what the Magistrate had had for lunch… Oh I do beg your pardon, I do, I do." He even suppressed his own guffaw.

Michael waited for Mr. Clerk to regain control.

"Unless the charge of theft is withdrawn by the plaintiff, he is most likely to be remanded in custody for a medical report."

"And if that report confirms a mental illness; what then?"

"Case dismissed."

"Thank you."

"Is there anything else I can help you with: the three thirty at Newmarket for example?" Oh I do beg your pardon; I really do."

Michael left, lighter of heart, but puzzled at the presence of this pantomime clerk, until he was passed on the stairs by a florid gentleman in bowler hat and pin stripes who burst into the room that Michael had just left, and shouted,

"What the hell are you doing in my chair, Smith; get out and take your damned sandwiches with you." Michael's interview had definitely been with the clerk to the Clerk. He hoped his advice would not prove to be so insubstantial.

Chapter Twenty-Nine

Guy's release from the navy in 1943, still in the darkest days of the war, had meant that he had no difficulty in finding a flat in London; it was not a safe place to live, and the population was substantially dispersed. Guy also, always seemed to have the right connections when it came to finding accommodation. Winifred still owned a studio in St. John's Wood, which nobody wanted to live in, because it was at the top of a house, and most of the roof was glass. This was perfect for Guy (who lived under God's protection) and paid no rent.

Derek, of course was still in the Royal Artillery, and surprisingly, still in England. After a very rough time defending fighter stations in the Battle of Britain, he had been posted to coastal defence in Plymouth. When he had originally joined the Royal Artillery, it had been with a jolly group of Bohemian artists who made up an artist's battalion, but that original camaraderie had been replaced by indifferent logistics. Plymouth's concrete blockhouses seemed to be occupied by equally unsympathetic human material. This unfortunately led him to seek solace in the sexual comforts offered by khaki clad ATS thighs. The solace was short lived because, being a soldier of principle, when she said she was pregnant, he married her and became the object of her abuse. She was no more likely to conceive than one of his artillery shells, and she had simply lied; she wanted his married man's allotment. She was a sadist. Undoubtedly, she had powerful sexual attraction which too often, Derek found it impossible to resist, but a mutual climax was a signal for her to punch his face and scratch his cheeks. Derek was reduced to inventing accidents in the blackout as explanations for his injuries. He was sniggered at and not believed, partly because her reputation had gone before her, and in some cases had been enjoyed. Her name was Betty, although 'Batter' would have been more apt.

Michael knew all this because he witnessed it in Guy's flat that night. Derek was there on leave. Unable to ring Guy, Michael had just turned up. Recognition of your caller was primitive; you announced yourself from the street by calling in the direction of the flat you hoped your friend was in. If your friend was at home, he came to the window and threw down a key, which either hit you painfully, or you caught, or it disappeared down a drain. If on the other hand you were trying to collect on an unpaid bill, you would not receive a reply. Michael advanced and was recognised; he even caught the key deftly and was able to open the paint peeling front door and start up the six flights of stairs to the glazed studio on the roof.

"Lovely to see you, Michael: whatever are you doing here, new posting?"

"Not good news I'm afraid: let me in and I'll tell you all about it." Guy let Michael into the wide open space of the studio only to be hit on the shoulder by a flying tube of paint launched at Derek by the screaming Betty. Now she was tearing to shreds a fist full of charcoal drawings. Derek was crouching in a chair with his head in his hands.

"Sorry about this," Guy muttered. "Come into the kitchen, I'll explain." Over a cup of stewed black coffee, Guy described Derek's disastrous wife. "They're spending a few days leave here."

"Well my news is not much better." And he brought Guy up to date about Leonard's troubles.

"Stay as long as you need to. I can only offer you a mattress on the floor. The lovers are still sleeping together: it's the only time they're quiet; and even then it sometimes ends in tears. Oh dear, oh dear, it seems we need to do some praying for a demonstration of harmony. It is in rather short supply in the world just now, isn't it?" Guy sighed.

"I think my dad's problem is that he has worn himself out praying for harmony." But nevertheless Michael did not go to sleep on his mattress, that night without affirming that "Thine is the power and the glory, for ever and ever."

The court house was seethingly busy with petty business, dishevelled, sober, drunks, who could now give their names and addresses and accept their fines, and shuffle off for their next drink. There was a black market case which was more complicated and had to be referred to a higher court, there was a hapless deserter, and then it was Leonard Godley. Leonard stood upright and dignified in the dock. He had not been allowed a razor and so was grizzled by three days growth of beard. By now it had acquired a certain solidity of distinction. The magistrate (fortunately Mr. Devine!) looked at him with some apparent surprise. Such dignity and presence was not common among the prisoners in his court.

The comic clerk of yesterday, now dignified in his gown, spoke out. "Are you Leonard Godley of 245 Manchester Road, Sheffield."

"I am." The clear projection of his deep voice engaged everyone's attention.

"You are accused of stealing a suitcase, the property of Mrs. Joan Wadsworth, at King's Cross Station on Saturday July

20th. How do you plead?"

"Not guilty."

"Call Constable Henry George." Constable George of the Transport Police explained the details of the arrest.

"Call Sub-lieutenant Anthony Michael Godley, RNVR." Mr. Devine, the magistrate addressed Michael, "You, I understand are the son of the accused and are here to represent him."

"That is correct, sir."

"What can you tell us that is relevant to the case?"

"My father does not contest any of the facts that Constable George has told the court. He is not able to do so because he has no recollection of any of the events after leaving Sheffield station on the train. My father is a Christian Science Practitioner of Healing and has, as a consequence of the wartime situation, been working under great pressure, in his healing work, his religious duties at Catterick Army Camp and his charity relief work. His explanation to my mother, as he left the house, without a hat, coat or bag, was that he must go and see his friend in London. My mother was unable to restrain him and I believe he boarded the train in a state of mental derangement. His actions on arriving at King's Cross were entirely unconscious and he took Mrs. Wadsworth's suitcase off the rack unconsciously as a reflex action. I hope that the court will deal with the alleged offence with this condition in mind."

"Thank you, Lieutenant Godley. Do you wish to question Constable George?"

"Thank you. Yes sir. Constable, did the prisoner make any attempt to avoid arrest?"

"No, sir."

"Did he have a valid ticket?"

"Yes, sir."

"Did he make any reply when charged and cautioned?"

"He just said, thank you."

There followed a few moments of muttered conversation on the bench which ended, to Michael and Leonard's great relief, with the decision to remand in custody for a medical report. Michael rushed round to the desk sergeant to find out what this exactly meant.

"It means that your father will be taken to Wandsworth prison, where he will be accommodated in the infirmary and examined by the medical staff and the report will be submitted to the court for a sentencing decision."

"How long will it take?"

"I should think a week."

"Can't he be bailed?"

"Bail was not mentioned and would have been unlikely, as they need him to be under observation."

"Will I be able to see him?"

"Yes, apply to Wandsworth; he'll be there this afternoon."

"Can I see him now?"

"Not now, sir, we're getting the transport ready for him and the other prisoners but he knows you are here and we will tell him you'll be at Wandsworth as soon as possible."

"Thank you. I suppose that will have to do." Michael went off to ring Edith and let her know what was happening. Again it was Doris who answered the phone, which was a relief. He told her the story and she was comforting.

"Well done, Tony. You did well. They'll let him off now."

Let him off, let him off: how pitiful to think of his dear loving father having to be 'let off' anything, except perhaps the huge burden of his work. He was such a good man.

Chapter Thirty

The Gothic gates of Wandsworth Prison frowned their Victorian scowl over all those who entered there, both the warders and the confined. Although the same architectural period as the King's Cross police station, it appeared to threaten more. King's Cross allowed the guilty to remain innocent until judged: Brixton dealt only in the condemned. Victorian institutions were all about authority, perhaps this is why their architects were attracted to the medieval.

Visitors too had to accept their atmosphere: Michael felt it weigh upon him as he pressed the bell push beside the massive door. There was a pause that tempted him to ring again. He considered it, but feared it might offend. Then the wicket gate was opened by a warder whose bulk all but filled it. His expression was impassive and lofty; narrow eyes assessed the closeness of association with criminality, of this visitor who challenged the inviolability of the prison. Seeing the gold braid of a naval sub-lieutenant, his eyes relaxed slightly.

"I have an appointment to see Leonard Godley – a prisoner," he added reluctantly. The massive warder referred to a clipboard he held under one arm like a swagger cane; his military connections were evident.

"Follow me, sir," he conceded. He found himself in the guard room; identity was established, a telephone call was made and Michael was directed across the parade ground towards a nurse waiting at a side door.

"Your father is in the hospital ward." She seemed fully familiar with the case, which reassured him. "He is under heavy sedation; he has violent dreams and disturbs the rest of the ward at night, so we've had to sedate him. We would move him but there is nowhere for him to go."

"Will he know me?"

"That's up to you."

"Has he been examined by the doctor, mentally, I mean?"

"Yes, and he is being kept under observation."

"Have they reached any conclusion?"

"That, I cannot say. This is the hospital ward."

They were now in, what appeared to be a warehouse, with a glass roof, that had been partially obscured by wooden planks laid across the tension bars, this, to catch the falling glass from the bombing. Michael was glad to think that that danger, at least, was past.

"Here he is. I'll leave you with him, when you want to leave, come to me at my desk at the end of the ward."

Michael looked down at his still unshaven father; his head half hidden in the course linen pillow, like a profile on an ancient coin.

"Dad. Daddy. Leonard." Michael touched his arm; squeezed his hand that lay across the sheet as if severed. His eyes opened; the mist cleared and the grizzled beard stirred in a weak smile.

"How are you?" How banal is that inevitable greeting, to which you should always reply with bland untruths, putting the questioner at ease. On this occasion there were no platitudes.

"I'm frightened. I can't sleep, they sedate me, but drugs have no effect on me. I wish they did." He began to cry; this was a sinful spiritual failure for him.

"It won't be long now, and we'll have you home again, then you'll sleep peacefully; we'll look after you. Mum will be there to comfort you."

"Yes; I'm sorry, I mustn't despair; I can trust in divine mind and the power of good; and you." He began to relax and within ten minutes was asleep. Michael gradually withdrew his hand from Leonard's hand; checking his pulse as he slid over his scrawny wrist, because his breathing was hardly visible or audible. He went over to the ward nurse, past the rows of sick prisoners, past their gurgling coughs, their mumbled expletives, their blank stares.

"I'm leaving now. I'll be back tomorrow; he's sleeping now."

"Good; he needs it. We all need it; he had a terrible night. If it goes on like that we'll have to move him out."

"Where to?"

"That's the problem, where to. We'd have done it already if we had any space to go to. Keep coming, you obviously have a calming effect on him."

"I will; thank you. See you tomorrow."

***

There's a telegram for you." Guy called from the window, as he threw down the key.

"It'll be from Crail: I sent them one to tell them what was happening." He opened it as he entered the flat. *"Carry on. Keep in touch. No news yet on joining ship. Lt. Cmdr (A) R.G.Haigh RNVR."*

"All right, is it?"

"Yes; good news. No recall."

"How are things with Leonard?" Michael described the gloom of Wandsworth and Leonard's depression.

"Should I go and see him?"

"No; he wouldn't want you to see him like this; your help will be needed when he comes out. I shall have to go back to flying, and probably the Pacific. Mum, bless her, is loving, but not very resourceful; got any ideas what we could do?"

"As a matter of fact, I have. Do you remember Peg?"

"Peg; I don't think I've met her; only heard Dad talk about her."

"Oh if you'd met her, you'd remember her; she's a great character. I first met her a year or two ago, when I was still in London; met her at the Christian Science church in Chelsea. She was going through a very sad time. She was a widow who had lost her only son in the R.A.F.: disappeared over the North Sea, coming back from Germany. She was convinced he was still alive and grasped at any religion that could give her hope and comfort. I found her in tears coming out of church and I (don't know why) put my arm round her. She clutched me like a life line, since when she has never let me go: even asked me to marry her at one point. As you know I'm not the marrying kind, but even if I was, she wouldn't be for me, she is too overwhelming with her frustrated affection. But she has a great generous heart and she adores Leonard. I know she would love to nurse him back to health. She's very earthy, which would be good for him; she'd feed him up and make him laugh. She has a rambling farm house in Buckinghamshire and plenty of room; and she is not short of money, having been a good business woman since her husband died in the troubles in Ireland. I'll talk to her about it; you can consider it done. By the way, you can sleep in a proper bed tonight, the honeymoon couple have gone back to Plymouth."

"Still together then?"

"Not for long I think."

"Oh dear: the fortunes of war. I suppose."

Michael returned to Wandsworth next day a little lighter in heart, knowing he had a solution to Leonard's next move. That heart quickly sunk when the nurse greeted him by saying that Leonard had had such a bad night with his nightmares that they simply had no option but to take him out of the ward to the only single space they had, which was a condemned cell!

"You mean, where you put prisoners waiting to be hanged?"

"Yes. I am sorry but that is the only space available, and the way he was screaming in the night (even under sedation) made it bedlam in here for the others."

"Yes, I see. Can I go and see him?"

"Yes, of course. I'll take you to a warder who can lead you there."

Michael followed the warder along oblique corridors, and felt the despair of knowing that this was a journey from which no prisoner returned. The machinery of execution were an extension of the condemned cells; it being considered humane to shorten the journey. The only exit was death; the drop into the unknown abyss, or the revelation of the truth about life; depending on your philosophy.

"Here you are, sir. Mr. Godley, here's your son to see you." The grizzled guard tried to sound as cheerful as the matron of an old people's home, but avoided making eye contact, as he unlocked the iron door. "I'll leave you alone: I won't shut the door. When you want to leave, ring this bell." Michael could not stop tears coming into his eyes as he looked into the cell. His father was sitting on the primitive bed, clasping his knees under his chin. He looked up, his own eyes equally moist.

"Oh, Michael, I am in purgatory."

"I know, Dad, but isn't it better being in your own space." He stuttered over the 's' sound, avoiding the word "cell".

"No: this is a condemned cell. You know what that means, a death cell. A hundred years of dead men have spent their last hours in this place. I am an imprint for their terror. I try to sleep, but as I drop off, their nightmare smothers me. I feel the rope around my neck: I feel the trap open and the drop; the fearful crack, and the erection and ejaculation. Did you know a hanged man ejaculates at death: is it the last desperate scattering of seed to perpetuate the race? Twice this has happened to me, now I try to stay awake."

"Oh, Dad; have you told anyone about this?"

"Yes, I told the young doctor who came to see me. He just made a note in his report."

"At least he is making a report; that's good; that's what we want to get you out of here. I'll try to see him."

"There are two other cells occupied along here. Those two traitors, Joyce and Amery. One of them was hanged this morning. I don't know which one."

Traitors, hanging; are we still in the middle ages? Michael felt the claustrophobia of history about him. He desperately wanted to leave but knew he could not abandon his father. He stayed another fifteen minutes and tried to bring some normality into his world. He talked about Peg, and Leonard seemed to respond at this gleam of hope.

"God's love is ever present, I mustn't forget that. A way is being prepared. Is Mother all right?"

"Yes, she sends her love, and so does Doris: they are knowing that you are free in truth. It won't be long now. I'll leave you now until tomorrow, and talk to the doctor. Peace be with you, Dad," and Michael kissed his still growing beard.

The conversation with the doctor was encouraging: he had completed his report and sent it off to the court. The conclusion was that the prisoner was not responsible for his own actions, was suffering from a severe mental breakdown. He had also added that he was of no danger to the public. Release looked promising.

Michael left the prison to visit the King's Cross Court to see if he could find out when the next hearing would be. His Alice in Wonderland clerk cheerfully gave the information that it was down for Friday, in two days' time. He would save the good news for the next day and his Thursday visit to Leonard. Surely he would be able to sleep on Thursday night.

He did: and on Friday the hearing was over in fifteen minutes; a wished for anti-climax. They didn't even ask whether he was going to be cared for, but Sub-lieutenant Godley assured the court that arrangements had been made for his treatment and there would be no more King's Cross incidents. Leonard was gathered up with gratitude, helped into a taxi and taken home to Guy in St. John's Wood for a shave of restoration.

Chapter Thirty-One

Michael left Guy to make the arrangements with Peg and returned to Crail and the squadron. He felt a shudder of guilt at his relief to be back with his chums and planes. He had no more human responsibilities than to his crew. He was part of a machine again, and the numb comfort that brought.

"Have you heard the news? They've dropped an atomic bomb on the Nips, they reckon it'll end the war." Ted looked blank and made the report without elation. They both felt deflated and knew that this was the wrong response. The death and destruction would now be ended; that was good, but all their training had been for nothing. They hadn't been allowed to pass their final test; the test of facing fear, but they had escaped the evil of killing.

"Do you think we'll still go on to "Illustrious?" Ted looked as if Christmas had been cancelled.

"I shouldn't think so. They'll just shut everything down to save money. I'm sure we're practically bankrupt, anyway."

"Will they just send us home then?"

"I'm flattered that you think I have all the answers, Ted, but the First Sea Lord hasn't had a chance to tell me yet."

"Sorry, Mike; come and have a drink and talk about the future."

***

Within two days Japan had surrendered and the war was over; time for celebration. The local Admiral ordered a 'Balbo', a massive formation flypast to impress those below. Rather quaintly it is named after an Italian Admiral who, though on the wrong side for half the war, was much admired for his bombasity. Aircraft from all over Scotland rendezvoused over Dundee and flew down the coast to the Firth of Forth and Edinburgh. It looked like a seasonal migration, and perhaps it was.

The squadron was disbanded and sent home on indefinite leave, which was wonderfully convenient for Michael and his now returning domestic responsibilities. He went to meet generous Peg in her ramshackle Buckinghamshire farm and to see if his mother and father were settled. But first he went to Sheffield and collected his father's car and some petrol coupons. Driving south, he felt a sudden sense of freedom, a freedom nonchalantly surrendered two years before. He looked at his gold braid and the wings on his wrist as it held the steering wheel, and suddenly thought how irrelevant they were, how incongruous, how already they were old fashioned.

As he pulled into Peg's overgrown drive and parked under a lime tree, weeping its intoxicating scent, he stepped out and sighed contentedly. A bearded collie approached him and as he bent to stroke its shaggy head it suddenly levitated into the air, did a half roll, which would have done credit to a fighter pilot, and fastened his jaws on the gold braid that a little while before had been the subject of his musing.

"Ouch! That hurts! Get off." Michael swung the dog in a circle, but he didn't let go.

"Scruff, Scruff! Down, down. Drop!" Peg's last command had an effect and 'Scruff' (as such appeared to be his appropriate name) opened his jaws and dropped to the ground. He hung his head and cringed his curled up body round Peg's stout legs. He didn't look her in the eye; he was clearly ridden with guilt.

"You bad boy: don't do that again. We'll send you back to the army."

She spoke in her broad Birmingham accent. This threat caused Scruff to shiver with dejection, and he cringed almost to extinction, allowing one bloodshot eye to be raised in pathetic supplication through his furry fringe.

"Sorry about your welcome, Michael. I'm Peg; this is Scruff. His problem is shell shock; you see, he was called up into the army a couple of years ago and we don't know exactly what happened to him, but they invalided him out. The rumour was that he lacked moral fibre and instead of going on his missions, he'd hide out in a convenient hedge until the firing died down. But when they de-mobbed him, they didn't de-militarise him. So, if he sees anyone in uniform, he disarms them. The postman won't come near us; we have to collect it from the gate." Peg laughed heartily, and kicked the dog affectionately. He fawned even more. She gave Michael a bear hug and with her arm round his shoulders lead him to the house. "I hope you've brought some civvy clothes."

"Yes I have. I hope my 'thank you' letter about Mum and Dad got through the postman and Scruff."

"Oh yes, it did, and thank you; but really it's a joy to me to have them here. Come and see them, I think you'll be impressed." She called out, "Leonard, Edie; he's here." The paint peeling door scraped open under the trellised porch and Leonard appeared. What a wonderful transformation; he was fat in the face and beaming, and so was Edie close behind. Peg's diet of roast chicken, fresh veg and strawberries and cream had worked a miracle.

"Oh, Dad, you look terrific; and you, mum." Michael kissed them both. The immediate past had already receded under Peg's embracing love and generosity.

Scruff weaved expertly between all their legs to bring from the dim interior the prettiest of young women, with an equally pretty baby girl cradled in her arms. "Hello, I'm Denise." She had a low voice; it bubbled with an irrepressible smile that flirted from her big brown eyes. "And this is Pod, the baby of the house." Pod was right, she was the image of her mother.

"Yes, meet Denise, another of my brood." And Peg smothered little Pod with kisses. The gaggle shuffled into the kitchen which throbbed with the heat of the Aga and reeled with the warmth of a Coq au Vin slumbering in the lower oven.

"Here, hold Pod, I'd better have a look at that." Denise bobbed down on her knees and clanged the iron door with a chequered glove. A waft of warm herbs, wine, and succulent meat, seduced the appetite. Denise lifted the lid and the aroma intensified. "Perfect!" she said. "Ready any time we like."

"You hungry, Michael?"

"Of course, with temptation like that." He handed Pod back to Denise who locked her eyes on his.

"All right; we'll eat; after all, it is tea time," Peg laughed. Indeed it was about four thirty. "Come on, Edie, set the table." Edie, who a month ago would have silently shaken her head to fend off this sensuality, now leaped towards the dresser and rattled at the knives and forks, and flicked at the chequered tablecloth.

"I'll put the vegetables on."

As if summoned by the scent of food there then appeared Bill, surrounded by four skinny dogs who glared at Scruff, whose moral fibre wilted into the background.

“This is Bill, she lives in the hut across the field.” said Peg quickly as if to excuse the cloud of tobacco smoke that followed Bill into the house, the limp fag dangling from her nicotine orange upper lip and once white short cropped hair.

“Hello,” gurgled Bill and then coughed comfortably at Michael the newcomer.

“Is that the lot?” Michael nearly asked but let it pass.

“I’ll show you to your room,” said Denise with Pod on her hip. “We’ve been looking forward to you coming; we’re a bit short of young men.”

Michael again suppressed the question which had already occurred to him, “Does Pod have a father?” He discovered later that she did; but he was still in the army in India.

“It’s a funny old house, it’s all on the ground floor and the rooms seem to join onto each other; you have to go through my room to get to yours.”

“Oh! Don’t you mind?”

“No, just whistle, or shut your eyes.”

“I think I’ll just whistle, then, as there’s a choice!” He couldn’t help flirting with her, she invited it.

The house was indeed an odd one, it was built of inferior materials, indifferently assembled, held together by metal window frames, an asbestos tiled roof, and the caution not to have risen above a single story. It gave the impression that a puff of wind would blow it away, and that impression was not false. It had no foundations and hoped to keep dry by being sited on top of a slight mound. It was surrounded by ancient trees that shielded it from that menacing puff.

Peg had, at first, rented, and subsequently bought the property, in the early thirties. She was recovering emotionally and financially, from the death of her husband. He had been a clever Birmingham production engineer, who became the

English Managing Director of Singer Sewing Machines, Dublin. As such he was the target for a Sinn Fein assassination.

The house had been on the market for more than a year, trapped in the slump, and Peg found solace from her grief by driving a particularly hard bargain: a very low rent and an option to buy within a year, by which time the price had fallen further. Then, with her only child and son, Dick, she used her insurance compensation to establish a chicken farm on the battery system. This thrived until the outbreak of war when the concentrated feeding stuffs were no longer available and she had to abandon her battery hens. Ingeniously she found another use for the battery houses. She rented them out to the newspapers, who needed storage away from the bombing, for their huge rolls of news print. Peg was a natural entrepreneur; she even made a personal friend of the bumbling landlord.

She was a passionate and emotional woman and the death of her son in the air force, so soon after the violent death of a loved husband, almost deranged her. She grasped at any philosophy that transcended the limitations of the flesh; Spiritualism, Theosophy, the occult, and finally Christian Science. Her mind was probably saved by her all-embracing sense of humour, so that when pushed to the limit, she would laugh, after she had cried. But she hated loneliness and found people she could help. The first had been Bill, the animal lover. The shack where she had lived, burned down. This was not surprising, because her lips never lacked a cigarette. Peg built her another shack, well away from her own house, which so far had survived. Bill earned enough money to buy her cigarettes and feed her innumerable tribe of cats and dogs, by walking and boarding for others. She did not agree with sterilisation and opening any drawer in her hut, revealed nests of kittens.

Peg had settled on Christian Science because it led her to people who calmed her. Guy she had singled out because of his handsome features, his gentlemanly charm, his artistic sensitivity, and need of money which she was happy to supply. She was disappointed, though not repelled, by his homosexuality, and enrolled him as her escort, when he was available. She loved him to drive her in her Ford Popular, which she always seemed to have petrol coupons for. The wheel base of that car was so narrow, that Guy feared it might tip over, each time peg's bulk mounted the other side. The other addition to her brood, Denise, was Guy's friend Derek's sister in law; the wife of his brother Teddy. Now she had welcomed Leonard and Edie.

"I love your dad, Michael, just being alongside him makes me feel better" Michael always remembered this compliment and felt that it summed up Leonard's quality, people felt better when he talked to them; that was how he effected his healing.

"I get a clear vision of their spiritual identity and guide them towards it." That is how he tried to explain it to Michael. Leonard was all spirit and so was Edie; Peg was all earth, rooted in nature; it made a good mix, and fortified Leonard's body, grounding him in human affection.

Michael didn't really want to revive the memory of prison, but when he sincerely congratulated his father on being so wonderfully recovered, Leonard referred to it himself.

"I'm sure it was God's love, expressed as your love, and Guy's love and now Peg's love; it melted my fear. I was able to let it fade away like the bad dream that it was. What I was seeing in my clouded mind, was a misunderstanding that life can be bullied by the limitations of matter. The truth is, that love and harmony will always deflect any arrow of envy, if you can keep your mind open to it. And then, of course there's prayer. Prayer is not supplication, it is affirmation; it is not specific; it's universal. Divine power is always there to be affirmed, if we make ourselves receptive enough."

Michael was able to leave for Sheffield with a light heart. They had decided to close up the house there and surrender the lease.

"Leonard, I need your help." Peg was always direct and she could see that he was wonderfully recovered. "Now the war's over the newspapers are taking their storage back to London, so I lose my rent. I need to find something else to live on. Will you ask Devine Mind for an idea?" Peg always approached Christian Science as a sort of Delphic Oracle; she was an executive, Leonard was the priest.

"I'll give it some thought," he said, rather defensively. He certainly knew he wouldn't have any commercial suggestions, which is what Peg wanted. Anyway he cleared his mind to affirm that abundance and development was the true birthright of man's activity.

A few days later, Peg said, "I can't wait any longer for you to come up with an idea, Leonard. I've seen an advertisement for a property in Bognor, with planning permission for holiday caravans. Let's drive down and see it; I reckon cheap holidays will be what people want." They all set off in the Ford Popular and wobbled down to Bognor. Michael set off in the opposite direction to Sheffield.

It was just as well that he did go home again and scoop up the mounted mail in the hall. One of the letters was brown, buff, and O.H.M.S. It was the end of his indefinite leave; 'report to RAF Hednesford, Staffordshire by 1400 hours, Monday, October 3rd'. It was now September the 27th. There was no time to be lost in ending his youth in Sheffield.

But first he switched on the electric kettle and sat in his

father's chair that looked out of the front window over Rivelin Valley. The reluctant hissing of that notoriously slow kettle encouraged nostalgia and recall. He knew that it was the end of an era, Sheffield would never be his home again; the ambition to leave its provincial limitation was about to be realised by a telephone call to 'Caudles' the removal people. Peg had plenty of storage room in her empty battery houses and the bridge would be burned. He was a Sub-lieutenant in the Royal Navy; he was going to Pembroke College, Oxford, when they released him and he didn't need smoky Sheffield. He was Michael now, not Tony any more. But what about Miss Robinson; Daphne, as he thought of her now. She was quite often in his affectionate thoughts. Would he see her again; did she miss him; was she trapped in that blue beard's provincial castle; did she want to be rescued? At last the kettle shrieked and hissed him out of his fantasies. No, he would not try to ring her: that ogre of an uncle would answer the phone and hiss him away like the kettle.

As he drove past the smoke blackened Town Hall, pitted with shrapnel wounds, he said goodbye with no regrets. As he headed up the Granville Road, past Stafford Road where they had lived before, he had no regrets. Then out towards Woodhouse and his grammar school; should he call on Daphne, Miss Robinson? No: write to her when you get to Oxford, she may have forgotten you by then.

Soon it was the A1 road to the south and north, and he was speeding south, loaded with all those memorabilia he didn't want discarded; the comfort blanket for his new life.

Chapter Thirty-Two

Peg was standing, legs apart, like a general surveying his campaign. Her new life was a five-acre field with planning permission for fifty caravans between April and October, suitable plumbing and refuse facilities to be provided. She calculated aloud.

"Fifty caravans at ten pounds a week, times four weeks, times six months, equals twelve thousand a year.

Asking price for land, £5000, bungalow for me, say, £5000, say £2000, site plumbing, say £2000, twenty-five vans at £250 each is £6250, the other twenty-five, they bring their own and pay rent, total capital outlay equals eighteen thousand two hundred and fifty, say twenty thousand, say a return of fifty percent per annum; can't be bad. Halve the return for labour, imponderables and miscalculation, and it still makes twenty-five percent: can't be bad. Len, I think you've done very well with that divine mind of yours: I'll have it."

"What do think you'll get for Lodge Farm, will it cover it?"

"I'll apply for housing planning permission; that'll put the price up. The house is falling down anyway. Oh yes, there'll be plenty to spare. Don't worry, Leonard; I'll find you another nice house." And so she did, in Chipping Camden, near to Oxford, for when Michael went there.

***

R.A.F. Hednesford was a dismal posting compared with R.N.A.S Crail. Crail itself was a pretty little fishing village; Saint Andrews, Dundee and Edinburgh were easily accessible at the weekend. Hednesford was a mining village on the bleak moor of Cannock Chase, and Rugely and Birmingham were no substitute for Saint Andrews and Edinburgh. Moreover, it was an R.A.F. command, not naval, and there was a clash of cultures.

One month there was enough for Ted to say; "Mike, we've got to get wheels; we've got to have a car, we've got to be able to escape from this bloody place."

By the end of their Christmas leave, Ted had found a potential purchase. It was a 1936 Hillman Minx Saloon, suitably robust and capacious for companions, though tired. At the price of fifty pounds it was a possibility. They could raise that between them. Ted's parents lived in Ascot, that was where the garage was. Well, you couldn't really call it a garage; it was more a breakers yard; all right, a scrapyard. Michael took a bus over to Ascot; forty pounds burning a hole in his pocket and a steely determination not to be 'done'. He found Ted standing beside the stately Hillman, beaming with pride at his discovery. "What do you think, Mike?"

"Does it go; can we have a test run?" The greasy boiler suit, who was selling the vehicle, was quick to regret that the car was not yet insured, and could not leave the yard. He did, however, offer to start it up before they bought it.

He slipped an ignition key, worn almost to oblivion, into the dashboard; turned it, and then pressed the starter. The engine, as they say, 'burst into life'. Or rather gave an intimation of death. The mechanical sound was one of rearrangement, a sort of juggling of pistons and bearings without anything actually being dropped. Ted, who was standing at the rear of the car, was finding it difficult to speak because of the black smoke threatening asphyxiation. The salesman, or more accurately, the car wrecker, had a unique sales technique which was silence; do not speak unless spoken to, let the customer make the mistakes. After all, it was a seller's market and it would make good scrap if they didn't take it. He took a deep drag on his cigarette, and slowly exhaled to dilute the exhaust.

"What do you think, Mike?" Ted pleaded again.

"Well it sounds as if it will just about get us to the pub and back; but will it get us from Ascot to Hednesford, that's about eighty miles."

"It'll run as long as it's got petrol in it." The greasy boiler suit now spoke, sensing a deal.

"Petrol; yes," said Ted. "Fill her up and we'll take it for £50."

"Done," said the boiler suit, rather too quickly, thought Michael, but remembered the isolation of Cannock Chase, and supported Ted.

The money was handed over; the tank was filled. 'Tax Applied For ' was stuck on the windscreen with stamp edging; a cover note was torn out of a grubby book and stuffed in the glove compartment. They had their first car together; they were practically married.

"I'll drive."

"No, I want to drive." It was wedded bliss.

At least it was until they were getting near Banbury. There was freezing fog and the windscreen wipers wouldn't work. Michael propped open the bonnet on either side of the engine to allow the hot air (very hot!) to flow onto the windscreen.

But then the car ran out of fuel and spluttered to a halt.

"That bastard couldn't have given us a full tank," fumed Ted.

"Yes, he did; I checked it. It must be something else; a blocked fuel line, a failed fuel pump, I'll have a look." And Michael disappeared under the bonnet. He hand primed the fuel pump and the carburettor filled with petrol. "Try the starter, Ted." It started.

"What did you do: you're a genius."

"It's a duff fuel pump; it'll probably happen again."

"Oh great! I'm glad I'm not flying this thing."

It did happen again and again and again. They limped along, alternately pumping and stalling and starting. At last they reached a gentle hill which coasted them down to Banbury Cross, and one more pump spluttered them to a garage on the High Street. By now it was dark, it being mid-winter. The garage was closed, in fact, it looked as if it had never been open. Ted banged on the folding doors, but there was no response.

"Looks as if we're stuck for the night; we're not going to get to Hednesford."

"Well, the War's over, they can manage without us, but I suppose I'd better try and ring them, or we'll be up before the Commander, there's a hotel over there, if we can afford it." They crossed the deserted road, leaving the Hillman in front of the garage. The night cost them almost as much as the car but they were quite glad to have some warmth and comfort, rather than breaking down on Cannock Chase and walking the last three miles.

"It could have been worse," said Ted, as they woke the next morning to bright crisp sunshine and bacon and eggs. Life was even sunnier when they looked across the road to see a comforting cloud of smoke belching out of the Hillman's exhaust.

"You the lucky owners of this scrap heap, then?" The proud lieutenants reeled at this and were inclined to protest until, 'Jolly, Motor Engineers, Banbury.', continued; "Tired fuel pump, you see. I've put a new gasket in, but you need a new pump; sorry, but I haven't got one. Where you going?"

"Hednesford."

"You'll get there all right."

"Thanks very much: what do we owe you?"

"Go on; have it on me. If this is the only car you can afford, you must be broke." And he laughed and gave the Hillman an affectionate pat on the bonnet.

"Well, you don't meet many like that," said Ted as they chugged away, and he turned and gave him a salute.

The Hillman didn't last terribly long at Hednesford but it ferried them backwards and forwards to the Shrewsbury Arms in Rugely for a few months, obliterating their boredom. But she was abandoned when a rich young subby pilot joined the station with a 1933 Bentley. But that was another story.

Chapter Thirty-Three

Peg was as good as her word and when she had wheeled her deals, bought a house in Chipping Camden for Leonard to rent. Chipping Camden was about an hour from Oxford by car, and Leonard and Edie were very contented. Michael had to wait another four months until he was demobilised. That meant he had spent a year being totally redundant with five other pilots, pretending to be Divisional Officers to two hundred trainee mechanics, and riggers. They were reduced to taxiing wingless planes, teaching the trainees how to park an aircraft. Ted said they took the wings off to stop us flying away. Michael was the envy of the rest because he was released early because he had a place at Oxford in October. Poor old Ted had to endure six months more boredom; no wonder he got WAAF Sergeant pregnant!

Suddenly all that wasted world was behind him, and with an ill-fitting grey striped suit issued at the de-mob centre in Warrington (which he never wore) he was an Oxford undergraduate ordering 'commons' from the Buttery. Oh the delights of otiose terms to sustain elitism. In the navy it had been 'sippers' and 'gulpers'. Then it was large or small tots of gin; now it was 'commons' of toast. As the Oxford Dictionary defined it, 'a definite portion of victuals, supplied at a fixed price, 1641', two full slices of toasted butter to anyone else. The anyone else in this case was a visiting 'popsy'.

She could only be described as a 'popsy' because she was blonde and buxom, with pouting lips, and had already aroused the envious glances of those undergraduates who had had the pleasure of brushing against her as she waited for Michael in the porter's lodge. She seemed to attract 'brushing', which released wafts of Californian poppy perfume, arousing the basest instincts.

It was the earthy Aunty Peg who had organised this meeting. She was firmly of the opinion that if he became too immersed in academia he would suffer, like his father, from a lack of grounding. Sophie was the answer. Peg's farm was not very far away from Pinewood Studios and she had made friends with an attractive cameraman, abandoned by his wife and left to bring up his only daughter, Sophie. This he had done in the traditions of Pinewood and the film starlet. She had responded perfectly and had the figure to prove it. She had come to Oxford for the weekend and Michael was already wondering how he would fill in the time between kissing her Revlon lips. For the moment the time was to be filled with 'commons' of buttered toast.

"Oo! I'm all covered in butter; can I wipe my hands, is it through there?" And she opened the door into his bedroom, which was all bed except for a jug and basin on a wash stand. The basin was covered with a cotton towel as if discreetly hiding some sinister obstetric instrument. This did not deter Sophie from crunching it up with her scarlet finger nails and smearing it with lipstick from her scarlet mouth.

"That's better; how do I look?"

"Paler, but still lovely." (Why do I flirt so outrageously with her?" Michael asked himself. Because you're trying to get her into that bed in there. You be careful, or you'll be sent down before you've been up. You're still thinking like a Sub-lieutenant, stop it.)

Now she was pouting at her cherry lipstick and inviting further destruction of its sensual gloss. Suddenly, she was looking straight into his eyes and her own were brimming with tears. "I'm not clever enough for you, am I?" She glanced towards a book open on the desk. "I can't understand a word of that."

"Nonsense, Sophie; neither can I, it's Anglo-Saxon." But he knew she was being perceptive behind her splendid breasts: he must not toy with her; she was eighteen and he was the whole of twenty-one. It felt like a gap of a generation.

"Come on, I'll take you to the Randolph Bar and then out to dinner, by taxi, to The Bear at Woodstock, that's what a girl like you deserves."

And he did, and she loved it, and her eyes were quite dry with delight. How he kept the conversation going he never could remember, but it was a triumph of inanity and she felt like the brightest girl in the world. It all made a serious dent in his demob gratuity, but her pleasure was a joy to behold and he never spent a penny on a girl again, until he bought his future wife a sausage at the British Restaurant for one shilling and sixpence, and she loved him for the rest of her life; but not because of the sausage. Sophie went back to Pinewood and the life of glamour, which she was destined for, and thanked her Michael for assuring her that intellect was not necessarily an attraction.

"Now, back to the Anglo-Saxon and some serious acting, uncluttered by girls except; I wonder how Miss Robinson is getting on? Daphne, now she really is mature."

Chapter Thirty-Four

The 'Brew House' at Chipping Camden was as seventeenth century as Pembroke College, Oxford, but the atmosphere was different. Pembroke was about enlightenment, the Brew House was about brewing. It was a terrace house with no garden, and sunken low into the High Street, so that the sill of the living room window was level with the pavement. To a provincial lady like Edith, this was exposure that even a thick net curtain could not protect her from, and the curtain made it gloomier still.

The house, at this time, was dominated by "Puggins", the Spaniel bitch, who had just given birth (and not for the first time) to four sausage like puppies, the bastard offspring of a street roving mongrel. Puggins had been presented to Leonard and Edith by Bill, as a parting present. Bill believed in procreation, (perhaps to make up for her personal lack of contribution to it), and never had her animals neutered; thus Puggin's fecundity. There was not a lot of room for fecundity in the Brew House: one living room, a dining kitchen, up four steps to the rear of the house, past the stairs that curled up to two bedrooms and an attic in the roof beyond. The whole house seemed to be filled with afterbirth, but it wasn't, they were the puppies, growing larger every day. Edie's insistence that the animals were an 'idea of God's', was rapidly beginning to weaken.

"We'll just have to send for the vet," said Leonard, voicing her own thoughts.

"Yes," said Edie with relief.

The vet came and despatched the four puppies violently with an injection of prussic acid. This transformed squirming fury life into rigid, rictus, gargoyles to be stuffed into a bag and incinerated for five shillings.

The death of the puppies had a bad effect on Leonard; it precipitated a deep depression; a deep depression that had not left him by the time Michael came home on vacation at the end of his first term. It was the Christmas holidays.

"This is ridiculous, Dad, you're just being paranoid. You know better than that. Where's Devine Mind?"

Leonard looked ashamed and grasped Michael's hand. "Oh thank you for being here, you give me truth." Leonard had been insisting that he was being spied upon and being persecuted by the priest at the Catholic church on the opposite side of the High Street. "They know I'm a Christian Science Practitioner, and you know that Science and Health is a proscribed book by the Vatican."

"No, I didn't know, and it doesn't matter, because according to you, the power of God is universal and omnipotent." Leonard looked ashamed again.

"And have you seen this Priest you're afraid of. He's half blind and his cassock is smothered in snuff. Fortunately for him, he can't see just how fast his flock is fading. I think you should give him a prayer to help him in God's work." Michael knew he was going a bit far, but it did shake Leonard out of the worst of his depression.

"I think you are suffering from nostalgia for your dear old Sheffield. Why don't you go and stay with Doris and Fred, they've got a spare room, and they'd love to see you for

Christmas. Then you could survey Sheffield for a possible return." Michael suspected himself of avoiding spending Christmas in the dungeon of the Brew House.

"What about Puggins?" Ah yes, what about Puggins? Well at least she wasn't on heat anymore; the vet had seen to that after disposing of the puppies.

"Take her with you; she's very domesticated, and Doris loves animals."

"What about Doris's cat?"

"Puggins is scared of cats."

"Look, I'll drive you there. You're not fit enough to drive, are you?"

Leonard suddenly brightened. "Yes, I will be; it's another three weeks yet."

Michael's relief was evident; not too evident to his father, he hoped. "Good, that's settled then. I have got myself a Christmas job at Harrods. I've arranged to stay at Guy's."

"Oh!" Leonard was obviously disappointed.

"I have to earn a bit of money, Dad, you see."

"Yes, of course you do, and so will I quite soon."

Chapter Thirty-Five

Harrods was a lark. It was the second Christmas after the war and the shops were beginning to fill up again. In the china and glass department, anything nice and coloured went for export, anything white and dull stayed at home, but as Harrods attracted Americans and other foreigners, at least they could display Coalport and Derby with a frustrating notice, 'Export Only', so the department looked pretty.

The temporary staff turned out to be something of a new boys and girls reunion. At the training session, Michael saw several familiar faces across the room. One was an attractive girl he'd met at the first meeting of the Experimental Theatre Club that term. She had asked him to a coffee party, and he'd never gone; she seemed predatory. He preferred the cosy, undemanding friendship of his best friend Humphrey, who saw girls as something to draw (preferably in the nude). He wanted be an artist, which was why he was reading Politics, Philosophy, and Economics. But that was his father's idea.

They were trained in the intricacies of invoicing, the proper destination of an infinite number of copies, and the checking of credit. The trainer was insistent that if the account customer had a title, then particular care should be taken to check (with the greatest delicacy) that the customer was not over their limit. They invariably were!

She didn't have a title, and she didn't have an account, but she had wonderful grey-blue eyes shining out of a pretty face that blushed easily, making her even more attractive; and she was trying to buy socks for her father's Christmas present. Michael was serving on the sock and handkerchief counter; it being the busiest Christmas present department in 1946. Their eyes met; they both blushed.

"Oxford isn't it, Experimental Theatre Club?" Michael asked.

"That's right; you were talking to Ken Tynan, and I didn't dare interrupt."

"Oh! I'm sorry, I didn't notice you."

"Oh!"

"No, I didn't mean that. I mean you weren't in my line of sight; but I did notice you later."

"That's all right then."

"It's Heather, isn't it?"

"Yes, how did you know?"

"I asked that girl who asked me to coffee."

"Ah yes, Toba."

"Yes that's right, Toba."

"Why didn't you come to the coffee party?"

"Too scared. But I'm not scared now. It's my break in a minute; can we have coffee now?"

"Yes, all right."

"I say, did you want some socks. I can see the supervisor giving me a black look."

"Oh yes, sorry: two pairs, grey, size twelve: and six khaki handkerchiefs."

"Six khaki; that's good; not selling many of those these days."

"They're for my father; he takes snuff, it makes him sneeze."

"God bless him, then."

The transaction was completed quickly, the supervisor's frown relaxed into a beam, and with a quick,

"See you, ten minutes, coffee shop corner of Montpelier Square, yes?"

"Yes." And with a flash of brown hair over her emerald green coat, she was gone. And that was the start of something life long.

***

For Leonard in Sheffield it was a different kind of life long; it was a life past. Michael had been quite right, Leonard had a nostalgia for Sheffield, the place of his birth, his growing up, his epiphany, his fulfilment; a fulfilment that had suddenly become incomplete with his mental breakdown and flight to the south. It was an unfinished business. But could he carry on where he left off; did he have physical and spiritual robustness to continue healing work again? Could he face going back to his old church to receive the sympathy from the people he knew and had helped, or worse, feel their loss of faith in him: was it a case of 'physician, heal thyself.' Or still another feared possibility, being swamped with appeals for healing work, taking it on, only to bring his insomniac head to boiling point again, unable to switch off the light.

But still he felt he wanted to return to reach out to his roots, to regain control of his mind, to feel secure in himself, not exposed to the ills of others which his sensitive soul could never resist responding to.

But what work could he do, what was he qualified for at the age of forty-seven and of 'unsound mind'. No; he was not of unsound mind, that he knew; he had confidence in his intelligence, he had an impressive presence, he inspired trust.

He would just be receptive and the right opportunity would present itself. Oh! He felt better for that process of thought, that prayer, which in fact it was.

Doris's little terrace house at Hunter's Bar was like thousands of others in Sheffield, built at the turn of the century when the city was thriving on Imperial and world trade. Steel for battleships, the merchant fleet, forgings for great engines, shining cutlery for the rich and poor, and the soot and noise and filth that goes with it.

But not at Hunter's Bar. Hunter's Bar was to the west of the city, and the wind blew towards the east. These little terrace houses were built to house the clerks of the commerce, just like Fred. Fred was a human calculator; it was a gift he had with figures, and he was never bored with them; they danced in his head and always came down in their right columns. Leonard envied Fred's simplicity; his pipe and billiards, and apparent complacency. Yes, there was a peace to be had in arithmetic with its logic and its rules.

There was also a simplicity about Doris's house (Leonard always thought of it as Doris's house because she had found it, and she had leased it, and she had decorated it). It had two rooms downstairs, a front room and a kitchen. The front door opened straight out onto the street, which fortunately was a cul-de-sac, and the only hazard was the two steep steps onto the pavement. There was no bathroom, only a sink in the kitchen and a tin bath under the draining board; the lavatory was in the common back yard, but at least it was individual to the house.

Up the steep stairs, which lead from the kitchen, were two bedrooms, one on either side of the top stair. Below the stairs there was the cellar, which was why the steps at the front were so high, and that was it, and Doris loved it. It was freedom from her father, it was her castle. The black iron stove in the front room was warm and wholesome with the smell of steak and kidney pie, behind the clanging iron doors with their crisp steel ratcheting 'snecks'.

It reminded Leonard of the house where he was born and brought up. That was at the other end of the city, nearer the steel works where his father worked as a mould pattern maker; but it had looked out onto fields. His eldest brother Ernest, lived there now, and the fields were houses. They didn't speak much, he could never understand Leonard and was a bit afraid of him. His other brothers weren't afraid of him, they admired his brain and asked for advice. But then they had escaped from Sheffield. One was a pumping engineer for the water works in High Wycombe, the other was a sub-postmaster near Ipswich. That was Willis, and he was grateful to Leonard for having helped him get the job, under rather strange circumstances. Willis, like Leonard, had joined up during the war, but he found himself at the mercy of a brutal sergeant. So he deserted and joined another regiment under a different name. Shortly afterwards, he won the Military Medal. When he applied for the sub-postmaster's position, he had to fill in a complicated form where the truth had to be told. How do you explain that Willis Godley, deserter, had won the Military Medal as Willis Cooper (his mother's maiden name). Leonard wrote a careful letter and resolved the problem; Willis lived happily ever after in his post office with his lovely wife and son. The other member of his family was Agnes. She still lived in Sheffield, in the east end, and was married to a miner, who was prospering under nationalisation of the coal industry. Leonard would visit her and be reminded of his loving mother.

Leonard sometimes wondered if he should have tried the

simple life; the rest of the family didn't have the agonies of his spiritual strivings; but then he had had some glorious revelations, both human and spiritual. The world had opened out to him. It was a different world, and we make our own worlds and we live separately within them, in our own bubble of consciousness. He knew the journey was not yet complete, but he was not afraid to look at the past. It told him he really never had a choice, he must go forward.

"Let's take Puggins for a walk in the Botanical Gardens; we can keep her on the lead," Leonard suggested to Edith.

"Yes, yes, let's. I see God in flowers."

"You won't see much of him in the gardens at this time of the year," said Doris.

"Oh yes, there'll be the hellebores," said Edith.

"If you say so, Edie," sniffed Doris.

"Do you want to come with us?" asked Leonard, always sensitive.

"No thanks, Len. I've got to take Beano to the vet; my Spirit Guide told me to."

"What's wrong with Beano then?"

"Nothing; but there might be."

"Well, I'll give him a good thought, anyway."

"Thank you, Len; see you later."

***

The Botanical Gardens were indeed rather forlorn after six years of war, neglect, and a sprinkling of winter snow, but Leonard and Edie had happy and peaceful memories of them in their courting days. The glass conservatories were intact then, a minor Crystal Palace, with secret seats under chaperoning palms, where lovers promised eternal love. Too many promises had shattered like the glass over the years, but not the bond of love between Edith and Leonard; their love had survived their struggles and sustained their faith.

"Let's cross the road and walk round Rutland Park; they're nice houses." Puggins lead the way, straining at the lead; she stopped at one house and sniffed at the weeds sprouting from the base of the front wall. The rusticated granite blocks supported a rising bank to three stories of a substantial Edwardian terraced front, and a generous bay window painted a faded dark green. The house was empty, as was the house next door. They appeared to have been used for some sort of council office. Propped in the window was a post card. Leonard climbed the steps to read it and satisfy his curiosity as to what this tiny notice might say, it certainly could not be read from the street level. It said 'For Sale. Apply at number 15.' It didn't even say Rutland Park; it seemed to want to keep its secret.

"Edie, come and look at this; it says it's for sale, apply at number fifteen."

"Oh, yes, I expect it is; nobody wants these big houses, too many stairs and a lot of work."

"But it's for sale; we could buy it."

"What with; we haven't got a house to sell." Edie could be quite practical at times.

"Well, I'm going to find out; come on," and with Puggins pulling ahead to number fifteen, they soon arrived at a similar house. Leonard knocked the knocker firmly without waiting for Edie to catch up and restrain him.

A few moments later there was a shuffling in the entrance hall and a shadow on the hammered glass, which opened the door. In the entrance was small old man not unlike an elf; he blinked behind gold rimmed glasses and raised his faded eyebrows in enquiry.

"Excuse me," said Leonard, "But I came about your 'For Sale' notice." Leonard spoke quickly, rather expecting the whole episode to vanish in a puff of smoke.

"Oh yes; are you interested then?" The elf seemed to be surprised that anyone would be interested; he didn't disappear in a puff of smoke but said, "Would you like to see it then?"

"Oh yes please." Leonard felt like a little boy being offered a ride on a bike he longed to own.

"I'll just put me coat on, then." He was in his waistcoat and shirt sleeves; he withdrew into the back of the house.

"We're going to be shown over the house, Edie." Edie was hovering on the pavement looking embarrassed.

"Oh Leonard!" is all she could say.

The elf reappeared dangling a key from his right hand thumb and forefinger, as if offering a jewel. The key slid comfortably into the lock and turned like the answer to a problem. The elf preceded them into the spacious hall and conducted them round the ground floor rooms, drawing room front, dining room back, kitchen, back door to a small jungle of a garden.

"You'd like that garden, wouldn't you Edie?"

"Sun in the morning; faces East; drawing room gets the sun in the afternoon and the sunsets; front garden good for geraniums," enthused the elf, and Edie blushed with anticipation. Leonard and the elf continued up stairs while Edie planned her garden. There were three bedrooms on one floor and two more attic rooms with dormer windows: it was a substantial residence.

Then Leonard had to ask the question, "How much are you asking for it?"

The reply from the elf was quizzical, "Do I know you,

could I know your name?"

"Mr Godley, Leonard Godley."

"Ee! Len; I thought it was you, but I haven't seen you since you were twenty. Don't you know who I am?" He grinned, more elfish than ever; like a riddle in a fairy story.

Leonard dug deep into his memory and haltingly suggested, "It's not Mr. Mather, is it?"

"Yes it is, and that's Edie isn't it? Ee! Len, I'm that glad to see thee again, I've always liked you." And he almost danced with glee.

"Edie, Edie, it's Mr. Mather; do you remember him from the pawn shop, where we first met, before the first war?" Edie blushed as if she wanted to forget the pawn shop, but she smiled nevertheless.

"Ee! Come and have a cup of tea and talk about it," grinned Mr. Mather, and lead them back to number fifteen.

The reminiscing over cups of tea (that could have been used for tanning leather) led to a quite phenomenally generous agreement by Mr. Mather. He would lend Leonard the whole sum of twelve hundred pounds with which to purchase both houses. He asked for interest only, at the fixed rate of two and a half percent. "What do you think, Len; could you manage that?"

"Yes; you'll be quite secure on that arrangement, it's very generous." Leonard had already worked out that he would convert the second house into three flats and let them to post-graduates from Sheffield University, which was only a short walk away; this would cover his borrowings and give him an income.

"It's not so generous, Len; I like to think of you having them, and I only paid five hundred pounds for them in the middle of this war. I've been lucky; I suppose I'm what people call a ‘little mester’, with my little bits of property all over Sheffield. But what’s the point of money if you can’t use it to help someone who helped you. There’s something about you, Len, when you were around, things went better, and my business prospered. I was so glad to know you survived our terrible war, and married Edith.”

“Well, it does rather look as if it was meant, our meeting like this, you’ve certainly solved my problem; perhaps we should thank ‘Puggins’ here, for sniffing at your weeds: which I shall soon clear up.” He added with a joyous grin, checking himself from becoming too pious, but he knew his prayers had been answered. And to be able to grin, joyously, was almost a forgotten experience.

As they walked away down the hill in a daze of joy towards Hunter’s Bar, they passed Weston House; the sometime home of the Saville family, where, in 1934, Guy had come to work, and horizons had expanded. It was now the headquarters of an insurance company, and none the worse for that; it had been a kind of insurance to Leonard, he hoped it would be to many others.

“Ee! It’ll be lovely having you live near,” said Doris.

“Ee! It’s posh up there,” said Fred. And Leonard felt a wicked pride, he liked the idea of being posh.

Chapter Thirty-Six

Oxford was living up to every expectation. Michael was sure his father would have been taking this wonderful academic opportunity more seriously, had he been offered it, but Michael was in love and got over his guilt. He was in love with Heather. Heather who had coffee with him at Harrods, Heather who was dumping her aristocratic fiancé for Michael the actor and romantic, Michael who wrote poetry and was elusive, Michael who kept quiet about his parents that Heather was convinced were a retired admiral and his dragon of a wife. They must be if they lived in Chipping Camden. They had fallen in love because they were in a play together and the sight of someone else kissing her had made him declare his love out of sheer despair.

"Of course I love you, silly," was her bubbling reply, and as all this had happened on tour in Paris, they began to plan their lives together. He was to be a brilliant and successful actor, she was to be a brilliant hostess. But first they had to get their degrees, which they did; then they had to get started on being a brilliant success so they could get married. The bottom rung of the theatrical ladder was an indifferent comedy in the West End which lasted all of six weeks, but did produce a rented flat through a friend in the cast. It was an early Victorian house in Hugh Street, Pimlico, backing onto Victoria station. Here was somewhere to hold brilliant parties. Heather needed a Crown Derby dinner set and loopy loo curtains, so she became an Air Hostess and went to New York. They were married in Heather's pretty village church in Ashstead, leafy Surrey. This was only after Michael agreed to be baptised and confirmed because the vicar said he would rather marry a Hottentot than a Christian Scientist. Michael told him he didn't want him to marry him, only perform the ceremony, but he got a funny look.

The next step towards brilliance was when Harold Hobson, now an established drama critic, and Leonard's friend from the twenties, got Michael a part in the Alec Guiness Hamlet. But brilliance once more proved elusive and the production was a disaster. Brilliant bottle parties there were, hosted by Heather but now she was pregnant and soon she would not be able to work. Something had to be done.

"I know, I'll be a graduate trainee."

"But you're twenty-eight," Heather reminded him.

"Ah yes, but I've done my research and found that John Lewis Partnership have an upper age limit of twenty-eight; so there's not a moment to be lost. I'm having an interview on Tuesday."

"Are you sure you want to do this? It's not how we planned it, is it?"

"Darling, I've seen enough of the profession to know that the best advice is: 'If at first you don't succeed, give up.' If you wait too long to get the message, it's too late, and it can seriously damage your life. I don't want to end up divorced and embittered in my dingy bed sitter in Maida Vale."

"All right, darling; but don't say I made you give it up."

"I'll never say that, because I know it's not true; it's just that little girl in there that has something to do with it: I'm sure she is a little girl. Perhaps she'll make up for it one day."

"How did you get on, then?" Heather was keen to know; she was looking forward to a steady income for a change.

"I think it went rather well. It was a rather odd interview. The Partnership seem to retain a retired head of the Civil Service to chair the selection board. After a few preliminaries about education and war service he stunned me by asking me to compare and contrast Marlowe with Shakespeare. That was right up my street and he had to stop me in the end. "Perhaps you could write a monograph on the subject," he remarked from below drooping eyelids. They said they would let me know: it's just like the stage, you see, except the runs should be longer; I hope!"

"What has all that got to do with working in a department store?"

"I really don't know: do you think it was a trick question; should I have analysed which, Marlowe or Shakespeare, would have made the best shopkeeper?"

"Yes, I think you should."

"Oh dear."

Michael's perception about Marlowe and Shakespeare proved to be just the sort of intelligence that the John Lewis Partnership was looking for. In a few days an offer came in the post, to join their graduate training scheme at the rate of eight pounds a week plus Partnership discount on all purchases; Michael accepted.

"I was getting twice that in 'Cry Liberty' at the Vaudeville Theatre," sighed Michael.

"But it only lasted six weeks, and you didn't get paid for three weeks rehearsal, That equals eight pounds a week, darling." Michael brightened up.

"The training course alone lasts twenty-four weeks, so even if they find me out by the end of that, I'll have done better. We could buy a house, if we had the deposit, if there were any for sale, if Abbey National would approve it."

But they were unlikely to find a deal as generous as Leonard's in Sheffield. Mr. Mather had been as good as his word, and they had moved into Rutland Park, decorated and converted, and attracted nice tenants. Leonard had even found a congenial job as a book keeper at a small paint wholesaler. Trade price paint eased considerably the cost of converting his flats. All this physical work and mental arithmetic took his brain off the boil and 'grounded' him, as Peg would say. Things were going well and they were about to be grandparents.

Yes, Julia (she was indeed a girl) safely arrived, and went off to Heather's mother to be fluttered over for the first two weeks, and to avoid the choking fog that descended over London. Michael, selling dress velvets in John Lewis, Oxford Street, could not see across the department. It stayed like that for almost two weeks. It was eerily quiet; the fog muffled the sound of the sparse traffic, only the tortured coughing from invisible bronchials indicated passing pedestrians.

Twenty-eight Hugh Street was no healthier. The atmosphere was further aggravated by the steam engines who would park the other side of the back yard wall and proceed to clean their fire boxes. This meant throwing a phosphorus flare into the fire which generated enough heat to burn off all the soot in the funnel. Most of it descended into the romantically pink painted back yard, and on to Julia when she returned with Heather from her mother's.

"It won't do," said Heather, protecting her child. "We've got to move. And another thing, that old tart next door keeps me and Julia awake all night."

She certainly did: us, and everyone else in the street. Julie, yes Julie; pity she had the same name as the precious-adored. Julie had had a rather good war. Hugh Street was conveniently near Victorian Station, and initiating the business with her own body, she had developed a brothel, which offered sensual comforts at non-commissioned prices; this, without missing your train. She had now retired from commerce, bought the house outright, adopted the pub at the end of the street and noisily entertained anybody who remained in the pub when it closed each night. One person who could be relied on to be there was an inept accordion player who had one tune only in his repertoire, this was 'There's a pawnshop on the corner in Pittsburgh, Pennsylvania'. The tune had polka rhythm which hammered your head for years at a time. Calls to the police only increased the size of the party when they knocked on the door.

"Oo! Hello, Gerry; come on in, darlin'."

Michael's actor friend, living upstairs, would frequently throw his bath water on her steps, as her guests arrived. Unfortunately, he did this the night the police responded, which ended any support they could expect from the law.

"Yes, darling, I agree; got any ideas?"

"Yes, let's move to Putney."

"To Putney; we'd have to go by sleeper!"

"Now, don't be silly; you know, where my aunts and my grandmother live."

"Yes, I know."

"Well, what's wrong with it?"

"Nothing, it's very nice; it's just a bit far, and near your aunts."

"Well, I've been in touch with my old friend Ann, and she lives in a flat in a lovely house that was built by the Jaeger's, you know the nice woollen people."

"That's some time ago, isn't it?"

"That's why it's so nice: anyway the ground floor flat is vacant and it's only five pounds a week."

"That's half a week's pay!"

"Well you'll have to get a rise, won't you." This must be what his doubtful father-in-law must have meant when he muttered something about family responsibilities. Ah well he was just coming to the end of his training, perhaps they were about to make him General Manager of the Oxford Street store; but he doubted it.

"All you have to do is go and see a Miss Beamish at the offices of Radio Luxemburg in Portland Place; she's expecting you."

"You mean I'm getting a job as an announcer?"

"No, silly; she is company secretary there and owns the Jaeger house; she only lets to nice people."

"How does she know I'm nice?"

"Ann said you were."

"Oh thank you: five pounds a week, you say?"

"Yes; off you go."

Miss Beamish was lovely: she beamed, had a cherubic face and a twinkle. She dressed in black bombazine in the fashion of some fifty years earlier, but yet was as youthful as a robin.

"So, you'd like the flat?"

"Yes, we would," said Michael trying not to sound doubtful.

"Well, you can have it: five pounds a week, monthly in advance, by standing order. I understand you work at John Lewis, just round the corner, same journey as me, except I now live in a flat upstairs here; very convenient. Well that's settled then; I'll send you the lease, you send me the money." And she laughed heartily, Michael tried to join in.

And so it was, they left Hugh Street that had been so convenient for acting in the West End (for just six weeks at a time) and went, not by sleeper, but by hired van to Putney and splendid it was with its Art Nouveau arabesques set in every fireplace, door handle and finger plate, window glass, mouldings. The bath in the spacious kitchen was perfect for a Levee or watching your lovely wife bathe when it was your turn to cook. There was even a grand piano in the drawing room on which Michael could elegantly lean. It was bliss; especially when he was made buyer for plastic handbags at eight hundred a year, and could afford it all. Have the vision and the rest will follow; that seemed to be father and son's philosophy of life. So far, so good. The 'runs' were getting longer, but not unlimited, he found.

Ironically, it was Sheffield that brought this run to an end. But that was some little way into the future, first it was: "We need a car, we're having another baby, and we need a car to get about and go on holiday."

"You're absolutely right dear, and I have just the perfect vehicle about to be delivered, as soon as I can find the fifty pounds to pay for it. It's an ex London Taxi, vintage 1938; landaulette body, which means you can fold the back down and wave like the queen."

"I've got fifty pounds: it's a one-hundred-pound War Loan Bond, my granny gave me. It's only worth fifty pounds, so let's sell it; it's all meant."

"Done," and it was, and collection was arranged from the tearful taxi driver who was retiring from the 'knowledge'. It was still in its modest black and blue livery when he drove it home. As he slowed in heavy traffic in Park Lane, a Commissionaire leaped on the running board, shouting, "Arlington Street and then Waterloo!" Michael could have done with the fare, but had to disappoint. Shortly afterwards he painted the blue, yellow, to avoid embarrassment and give the vehicle a more theatrical air.

"It's wonderful," Heather was thrilled and shrieked with delight when Michael demonstrated how it was possible to manoeuvre the grand Marmet pram into the rear compartment, and leave room for the legs of the passengers. "We'll never get rid of this, will we? We'll buy a country house and keep it in the orchard for the children to play in it, won't we?" But he orchard turned out to be Derby!

***

It happened like this: there was a tax, called the luxury tax. This was applied to all goods sold which were regarded as non-essential. This applied to handbags but not to 'shoppers'. The theory must have been that the shopping bag of the working class mum was a necessity, but the handbag of the lady who lunched was not, or if it was it was a luxury, and attracted the tax. It therefore followed that any bag which had no form of 'closure', was a shopper. This set the designers into a frenzy of ingenuity. The 'Bucket bag' was invented. It was elegantly designed, but was, after all no more than a floppy fire bucket, and was a favourite of pickpockets! It sold as if there was a fire; it was some twenty percent cheaper than any other holdall and, furthermore became a fashion item.

Departmental sales figures rocketed in Oxford Street and the south generally. Top management beamed at Michael.

The marcel waved, mink-tippeted, crafty old buyer of leather handbags (the position that Michael was expected to succeed to, when she retired) shook her head gloomily. "It'll do us no good; there will never ever be anything to replace it, and they'll say we're getting it wrong when the figures go down and stay down. It's like I told you; just keep a steady rise of two and a half percent a year and you keep your job; dramatic downs they don't like; explanations they don't want to know. Thank goodness I'll be on my Partnership pension next year. I'll suggest your only chance of surviving is to get moved to another department while they still think you're a genius. Let some other poor bugger take the rap."

"Thanks," said Michael, I see what I can do about it. But of course there was nothing he could do about it and economics took its predictably unpredictable course. Actually, in this case, it was predictable, but it didn't help; it was management that was unpredictable.

Michael was responsible for sixteen stores altogether and half of them were in the midlands and the north. In the mid 1950s there was a predictable time lag in the spread of fashion from south to north of twelve to eighteen months. Experience in the south told you when to stop stocking for the north and so avoid marking down unsold stocks. This he had done for Cole Brothers, Sheffield, which aroused the wrath of that terrifying gorgon, the female General Manager in Sheffield.

"What's happened to the handbag sales; they're down twenty-five percent?" Miss Gorgon's glasses were glinting like fire. "I'll tell you what's happened," she crashed on, "You've failed to order enough bucket bags, that's what's missing; there are only three in the department."

"And they've been there for four weeks; the fashion is over." Gorgon was not used to explanations and opposition, and didn't want it. Michael had made a tactical error; she had no opinion of graduate trainees. Michael was beginning to agree with her.

"I shall complain to the Director of Selling."

Now the Director of Selling was a retired Air Commodore who had had a good war as the senior officer responsible for protection from gas of all U.K. airfields. This, for some reason, had recommended him to Spedan Lewis, the Chairman and creator of the Partnership. Unfortunately, this splendid achievement had engendered a megalomania that led to the employment of many high ranking military, which then satisfied his lust for domination. Knowing nothing about retailing, these admirals, generals, and air commodores, while scanning the unfamiliar horizon for a landfall, a salient or a target, wisely relied on their warrant officers, like Miss Gorgon, to advise them.

Air Commodore Gas accepted Miss Gorgan's complaint as valid and Michael was sacked. Fortunately, the sacking was generous and gentle: the Partnership was schizophrenic, as was its Chairman; it was liberal, cultured and ruthless; it counted cotton reels but sponsored operas. When Spedan Lewis was preparing to retire (over which, took as long as a Diva) he placed a series of advertisements in the appointments columns of the broadsheets, profiling the qualities needed in his successor. As one wag put it; he was looking for a combination of Winston Churchill, Henry Ford, and Jesus Christ!

Michael felt the Christian benefit, and was given six months' pay to resettle himself.

Heather was depressed but brave. Little Georgina was now solemnly scanning the world from the pram that Julia had vacated, and they were homeless. Their lovely Jaeger flat had been snapped up by a smooth developer whose name was Sole, not Soul, of which he had none. He regretted dispossessing them, but found it inevitable unless they could afford six thousand pounds for their ground floor flat. The dear Miss

Beamish had offered to sell it to the three families living there for eight thousand pounds including the furniture, but she had to have a mortgage of one thousand pounds paid off first. She even offered to lend them the balance at rate of two and a half percent. But no bank or building society would consider an old house and none of them could raise the thousand pounds; so it was sold to Mr. Sole, who regretted that he would have to cut off the services.

Michael, scouring the appointments pages, saw an advertisement for commercial contacts executives at Rolls Royce Aero Engine Division in Derby. The work will be concerned with the selling of the Dart Engine to overseas airlines. Applicants should have a degree, commercial experience, and a knowledge of aviation.

"I say, this is me. This is my chance to save the country by solving the balance of payments problem, selling Rolls Royce Aero Engines round the world."

"But we'll have to move to Derby, won't we. I wouldn't like that." said Heather quickly.

"But we could buy a house there. There, they're all 1930s houses that the Abbey National likes, and they're cheap."

This had certain attractions, living as they had been, up three flights of stairs in a furnished flat in Sutton, then in basement flat in Hampstead, which was an improvement; down ten steps, instead of up three flights, and in swinging Hampstead, instead of suburban Sutton.

"This is not how we planned it," said Heather.

"The money's good too," Michael pleaded. "I think it's all meant."

"All right, have an interview, and see what happens; there doesn't seem to be anything else turning up."

He had his interview; no questions about Marlow or

Shakespeare this time. There was no panel, just one rather nervous engineer who kept referring to a textbook on personnel management for his next question. Of course they snapped him up and he was employed. Heather got over her disappointment when she walked into her brand new house in Allestree, Derby, with its through room, its kitchen dining room, its three bedrooms and view over the empty field at the back. The yellow taxi looked a bit startling in the drive, and curtains started to twitch.

"Allestree," mused Heather. I can only see one tree in the field, where are all the others. The next day some men came and chopped it down and started to build houses!

Michael began to feel that perhaps it wasn't meant after all, when he arrived at the office on the first day and had to clock in: it was eight a.m. He was shown to his desk in a large open office; it had an in tray and an out tray and a telephone. The supervisor explained to him what to do with the orders and invoices in in his tray. It consisted of sending them off to other departments, waiting for them to come back, writing a standard covering letter, and sending them to the post room. The most exciting thing was reading the destinations: Canada, Saudi Arabia, Brazil, Belgium, India, South Africa, U.S.A.; all over the world, in fact, places that clearly Michael would never see. The six successful candidates eyed each other furtively across the room and soon organised an escape club. Within twelve months, they had all escaped.

Brave Heather had organised a nursery school at home which was a boon to the local mothers; she had had it closed down by the complaint of a jealous neighbour. She had become a local hero and been offered a place on the Hospital Board, but by that time they were escaping.

The day of the escape was a hilarious adventure. Derby

station was an Air Ministry station. Every morning at seven thirty, hundreds of engineers and accountants from Rolls Royce would be assembled on the London bound platform, heading for Whitehall. This meant that if you had a clandestine interview in London yourself, it was inadvisable to leave from Derby, if the secret was to be kept. This meant getting to Nottingham by car, some ten miles away and on a different line. There was, however, a further complication.

A democratic car sharing system had been organised with neighbours, all of whom worked in Rolls Royce, but who were not members of the escape club. They loved it there. Michael knew he mustn't let his neighbours down, so an elaborate subterfuge was arranged. Michael would rendezvous as usual at the bus stop and pick up his passengers. He would describe to them in great agitation that Heather had succumbed to the most horrific attack of dysentery (from her air hostess days, you know) and couldn't look after the children.

He would run them to the factory, he asked them to explain his absence, then he would return home: so he said, but then he drove off to Nottingham. Brilliant, wasn't it! Except for the fact that the community was suffocatingly close and hubbies always rang their wives on the office phone during the day. Such excitement as dysentery set the telephones buzzing even earlier. The result was that a well-meaning wife rushed round to Heather to offer help! Fortunately, Heather was still in her dressing gown and improvised brilliantly, by saying that Michael was down at the chemists, buying up the local supply of Kaolin, and would be back soon.

The secret survived, the job in Uxbridge was offered, and the triumphant telegram was sent to Derby. 'Escape complete; job secured; love Michael'. Heather felt her tummy rumble with joy; or was it the onset of dysentery.

As the yellow taxi rumbled south with Julia and Georgina and Heather singing, 'Follow the Yellow Brick Road', and Michael beating time with his heaving shoulders bouncing over the thick spoked steering wheel, the approaching metropolis promised social sophistication as the introverted provincialism of Derby withered behind them. As they said later at dinner parties with chattering friends: "It is no surprise to us that Bonny Prince Charlie, turned back when he got there."

Chapter Thirty-Seven

Leonard and Edith were now happily established in their new home and enjoying the freedom of a modest affluence; motor tours to see Peg at Bognor in her caravanserai. Guy had joined her there, accepting her offer of a free caravan site for companionship. With the proceeds of the sale of the short lease of the St. John's Wood studio flat, Guy bought a luxury caravan. Winifred had wanted to be free of the responsibility and had handed it over to Guy. Ten years into peace again it had a value, and now being sixty-five, the welfare state, old age pension gave him enough to live on. Peg was looked after by her favourite unmarried niece in her spacious bungalow. Guy was even adored by a pretty spinster who cared for her aged, wealthy mother. Peg had to smother her jealousy as they were all members of the local Christian Science Church, and met each week. Derek had also met his new bride in Bognor and was now teaching at Chelsea and living in Fulham. So everyone was cared for.

They all looked forward to Leonard's visits because they felt that it was through his pure thoughts that harmony surrounded them. His was a very simple approach, he just assured them that the power of God's love for them and all mankind, was eternally available to a receptive mind uncluttered by the myopia of materialism. Keep the vision of goodness in the mind and it would manifest itself.

They tried to keep the vision, and it worked and sometimes it didn't. A visit from Leonard helped to re-establish that vision.

When he returned to Sheffield, Leonard had to struggle very hard to retain it, because of what happened. Mr. Mather had died and his son was about to liquidate his little empire and turn it into cash Leonard Godley and his house in Rutland Park was an obstacle in his way. He tried to put the pressure on Leonard, but the mortgage deed was clear; two and a half percent interest with no repayment element, in perpetuity. Bank rate was now four percent and the value of the property had doubled. If Leonard were to raise a mortgage to pay off the twelve-hundred-pound loan, he would have to pay interest of six percent, and double his costs. This he could not afford to do: Mather junior said he could. Leonard began to lose sleep, the letters from Mather and his solicitors (which had no legal force) un-nerved him. He went to the doctor for sleeping pills; Mogadon was prescribed. He felt he was betraying his faith; his sleep was even more disturbed.

Then the pressure was increased when Mather junior's solicitor at Mather's suggestion, advised the Inland Revenue to inspect the sources of Leonard's income, which seemed inconsistent with his standard of living.

Leonard had always been conscientious about his income from healing work, which in recent years had been inconsequential; his earned income from the paint firm, had been pay as you earn; this left the income from rents which had been duly reported in the returns and the overheads claimed to give a net profit figure. To the outsider, Leonard's standard of living could seem enviously comfortable. They dressed well, they ran a car. They went for frequent holidays, they were visited by friends with expensive cars. What was not obvious to the outsider, was that Leonard had done all his own conversions and maintenance, that he did not smoke or drink, or go out to meals or spend money lavishly on housekeeping. The Inspector of Taxes, apparently having no other pressing business and being a member of the same club as Mather junior and his solicitor, came to visit, and the inquisition began.

"Mr. Godley, I know from your returns that your sources of income are from Stokes Brothers, paint manufacturers and wholesalers, and from your flats at number eleven Rutland Park. Do you wish to tell me about any other source of income?"

"No, I have no other source of income, except my state pension which I am now receiving, having retired from Stokes Brothers."

"I understand that you are a registered Christian Science Practitioner of Healing, are you not?"

"I have not been a registered Practitioner for some years now." Leonard looked straight into the accusing eyes of the Inspector, and began to understand the line of his investigation. Was this just professional zeal, or was it prejudice?

"And when did you cease to receive income from your healing work?"

"When I ceased to report it on my tax returns; I don't recall which year it was exactly, you would have to refer to your records."

"I can tell you exactly when," the Inspector sniffed like a hound hot on the scent. "It was the year ending May 1965. Do you deny having received any income from that source since then?"

"Yes, I do."

"Why is that?"

"I was ill during that year," he faltered. "I had a mental breakdown." He dropped his head, "I was unable to work in that capacity again." He fought back tears; he was unable to look the Inspector in the eyes.

The Inspector was enjoying his ascendancy, he released his hold slightly.

"I'm sorry." But he countered with a quick; "But I suppose you are still in touch with your patients: they must miss your services?"

"Yes, some of them."

"But you no longer charge them for the healing work you do for them?"

"No."

"So, you still do healing work for them."

"If I am able to, yes." Leonard realised he had fallen into a trap.

"But you never take any remuneration for that healing work?

"No."

"Mr. Godley, you have rather nice car outside your house; to buy it must have taken a rather large slice out of your savings, but you have no savings, have you: at least none that attract interest to be reported to the Inland Revenue. How did you buy it then?"

"It was given to me by a friend who was replacing it with a new one."

"Is this friend one of your ex patients?" Leonard paused, he realised he was being trapped again.

"Yes."

"I suggest, Mr. Godley that this car was in remuneration for your work as a healer, and should have been valued as such in your returns for that year: was it?"

"No… but it was a gift… from a friend."

"I suggest not. Mr. Godley I shall require a list of all your former patients, and their addresses. I may contact them to ask whether they have made any payments in cash or in kind for your services in the years since 1965."

Leonard went white with horror at this vindictive attack. He rallied enough to mutter that this information was professionally confidential and his solicitor would be dealing with it.

"That is for you to consider, Mr. Godley, but I shall be further in touch. Good day." And he snapped his briefcase shut and left, leaving the door open and a chill wind blowing.

"What did he want?" Edith had been reading and praying in the dining room. Her deafness meant she could not overhear.

"He says I've been cheating the Inland Revenue," Leonard said numbly.

"You'd never cheat anyone, Leonard, God knows that."

"I hope so. I must ring Michael, he'll know what to do."

When Michael made his weekly call to his father, he realised there was something seriously wrong; his father's voice had lost its usual confidence and slurred with depression.

"What is it, Dad; what's wrong?" And it all came out. "Don't worry; I'll come and see you just as soon as I can get away, just a few days." And he immediately began to arrange it.

Another wave of depression struck the household when Leonard's doctor arbitrarily announced that that Mogadon, the barbiturate sleeping pill, was now proscribed, and could no longer be issued to patients; it had proved to be addictive, and a non-barbiturate pill was to replace it. Leonard was numbly indifferent until after a week of withdrawal he became deranged. By the time that Michael got to Sheffield he found Leonard as mad as Lear.

He was sitting on the sofa with eyes wide, threading an imaginary needle. On his shoulder was perched a white dove, kissing his ear. The dove was not imaginary; it had been passed on to Leonard when Guy had moved into his caravan. 'Tooey' had become deeply in love with Leonard and would accept no affection from anyone else, Edith included. She seemed to be trying to comfort him; she cooed and chirruped, dipping and craning her neck in affectionate agitation, on his shoulder. The scene was surreal.

"How long has he been like this, Mum?

"For about three days."

"Have you told the Doctor?"

"Yes."

"What does he say?"

"He says he'll get over it; it's withdrawal symptoms." He did get over it but it left him shattered.

"It's the strain of this tax business, and the pressure from Mather junior. I'll sort it out, Dad. You've nothing to fear; your position is legally right, they can't harm you. I'll go and see them and tell them so."

The fear began to clear from Leonard's face, his eyes began to focus; even Tooey calmed down and flew back to her wicker cage.

Michael tackled Mather first. He tried to avoid him, but Michael tracked him down in his suburban house in Muskoka Drive; ironically, where Michael had been born; the house his father had had to sell at a loss in 1931. One of the swings and roundabouts of life. There was not any evidence that Mr. Mather senior had left him a lot of money.

"I've come to talk about my Father's mortgage, Mr.

Mather," said Michael standing on the doorstep.

"Oh yes," there was a blank reaction.

"Can I come in?"

"I suppose you can; come in then."

"We were sorry to hear about the death of your father; he was a great friend to my father."

"Too great, if you ask me."

"Yes, I understand that you are unhappy about the terms of the mortgage."

"Yes, I am. I suppose you think my father was a very wealthy man, well he wasn't. Having paid the death duties on the estate, and paying off my own mortgage I was hoping to be able to retire in some comfort, like your father seems to be; but it's not looking that way."

"But you do realise that my father's mortgage terms are legal and can't be varied. Unless the house is sold."

"Yes; I know; and that is what I'm hoping will happen."

"Is that why you're pressurising him?"

"I'm not pushing him, I'm just making my point."

"Well, I would be grateful if you would leave him alone; it's making him ill."

"I'm sorry."

"If you stop pressurising him I'll try to work out a scheme whereby we sell one of the houses and pay off the loan. That would solve your problem, wouldn't it?"

"It would; would you do that?"

"I'll work at it."

"Thank you." And so it was left and the pressure was off, at least from that direction. Now it was the tax inspector that had to be punctured.

This turned out to need no more than a firm telephone call.

"My name is Michael Godley; my father is Leonard Godley

and he has now given me power of attorney over his property. May I meet you to discuss the problem you have with his tax returns."

There was, what Michael took to be a gulp, a slight pause, and then, "I have had the opportunity to review his returns, and that together with my meeting with him, have satisfied me that they are in order, and that no further action is required," Michael stifled his desire to ask why had he stirred it up in the first place, then? And said simply; "Thank you; I would however be very grateful if you write to my father in those terms, as he has been distressed by your doubts." Another pause, and then a grudging; "Very well, I will do that."

"Thank you; that is very kind of you," you sadist, but he didn't add that!

All this relayed to Leonard had a calming effect and he began to regain control of himself.

When Michael arrived home in London again, Heather was sympathetic and said, "You can't keep dashing off fighting fires in Sheffield. I have an idea; why don't we combine our resources and buy a house here, large enough for us all to live together."

"Are you sure, you're willing to have my parents living with us."

"Oh, yes; they're completely self-effacing; if the house is big enough, I don't suppose we'll see much of them, and... I've found the house!"

"You've found the house; where is it?"

"Not far away, in Teddington; six bedrooms on three floors and on the river !"

"Sounds marvellous; can we afford it?"

"With what we've got from Derby, your father's house and a mortgage, I think so."

"How much is it, then?"

"Seventeen thousand, five hundred pounds."

"What's wrong with it; it sounds too cheap."

"I think people don't want six bedrooms on three floors and by a rat filled river."

"Is it rat filled?"

"No, of course not, but they think so. I like the original 1895 estate agent puff: 'Would suit fishing and boating gentleman'."

"Yes that's us all right: let me see it then."

It was all that Heather said it was, and the middle floor lent itself perfectly to conversion to a flat; main bathroom already there beside the main bedroom; kitchen dining room from another bedroom; the third bedroom on that floor, with balcony onto the river and garden, became a splendid drawing room. Then three more bedrooms upstairs for the family. Downstairs, a kitchen dining room, a drawing room onto a veranda, a dining room and a large hall; perfect for parties, said Heather.

What would Leonard think? Leonard thought it a wonderful idea; Edie thought so too, as long as she could bring her geraniums. Of course she could, and put them on her balcony. Leonard, once more felt that his prayers had been answered and immediately began to get better. Michael dealt confidently with the mortgages, sale, bridging loan, builders and removal. Within a few months it all came together. But it was a hectic time, particularly as, in the middle of it all, his employers sent him off to Egypt to negotiate a sale of aircraft starting equipment, and Heather was pregnant with number three.

Chapter Thirty-Eight

If Michael had suffered under air commodores in John Lewis, he did not escape them in his new appointment. He had been very impressed at his interview, by the Chairman/Managing Director of this private company. He seemed to Michael, to possess all the qualities that he, himself, lacked. They can be summed up by, ruthless business ambition, plus an outstanding personal greed. Perhaps there was something to be learned here, for survival in this material world. Anyway, he hoped so.

At the interview there had also been present a somnolent figure with a red face, who was introduced as Air Commodore Epsom, Director of Exports, your immediate boss. Subsequently, Michael would have thought it equally appropriate to call him Kempton Park, Cheltenham, or Aintree. The bibulous Air Commodore's main function seemed to be as consultant to Chairman A.J. Green, on the sport of kings. He kept his betting account books immaculately, and always showed a profit at the bottom of each page. It later turned out that this was not the case with the company's books after the Chairman had subtracted his tax free winnings. The Air Commodore did have another function, however, which was, to entertain visiting Arab generals when bribery became necessary. Bribes coming from a benign English gentleman were somehow sweeter.

If there were any civilised places to visit overseas, the Air

Commodore and the Chairman would go; if there were smelly places to do business with, Michael would be sent. Egypt was regarded as smelly; the firm's agent was alerted to receive Michael in Cairo.

Shepheard Hotel was not at all smelly; it was as luxurious and mysterious as Agatha Christie. Michael saw a lot of it. It was considered discourteous to make an appointment to see the official concerned with your business at the ministry; the correct procedure, as conducted by your agent, was to ring at about eleven o'clock in the morning, and ask politely whether it would be convenient to visit the official this morning. If the answer was no, it was considered rude to repeat the suggestion sooner than two days later. Michael saw a lot of Shepheard's, dhows on the Nile, the pyramids, the dusty Cairo Museum, and the Cairo nightclubs, before his business with the government was finished successfully.

Celebration of this triumph nearly lead to social disaster.

It had now been ten days since Michael arrived in Cairo, time enough to develop the famous 'gippy tummy'. By now he had such a delicate digestion that he was living on whisky without the ice: that had undoubtedly given him the tummy in the first place. However, it was a great relief to have completed the negotiations and his agent felt the same and insisted on celebrating at his favourite nightclub, at Michael's expense. A table next to the dance floor, had been arranged; this was where the cabaret was performed. It was not long after a slim slightly clad German chanteuse, (if that is not a sophism), began to sing to the clientele for which she had been tipped to ogle. Michael was her target. The medicinal neat whisky having provided the necessary anaesthetic, he responded when she took his numb hand and lead him onto the stage, inviting him to duet with her. Being of a conceited disposition where his voice was concerned, he sang romantically with the chanteuse and fell right into the trap. The next act, introduced by the chanteuse, was even more diminutive and scantily clad; she was a roller skater dancer, who, having been introduced romantically to Michael, took him by the wrist and ankle, and swung him round her head and feet. The centrifugal pressure on his digestive tracts, such as remained, threatened the front, and even the back row with an odious aspersion. Michael felt the honour of his country and the future of its overseas markets, depended on his muscular restraint. By a triumph of will over the frailty of matter, he closed all orifices and water tight doors. Nothing escaped; he landed safely on two feet to glorious applause which seemed, to his ears, to mourn the decline of the British Empire. He was still in a celebrity daze when he was poured into his seat on the BOAC Constellation heading for Heathrow.

***

Heather, meanwhile, had had had her moments of panic and indiscretion. The builders were everywhere in the new house; the cat had had kittens under the stairs, two of which had not survived. To a pregnant woman with her husband overseas, such a sight is un-nerving; she wanted it removed. Still in her dressing gown, early one morning, she rushed out into the garden and in extremity, addressed an Irish labourer:

"My husband's away, and there's something I can't do for myself... and by the way, bring your shovel!" Paddy scratched his head.

Chapter Thirty-Nine

Leonard and Edith were sitting among the packing cases and dust sheets prepared by the removal men for tomorrow's move to London. A large scrawled notice on corrugated cardboard leaned against the potted geraniums: 'Please take care'. There were tears in Edith's eyes.

Leonard took her hand. "I'm sure it's the right thing to do, Edie." She nodded slowly.

"It's better than the move south last time, isn't it?" She nodded again.

"Come on, let's go for a little drive and say goodbye; shall we?"

"Yes," she said, with surprising alacrity. Leonard had recovered well enough to drive again.

"We'll say goodbye to Derbyshire and then have tea with Doris.

Leonard lead the way to the car. He took the Ecclesall Road to Bents Green; Muskoka Drive, where their aspiring dreams had begun in 1924; in the stuccoed, semi-detached, three bedroomed house, on the new estate; built by a builder who had been out to Canada and returned a rich man. Muskoka was the name of an Indian tribe, whose lands he had acquired. They had both left behind the grimy brick rows of Sheffield east, and were now puffing out their chests in the fresh western breeze of Derbyshire, and Tony was born; a new life.

"It's thirty years ago, Edie, but it hasn't changed much, has it? I think that nice Mrs. Birkenshaw next door still has the same curtains up at the front window; the ones with the pattern outside, I don't think we'll call; we'd never get away."

Leonard continued up to the Round House, the old toll house that used to collect money for a short cut to the city. Now it collected money for ice creams and chocolate bars and bottles of fizz.

"Do you want an ice cream, Edie?" Edie shook her head.

"I think I will." And a boyish glee spread over his face; Edie laughed to see it and felt younger again.

They drove on, crossing Burbage bridge and its rushing stream dashing under, white with froth and brown with peat; it tumbled towards the Derwent River, scattering the grey-cropped sheep, as it went. Froggatt Edge drew a line against the rippling sky to their right. Froggatt Edge, black with granite, grinding hard, enduring, inspiring. "We'll come and see it again, Edie," said Leonard seeing the nostalgia in her eyes. On to Bakewell, where they bought a tart for tea with Doris, then to Chatsworth Park, with its remote grandeur; incongruous luxury, hiding from a savage land, suckling to the fertile valley and the coal of nearby Chesterfield. Back up through winding Curbar, cresting onto Sheffield, hidden in industrial haze, but only ten minutes from breathtaking beauty; that was the joy of the Sheffield they were leaving behind for gasping London.

"Ee, we shall miss you, Len; it's always a comfort to have you near."

"We'll come and see you, Doris, and there's always the telephone. Where's Fred?"

"He's upstairs in bed; I don't know what's wrong with him; he's just depressed. He's on sleeping pills; he hasn't been to work for weeks."

"I know what it's like, shall I go and see him?"

"No; I asked him but he went quite panicky."

"All right then, I'll give him a good thought." The perennially cheerful Doris was tearful when they parted. Edith hugged her brave sister hard and said, "God will take care of you."

"I hope so, love."

The journey to London, next day, was silent until they reached Buckinghamshire (they were staying the night at the Bull, Gerrards Cross, to let the removal men get ahead of them) when Edie remembered Peg and funny old Lodge Farm. She began to sing hymns.

"That's better Edie; we'll be all right now."

***

Their delight in their new home was a joy to see. Michael and Heather had supervised the placing of the furniture meticulously to replicate the arrangement in Sheffield; they had hung the pictures in the same places on the walls, paintings by Guy and Derek and Winifred, each telling a story in the episodes of their life. And the famous geraniums were glowing on the veranda. The new kitchen dining room gleamed with its view over the garden and river, and the expansive bedroom even had a safe in the wall (as left by the previous owners). Though they had nothing to put in it, Leonard felt himself a man of substance; spiritual substance. And so began a happy and peaceful ten years for Leonard and Edie. They were able to watch their grandchildren, Julia, Georgina, and Matthew, maturing under the social pressures of the 1970s. Edith was protected by her deafness from the loudest excesses of the audio revolution, and Leonard enjoyed the parties Heather gave in her grand Edwardian house, one of the earliest of which was in celebration of the golden weddings of all the parents; Michael's and Heather's, which happily almost coincided. Leonard was able to talk about the First World War at last; previously it had been screamed about in a trauma, now he discussed and commented on A.J.P. Taylor's recent History, and made marginal notes in his copy.

"If we are receptive to good, and keep the lines open to the power of Devine Mind, the vision will be made manifest. Isn't this so, Edie? I think we have arrived at a little bit of heaven."

Leonard sat in his familiar chair, now overlooking the riverside garden, and felt light as a spirit.

Pleasant memories seemed to be dominating, particularly when a remarkable coincidence arose for Michael.

There was an election in the offing and the Independent newspaper advertised in its columns for volunteers, with at least three generations in the family, who would be willing to confess their voting preferences over as many elections as they had been part of.

Heather's main concern was to keep her aged mother amused. This could easily have been a full time job. Sybil was voracious for stimulation. Heather saw the advertisement and regarded it as a godsend for Sybil, because Sybil had voted in every election since women had been given the vote. The response from the newspaper was immediate and enthusiastic. Sybil was interviewed like a star and loved it. Of course she had voted Conservative every time, but it was the bland submission to the males in her life that made her replies socially interesting: "My father told me how to vote and then my husband." The consequence was that they had produced a daughter who was a confirmed Labour supporter. The invitations to be interviewed were extended to the whole family, until the article covered a whole page when it was published just before election day. The article included photographs and biographical profiles.

A week later, a letter arrived for Michael from the journalist, enclosing another from a reader, it said: 'I would be grateful if you would pass on this letter to Michael Godley, featured in your article on voting, as I believe he was a pupil of mine some forty years ago', It was signed, Daphne Robinson, and her address was in Westminster.

It took Michael's breath away; he picked up the telephone and dialled her number; she answered; Michael spoke; "Hello, Daphne, it's Michael, how are you?" There was silence for a moment, and then, "How wonderful; I knew it was you." And conversation flowed as if time had stopped since 1946.

"We must meet; give me a few days, and I arrange it. I'll call you back; will you be there?"

"Yes, yes, I will." Daphne sounded like a young girl and Michael's heart beat faster; he almost felt guilt as he explained it all to Heather, but she was equally intrigued and sent him off to make the arrangements for their meeting. It so happened that she was committed to taking her mother to Paris in the next few days, so she risked leaving the lovers alone; she was not too concerned as Daphne was now over eighty!

"I'll come and collect you, Daphne, and bring you out here for lunch, and we can talk and talk and talk, and look at photographs."

And so it was, and they did talk and talk and talk, and fill in their lives in between. Daphne was now frail, but still a pretty, white haired lady, with flirtatious eyes that had lost none of their enticing intelligence. I could have married her; we would have been joyous companions; engrossed lovers, as I am with Heather. These were thoughts that rushed through Michael's head as he kissed her cheek. He longed to ask why she had shut him out of her life, but he felt he already knew, and he didn't want to criticise her husband, the forbidding Doctor Linfoot, who had died many years before. She was devoted to her step family, who were equally fond of her; it would be ugly to disturb all that. Let's just pretend there has been nothing in between. They looked directly into each other's eyes as they talked, and they shone with love deferred.

When Michael took her home, to be given tea in her Westminster flat (not her headmistress's study!) he saw again that romantic vision of her leaning back in her swivel chair, her hands clasped behind her head, her dark hair framing her pretty face and shining eyes, her soft pink cashmere jumper, kissed by a single row of pearls, her breasts reaching out to him. Michael said; "You know, I was rather in love with you."

"And I was with you." And she kissed him on the lips. The fifteen years of pitiful arithmetic between them melted away as they embraced.

They saw a lot of each other in the next two years, Heather was included and approved of. They would meet for lunch at Fortnums and go to the Royal Academy together.

But then one day Daphne's favourite niece rang to say that she had died quite suddenly and painlessly; happily, in fact, of a sudden stroke. Would Michael make the address at her funeral: of course he would; he was honoured and grateful to summarise her life and love. He ended with a poem written for her:

Is Death perhaps a meeting after fifty separate years?
A union of souls, matured in the world's long adolescence?
If so, you know this joy already, the judgement has been made,
Your innocence is guilty of no self-regarding gaze.
Still you are startled by beauty,
Astonished by joy;
Wondering and seeking, you have found,
That love is us in others, not lonely in ourselves.

The bubble of our consciousness, from a warm sea floor,
Rises to envelope,
The teacher and the taught,
The giver and receiver,
The lover and the leaver,
The future and the past,
Memory and oblivion,
All as one at last.
Death cannot diminish you,
Your consciousness remains
In the love you placed within us,
To ease our future pains.

It did ease future pains; it did give a feeling of completion that they had come to know each other again. It reinforced the harmony of their lives.

Chapter Forty

Indeed it was a bit of a pain when a take-over battle threatened Frederick Braby, the company Michael had been working for, since leaving Rolls Royce. He had not over-estimated A.J. Green's ambition and greed. He had succeeded in merging his vigorous, small but successful engineering firm with a moribund, but respected public company called Frederick Braby. He had appointed himself Managing Director of the group, while third generation Eric Braby (known as the thickest head in the City, and chairman of many a price fixing association) remained as company Chairman. This suited Eric Braby, as it meant that he didn't have to have anything to do with the running of the company; he was, after all, Commissioner for Scouting for the south of England.

A.J. continued to run this public company, as he had his own, like a personal honey pot. He was not used to the dangers and disciplines of the Stock Exchange; soon he was being hunted. The balance sheets showed mouthwatering property assets, practically no borrowings, and a pitiful return of five percent on the employment of all the capital being used. It was an asset stripper's dream, and the hunt was on.

It was not long before the most aggressive of the stalkers had a controlling interest and took over the company, using, of course, borrowed money, most of which had to be realised and repaid. Inspection of the books began in depth. By this time

A.J. had transferred most of the cash into his own former fiefdom, from where it had found its way into his personal account.

As General Manager of this main subsidiary, as it had now become, Michael was called into the new owner's office. He was a young, glistening entrepreneur, about the same age as Michael. 'Where did I go wrong?' thought Michael idly, as he admired the cut of the entrepreneur's suit and the pinkness of his hands, and indeed the smoothness of his voice.

"How do you dom my name is Peake; I'm your new boss." He was polite but brusque. "Tell me Mr. Godley, what proportion of these debtors are recoverable. He passed his plump hand over the accounts on his desk. The man was obviously a realist, he knew from experience, and no doubt from his own methods, that the debtor figures are easily the most manoeuvrable. Michael did not hesitate, "About twenty-five percent."

The new owner's fingers clenched on his gold pencil; his complexion subsided suddenly from pink to grey. "Christ," he expelled over a gasp. "I had allowed for fifty percent, but not seventy-five. What's the explanation, how come?"

Fortunately, Michael had never been made a director of the company, that was reserved for cronies of A.J., and it meant paying them more for the risks they were taking. He wasn't even a Chartered Accountant with his professional life at risk.

There were no professionals in A.J.'s personal company, only lowly book keepers and compliant managers, who obeyed his orders as to where to place the figures to tell the best story. Michael explained this to the shaken owner. ('Perhaps I didn't go wrong: at least I'm not in his position.')

"But how did he keep afloat?"

"He had the power to siphon it off from the parent

company."

"I see: thank you. I'll speak to you again."

The interview ended, but was followed by many others, including the auditors and solicitors, and an undertaking from Michael to give evidence in court. Their pressure on A.J. succeeded in him returning many millions of pounds to avoid a trial. For Michael it meant the disappearance of his job. Then came the question, what to do next?

Chapter Forty-One

'Next', came from an unexpected quarter. When Michael was at Oxford he had become involved with a rich old lady (at least he regarded her as an old lady, he being twenty-two, she being fifty!) her passion was Shakespeare. The Baroness, as she was known, (her grandfather had been ennobled by the King of the Belgians for the excellence of his acid drops!), undertook the production of a Shakespeare play, in her lovely garden near Wallingford. She had been doing this since 1929, when she had run away with a handsome actor-manager, whose responsibility thereafter was to direct a play of Shakespeare's each summer for the rest of his life. This, he was well qualified to do (as a boy actor he had appeared with Irving, because his father was playing Claudius) but Herby dreaded each summer because he hated actors who were 'bloody amateurs'. His red hair bristled with bad temper, as it turned white over the years, and he had to struggle against incompetence, absenteeism, and temperament. But it was after all only for three months of rehearsal each weekend which left him nine clear months to calm down.

Michael became involved when Paulise, the Baroness, approached her contact in Oxford for a new generation of actors. Michael was recommended by Neville Goghill and she gobbled him up as Demetrius in 'A Midsummer Night's Dream.'

Although he agreed with Herby's frustrations, he found the whole atmosphere magical and he appeared in the productions (together with Heather and the children) for the next twenty-five years, until both Paulise and Herby had died.

They became supportive friends and Michael was able to help Paulise during the scandal when her only daughter ran away with a married jockey in the village: but that's another story.

Julia had become infected by the theatrical bug and went on to drama school and later an assistant director in television. Her best friend from drama school had become a successful agent and had seen Michael acting in Paulise's productions. "Why don't you take on my daddy?" Julia suggested to her.

"I will," said Sharon, "I haven't got any old men on my books." Michael was fifty-five at the time! Paulise would have smiled, but she had gone by then. As the new owners were glad of Michael's co-operation, they gave him six months' pay to resettle himself, which was not going be easy at the age of fifty-five; he was lucky to have an old profession to fall back on.

"What do you think, Dad?"

"Well I encouraged you when you tried it first; I encourage you now: if it's right, It will work out."

"What do you think, Heather?"

"Well you were the one who said, 'If at first you don't succeed, give up.' You'd better make it succeed this time."

"I will, I will: at least I swear that I'll bring in the same money I've been earning with Braby's, even if I have to be a painter and decorator: It wasn't very much, you know, less than you are earning,"

Heather was by now a Deputy Head. If he had known just how much painting and decorating he would be doing, he might have changed his mind.

However, things started off well; he was put up for an Italian commercial. He found himself peering myopically through the Soho gloom, at the address he had scribbled on the back of a Barclaycard final demand.

He approached a not very young lady, whose eyelashes would have encouraged a forest fire; she smiled.

"Do you know D'Arblay Mews, number fourteen, The Today Film Company?"

"Oh! An actor," she scorned and turned on her stiletto heels, "Round the corner, past the dustbins, join the queue," was her parting shot.

There was no queue, only a shabby door and a ladder of names with bells beside them; Simone, Rachelle, 'Heavy Breathing Productions', then 'The Today Film Company'. This he pressed and a burst of static let him in. Seven flights of panting coconut matted stairs, brought him to reception.

"Michael Godley for the casting." Debbie, with a telephone growing out of her left ear, a little boy haircut, and unbuttoned blouse, gave him a clipboard, two forms and a biro, and waved him towards the other hopefuls. Each of these was practicing the art of nonchalance. That is, reading a script, carried for months in the briefcase, looking anxiously at your watch to give the impression that you have another appointment; talking loudly about the job you are currently doing, or just have done, (actually three months ago), or just plain reading 'The Times'.

He filled in the forms, telling the usual lies about age, size and recent work, then tried to remember his agent's number. The brief from his agent (never to be relied on) had been that they were looking for an Indian Army colonel type, riding an elephant to extol the delights of a famous Dutch chocolate, which had an elephant for its trade mark. The room was full of fierce moustaches and insecure monocles, that made the eye appear as if it had suffered a recent mutilation.

"Michael, how good of you to come." This was Lewis the casting agent. His oily charm guaranteeing a constant flow of actor fodder to his castings, where they would submit themselves to ritual humiliation and rejection.

"We are ready for you now. Thank you, Trevor, speak to you soon."

This, to the actor just exiting and suffering a severe loss of nonchalance, by stuffing his arm into the lining of his coat, instead of the sleeve. Michael blinked 'nonchalantly' as he entered the floodlit studio, genuflecting over a lighting cable.

"This is Michael Godley," said Lewis, as if presenting an award winner, "and this is Signore Gaspata, your director."

Signore Gaspata, living up to his name, exhaled in awe. "Il Papa, il Papa; you are the Pope."

Michael, when he crinkled his eyes and folded his hands, did have fleeting resemblance to the Pope. Signore Gaspata could not believe his luck; the Pope advertising his chocolates in Italy! After that Michael was not allowed to leave the room. It was, however, explained to him that the character had been changed from English colonel to French explorer.

"You will come to Milan on Monday, film on Tuesday, return on Wednesday; all expenses paid and £1000 in your hand, yes?"

"Yes," agreed Michael in a daze.

"Excellent; it is settled. We speak to your agent now; arrivadieci!"

So began the ride of an English actor on an Indian elephant, playing a French explorer advertising Dutch chocolates as eaten by a Polish Pope in Italy, speaking Italian, to be dubbed by an Italian actor with a French accent.

What was that? Speaking Italian? Nobody mentioned speaking Italian. Michael suppressed his misgivings as his taxi swept through the gates of a minor palazzo, where the Renaissance offices of the film company luxuriated.

"Michael Godley?" said the dark eyed beauty who rose to meet him.

"I am, Bella." Michael melted in her warm smile, then froze as she sat him down and said, "Here is your script."

"Script," he faltered. Bella was business like; "Here is a translation, here is a tape, you have plenty of time to learn it, we shoot at seven in the morning."

"Shoot. Yes!"

He was hustled off to his hotel in a sinister black Mercedes. The hotel was indeed splendid but marble columns suggested mausoleums, the glass doors, holy relics, the silk curtains, of shrouds, and the black coated waiters, undertakers. Upstairs in his room, the walls of which seemed to close in relentlessly, he played the tape. It sounded like Italian machine gunfire. He looked at the script; he looked at the translation; he could find no connection. There was nothing for it but to learn it phrase by phrase, putting it together like a broken arm. Two hours later he had learnt it, like Eliza Dolittle at her first act curtain. Wine, Italian wine would help him accelerate his accent. He went to the restaurant ant drank a litre and a little veal. Back in his cell, feeling in need of sympathy he rang Heather.

"I'm alone in this terrible hotel in Milan and they're making me learn this dreadful Italian advertisement, and they're going to take me out in Monza Park at seven o'clock tomorrow morning and shoot!"

"Darling, you'll manage perfectly well; you always do. Don't forget the perfume: and the car isn't starting properly!"

When he found he was remembering less at one o'clock than at eight, he decided to put in for a call at five o'clock, and go to bed, His head had hardly touched the pillow when the telephone rang, 'Ah that will be Heather ringing back with remorse at her heartlessness: or to remind me of that perfume again.'

"Pronto?" He was speaking Italian fluently now and well enough to understand that this was not Heather, but another woman, "Good evening. I am a woman, you are a man, and you need me as your paramour."

"Non gratzie, tropo tarde, labore domani, gratzie tanto." He hung up intellectually exhausted, but smirked at his fluency.

Before he could finish congratulating himself, the door opened, a hand connected to a naked arm came through, and switched on the light. She was definitely cross. "You could not have comprehended. I am a woman; you are a man; you need me for your paramore, paramore, paramore."

Why did she keep insisting she was a woman; he began to suspect she was a man; she certainly looked awfully strong. For one terrible moment he thought he was going to be violated, until he shrieked:

"I have no MONEY!"

This was the Holy Cross against the Vampire, the smell of garlic; she turned and slammed the door, uttering curses of eternal impotence. They forgot his early call and so after three double espressos he slumped silently into the black Mercedes with the rest of the crew and headed out for the killing grounds in Monza Park.

"Ciao, va bene?" Bella as bright as ever. Michael smiled wanly. She tripped prettily through the trees to where his white safari suit was laid out on a tarpaulin; there was no chair; he balanced like an acrobat in his underpants and slithered into his white trousers and tunic. He was told firmly not to sit down. As there was no chair and the tightness of the trousers forbad it, this was superfluous. Leaning against a tree was also forbidden. 'Whose side were these people on?'

"I will show you your elephant," said the now, sickeningly smiling Guilia.

She led him further into the forest to where a scaffolding had been built for further execution. Michael began to think. It was some twenty feet high, like a small railway trestle with a track on top. This was the 'elephant'. The howdah was a box with a chair on springs in it; its bogey wheels ran along the track. Six slaves stood round the scaffold. Four held ropes attached to the front, rear, and sides of the 'elephant'. One to pull forwards, one to pull back, and two to pull sideways against the springs. The other two held long poles, one pole had a withered palm leaf tied to the top; this signifies jungle. The other had a stuffed sock on the end; this signified the elephant's trunk.

The camera and Signore Gaspata were nowhere to be seen. He was twenty-five yards away, shooting head and shoulders in a long shot. His rasping voice came over the loudspeaker. "OK, let's go: get him up there."

It then became apparent that the ladder they had brought was not long enough to reach the howdah. A dwarf was pressed into providing the missing link.

"OK, action."

The two side men rocked the set, the front man pulled forward, the man with the pole and palm leaf swiped at Michael's head. He gabbled his Italian script and offered his cocoa beans as instructed; the man at the back miraculously pulled on his rope in time to stop the howdah skiing off the track.

“No good: take two,” growled Gaspata, and added some extra expletive that Michael didn’t catch.

“What’s he saying?” he asked Bella.

“He says he doesn’t like your accent.”

Action, action; and so it went on until take forty-two when Michael felt a thumping in his chest and was seeing double.

“What’s the matter with him?” yelled Gaspata

“I think he is tired,” said the perceptive Bella.

“OK. Break for lunch.”

Michael was taken from the scaffold like a Pieta and helped pale to the luncheon area. He was admonished not to sit down in his white suit. As there were no chairs and his trousers were too tight, the command was irrelevant. The lunch break passed in an attempt to digest the indigestible. A walk into the forest to relieve the pressure without splashing the suit, was successfully achieved, and then it was back to the scaffold.

“Action: I tell you what, Michael, you get this right first time and I double your money and put a women in your bed.”

“Could I have one without the other?” thought Michael, remembering his ‘paramore’. Of course he didn’t get it right until ‘take’ twenty-eight, when they almost ran out of the chocolate bars that had to be knocked out of his black and blue hand.

“OK, cut; we move to the elephant.”

Yes, there was a real elephant after all. She had been imprisoned in her cattle truck all morning but she was beautiful and patient, unlike her mahout, who was ugly and ratty, and had an iron bar with a spiked end. Her name was India. She was easy to mount, being shorter than the scaffold. Michael had no more words to say, he was sitting comfortably, sympathising with India, whispering advice, not to be bullied.

The camera crew now performed the pantomime of trying

to take a camera up a tree on which the lowest branches were higher than their only ladder could reach. Their problem had to be solved by the luckless dwarf who was sent up the tree as if collecting coconuts. The camera man in the tree proved to be as inept as Michael in satisfying Signore Gaspata. India did not mind because each failed take provided her with a chocolate bar to eat; until they were in danger of running out of chocolate bars, (the subject of the advert). The mahout then resorted to bashing his elephant's trunk before she could eat her choc bar; he made her drop it and it was offered again for the next take.

Then India realised she was being exploited and abused. She had an answer. She stopped responding; she spread her back legs wide and peed until her bladder, (which had the capacity of a brewer's tanker), was relieved. She then filled the now steaming forest with the earth shaking thuds of seven deposits. For a few awesome moments there was a silence of respect: then everyone burst out laughing, including Singore Gaspata, who called 'It's a wrap'.

The rest of the evening was bliss; Michael's money was doubled, and he didn't have to have the 'paramore'; he was able to buy a gallon of perfume and come home to Heather who kissed him and said, "There, you see; I told you you'd be all right."

"You smell gorgeous," he replied.

It was not exactly the realisation of Michael's ambition to be a fine classical actor, but it was the beginning of a sort of living, doing what he enjoyed; in spite of the Senior Gaspatas. It did, after all, underline the ephemeral follies of human existence.

Chapter Forty-Two

Leonard seemed to be happily rounding off his life and memories by visiting his friends. He and Edith were away in Bognor, seeing Peg. Peg was well looked after by her loyal niece; the bungalow did creak under their combined weight, but the single storey spread the load. She didn't go to her Christian Science church any more, partly because she was too immobile, but really because her beloved Guy had left his caravan and married the beatific Christabel; she who had devoted her life to her mother, her mother who had died, and left her with the need to look after someone else; and the money to do it.

"When I think what I've done for that Guy!" she complained to Leonard. "I've pulled him out of every financial hole. I've given him a home. I've ferried him about."

"No, Peg, he did the driving. Unconditionally, Peg, is how we have to give; if we want to receive: and we never know where our receiving will come from, except we know it is from God."

Peg pouted a bit, but said, "I suppose you're right, Len."

"He gave you real friendship, companionship when you needed it so badly."

"I suppose Cristabel knows he's no use as a man."

"Is that what you're really grumbling about, Peg?" Peg pouted again. "Fortunately these things fade with age, I hope it has with you; let him go, Peg, you are not alone, you've got Betty, your niece, and she is so glad to be with you; it is truly mutual, and she knows her future is secure."

"Yes you're right. How do you feel about living with Michael and Heather?"

"Totally happy; at peace: and you know it was Heather's idea. Michael told me so when I was worried about what she would think. It is a mutual good, as all goodness is, by definition. They love their house, and we can watch all that youthful life going on without having to be involved in it, unless we want to. They gave us a wonderful golden wedding party, combined with Heather's parents; there was a music hall, her father performed: I didn't, but I enjoyed it, we felt surrounded by love."

"You're so lucky to have your son, mine was ripped away from me." She dropped a sideways glance at the sliver framed photograph of Dick in his R.A.F. uniform, the silver of the frame reflecting the silver of his wings.

"There is no separation in spirit, Peg; you know you can draw strength from him still and you have done, haven't you?"

"Yes, I have; but I still ache to have him with me." Leonard knew it was better to let it go with that; Peg was a very passionate and possessive lady.

"Yes, I miss Bill too, and her bloody dogs; though not her clouds of smoke: those did for her in the end, didn't they. She coughed herself to oblivion; pity!"

***

Leonard's next journey was to the heavens, or more specifically the Isle Ornsay on the Isle of Skye. There Guy and Cristabel had built their ideal house that watched the changing light over the Cullins from its veranda. They both had Scottish roots and savoured its spiritual beauty, so remote from the brutalities that had grown the money in the first place, and made it visible to them now.

"Did you ever think that life would lead you here, to such comfort and beauty?" Leonard was thinking of Guy's early life of sensual delights and social superficialities.

"Only gradually, as indulgence was stripped forcibly away. Then it became a vision and it has come true. I owe it all to Cristabel, not just her money, but her calming presence. She seems to have been waiting and expecting this moment and I am part of it."

"You were both receptive; not striving, that's what we need to be, 'receptive' to good; not striving for it, not demanding of it, not assuming it is ours by right of religion or power; be submissive to good; to love, and fear no evil. But you have to be pure in heart so perhaps you are, Guy, at last!"

Leonard smiled, and sipped the single malt that Guy's fading sensuality had handed to Leonard in the setting sun.

"Drink up, Leonard," as Edie would say, 'It's just an idea of God.' Edie shook her head in the fading light, but was smiling.

***

Their last call was with Doris in Sheffield. Doris was now in a home for the old, not far from where she had lived for half her life. She was confused, but as ebullient as ever, when not asleep among the lolling ranks of television junkies.

"Hello, Tony, hello, Heather." It was Leonard and Edie. Michael and Heather were her usual visitors, so it was a perfectly logical mistake. Leonard did not correct her.

"How are you, Doris?"

"I'm all right; just worried about Beano."

Leonard knew what she was referring to. Doris had had a hard time surviving the death of bland Fred, who suddenly declined into a deep depression and took an overdose of sleeping pills. She remained in the same house they had lived in since their wedding; continued a running battle with the landlady who tried and tried to increase the rent. This provided welcome stimulation every week. For a short time she had a pernicious boyfriend; but her emotional life was centered on 'Beano' her un-neutered ginger Tom, the scourge of the district when the females were on heat. He would return home bleeding about the face, teeth missing from the projectile milk bottles skillfully aimed by furious insomniacs, desperate at Beano's sexual squalling.

"How could people be so cruel?" Doris wailed to Michael when he visited, pointing to Beano's battered beauty.

"Perhaps you should have him neutered, Doris."

"Oh no, I couldn't do that: it's against nature, and my Spirit Guide says so."

"Oh, I see."

Then Doris had a stroke and had to go into the home. Her loyal nephew Tony had been given power of attorney and so ended the lease and closed up the house, handing it back to the greedy, and now exulting, landlady. But what to do with Beano?

Michael went to Doris's local vet, where she was well known; they were always patching up Beano's nose and extracting broken teeth. "My auntie has had to go into a home, so we'll have to put Beano down."

"Oh, no; oh no; you can't do that; he's a ginger. I love gingers." This was the ginger haired receptionist speaking in alarm.

"What shall I do then?"

"Bring him in here, and I'll take him home."

"But he's an un-neutered Tom; he's a menace."

"He's not, he's a love; bring him in; here, here's a basket."

Now, how to catch a Beano. For some time now, ever since Doris had been ill and living downstairs, Beano had been living feral upstairs in Doris's former bedroom. It was also his lavatory; crunching coils crackled underfoot, or sometimes squelched if you were unlucky. Michael tentatively opened the door, just enough to let himself and the basket in. He shut it behind him and was relieved to see Beano curled up on the bed (no doubt exhausted by his nocturnal successes). He crept over to the window and closed it quietly. Beano raised one battered eyebrow, saw the basket which he associated with tooth extraction, and immediately levitated to the top of the wardrobe, from where he threatened to scratch out Michael's eyes. Michael wrapped the stinking eiderdown round his arm and tried to smother the flailing paws of the ginger whirlwind. He only succeeded in toppling the whole wardrobe on top of himself and catapulting Beano onto the bed. Michael began to foresee the grisly outcome. He would be discovered some pungent weeks later, pinned and suffocated, under the wardrobe, half eaten by Beano.

Fortunately, the wardrobe was nineteen thirties flimsy, and empty; he was able to throw it off and escape. His next tactic was to net Beano under the eiderdown and gradually squeeze him into the open basket, like toothpaste. This worked until the last slamming of the lid, which was not achieved without a dramatic laceration of the wrist. Dripping blood, but triumphant, Michael returned to the vet.

"Oh he's lovely," said the red haired receptionist, very

pleased with her latest pet. Beano scowled. "I expect he's missed his loving." Redhead was not to be rejected and took him away like a conquering Amazon.

Doris, of course, never knew the full story; she only knew Beano had a good home.

"Nothing to worry about, Doris; Beano's quite happy. Are you happy, Doris; is it all right here?"

"Yes, come up and see my room." They did, and it was lovely.

A few days after they had left her, Doris died in her sleep, smiling, and her humble life faded away, all bagged up.

The van backs up to the back to back.
Exhausted diesel splashes rotting brick.
The driver belches, 'Bag it up, it's all for t' dump.'
And ninety years of rented life is jumbled into blind black bags,
Jumbled like the mind that once arranged them.
The beauty mocking curler,
The heartless lover's Christmas card with sorry sentiment:
The Spiritualist message; a promise from beyond:
The tipsy crucifix on the mirror, leering
At the spent brass lipstick's traces.
The empty bottles of the cures that failed;
The television statement for rented entertainment;
Vi-Deo, the sight of God, promised at a discount.
A rumpled mind in a moaning home.
Like paper weighted snow tumbling in a trapped false scene;
And successive shrinking Zimmer frames showing life's diminishing perspective.
But see, the catkins burst against the cold,

And snowy clouds withhold their white confusion,
A horizontal winter sun, cleaves the eternal hills,
And golden light washes the dancing cripple.
Death is her renewal.

Epilogue

It was June and it was Julia's birthday; she was twenty-one. The garden was throbbing with her theatrical friends; it was (as always) a dressing up party: the theme was the Twenties. Why? No one knew, except that the dresses were pretty if your body was slim, as they all were. Handkerchief points and bandeaux pinked and blued and purpled over the green grass: chatter gurgled with clinking glass. Roses climbed to the balcony, where Leonard and Edie stood, with Michael and Heather on either side.

Suddenly, Julia saw them looking proudly down, swung her glass in the air, spraying the revellers around her, and shouted, "A toast, to Granny and Grandpa!"

The whole party took it up; Edith clapped her hands together; Leonard beamed; and turned to Michael and said, without a tear in his eye,

"You know, Michael, these have been the happiest days of my life!" Then he sneezed and laughed.

That evening he felt a summer cold coming on and went to bed. The cold took hold; it became benign pneumonia, and three days later, he slipped into a coma and died.

***

The brilliant sun gleamed from the little cortege of two black